STRANGE TALES OF AN ORIENTAL IDOL

BUDDHISM AND MODERNITY

A series edited by Donald S. Lopez Jr.

RECENT BOOKS IN THE SERIES

A Storied Sage: Canon and Creation in the Making of a Japanese Buddha
by Micah L. Auerback (2016)

Rescued from the Nation: Anagarika Dharmapala and the Buddhist World
by Steven Kemper (2015)

Grains of Gold: Tales of a Cosmopolitan Traveler
by Gendun Chopel (2014)

The Birth of Insight: Meditation, Modern Buddhism, and the Burmese Monk Ledi Sayadaw
by Erik Braun (2013)

Religious Bodies Politic: Rituals of Sovereignty in Buryat Buddhism
by Anya Bernstein (2013)

From Stone to Flesh: A Short History of the Buddha
by Donald S. Lopez Jr. (2013)

The Museum on the Roof of the World: Art, Politics, and the Representation of Tibet
by Clare E. Harris (2012)

STRANGE TALES OF
AN ORIENTAL IDOL

**AN ANTHOLOGY OF
EARLY EUROPEAN
PORTRAYALS OF THE BUDDHA**

Edited by Donald S. Lopez Jr.

The University of Chicago Press | *Chicago and London*

The University of Chicago Press, Chicago 60637

The University of Chicago Press, Ltd., London

© 2016 by The University of Chicago

All rights reserved. Published 2016.

Printed in the United States of America

25 24 23 22 21 20 19 18 17 16   1 2 3 4 5

ISBN-13: 978-0-226-49318-3 (cloth)

ISBN-13: 978-0-226-39123-6 (paper)

ISBN-13: 978-0-226-39106-9 (e-book)

DOI: 10.7208/chicago/9780226391069.001.0001

The University of Chicago Press gratefully acknowledges the generous support of the University of Michigan toward the publication of this book.

Library of Congress Cataloging-in-Publication Data

Names: Lopez, Donald S., 1952– editor.

Title: Strange tales of an Oriental idol : an anthology of early European portrayals of the Buddha / edited by Donald S. Lopez Jr.

Other titles: Buddhism and modernity.

Description: Chicago : The University of Chicago Press, 2016. | Series: Buddhism and modernity | Includes bibliographical references and index.

Identifiers: LCCN 2016000231 | ISBN 9780226493183 (cloth : alk. paper) | ISBN 9780226391236 (pbk. : alk. paper) | ISBN 9780226391069 (e-book)

Subjects: LCSH: Gautama Buddha—Christian interpretations. | Gautama Buddha—Early works to 1800. | Gautama Buddha—Cult—Europe—History. | Buddhism—Study and teaching—Europe—History.

Classification: LCC BQ894.S77 2016 | DDC 294.3/6309—dc23 LC record available at http://lccn.loc.gov/2016000231

♾ This paper meets the requirements of ANSI/NISO Z39.48-1992 (Permanence of Paper).

Truth is uniform and consistent, but fiction is variable and incongruous; and therefore it is no wonder that the accounts of Boodh, which are a tissue of fables, should be very dissimilar and inconsistent.

ROBERT FELLOWES (1817)

CONTENTS

ACKNOWLEDGMENTS

This book was written with the generous support of a fellowship from the John Simon Guggenheim Memorial Foundation, augmented by funding from the College of Literature, Science, and the Arts at the University of Michigan. Initial research on the project was conducted while I was a scholar in residence at the Getty Research Institute in Los Angeles. Among its excellent staff, I would like especially to thank Sabine Schlosser, Jasmine Lin, and George Weinberg. My research assistant at the Getty, Candace Weddle, provided invaluable and uncomplaining support in accurately transcribing long passages from arcane texts. At the University of Michigan, Anna Johnson checked the accuracy of those passages and offered useful suggestions for the headnotes.

About his origine and native Country, I find the account of those
Heathens do not agree.

ENGELBERT KAEMPFER (1727)

After a Christian uprising in Japan in 1637, the shogun banished
all Europeans from the country except the Dutch, who seemed interested only in commerce. But he severely restricted their movements, forcing them to live on an artificial island in Nagasaki Bay
called Dejima, constructed for this purpose just three years before.
The Dutch were the only Westerners allowed on Japanese territory
until the arrival of the American commodore Matthew C. Perry's
black ships in 1853.

On September 24, 1690, the Dutch ship *Waelstrom* landed at
Dejima. Among its occupants was Engelbert Kaempfer, a German physician employed by the Dutch East India Company. He
remained for two years, confined to Dejima except for an annual
trip to Edo Castle and an audience with the shogun.

Kaempfer's voyage from the Dutch East India Company's headquarters in Batavia (modern Jakarta) to Japan had included a stop
in Thailand. Having seen statues of the Buddha in both that country and Japan, Dr. Kaempfer came to the conclusion that the idol
worshipped by the Thais represented the same figure as the idol
worshipped by the Japanese. Despite the fact that references to
the Buddha by Westerners extend back to 200 CE, Kaempfer was
among the first to make this startling discovery.[1]

Today, the Buddha is familiar to us as an Indian sage, the
founder of a religion so profound that it seemingly transcends the

category of religion; perhaps it is a philosophy or simply a way of life. We have forgotten, if we ever knew, that for many centuries Europeans regarded the Buddha with profound suspicion. He was an idol worshipped by heathens, and the man who became that idol was himself a purveyor of idolatry, spreading its pestilence across Asia. And the Buddha was not just one idol. He was many idols known by many names. In retrospect, the reason for the Europeans' error is understandable. In the various Asian lands, the Buddha is depicted according to local artistic conventions, and so the Buddha in Thailand looks different from the Buddha in Japan. He is also known by different names in a range of local languages. In the course of this study, I have collected over three hundred European names of the Buddha from the period 200–1850—names like Bubdam, Chacabout, Dibote, Dschakdschimmuni, Goodam, Nacodon, Putza, Siquag, Thicca, and Xaqua. And the religion that these various idols taught was not called Buddhism—the term did not appear in English for the first time until 1801; it was called idolatry.

Sometime in the late seventeenth century, European missionaries and travelers began to realize that the many idols seen in many nations and the many names recorded in many languages all somehow designated a single figure, though whether it was a figure of myth or of history remained undecided. By the end of the eighteenth century, his identity (and gender) was well established, and it was generally accepted that he had been a historical figure, although his origins were debated. In the nineteenth century, empowered by the new science of philology, European scholars began to decipher Buddhist texts, and the Buddha that we know today was born. We should not immediately conclude, however, that because Europeans now had texts, the Buddha they described was the Buddha of those texts. Indeed, it might be said that in the early decades of the nineteenth century, the Europeans found their own Buddha.

Western references to Buddhism date to the first years of the third century CE, and during the sixteenth, seventeenth, and eighteenth centuries, European contact with, and writing about, Buddhism was extensive. Because much of what European writers wrote about the Buddha and Buddhism during this period is considered wrong today, these accounts have largely been forgotten or dismissed. However, they are of great importance for understanding the evolution of our view of the Buddha. This volume, then, is a sourcebook of this fascinating literature. Although it deals only with the figure of the Buddha and not with Buddhism more generally, the available literature is vast, and what is provided here is merely a sampling. It is an anthology of European writings about the Buddha, beginning with Clement of Alexandria around 200 and ending with Eugène Burnouf in 1844.

The descriptions of the Buddha presented here are diverse. European authors gleaned their knowledge about the Buddha from a number of Buddhist lands, in a variety of settings, with a range of linguistic skills, and over the course of several centuries. A Jesuit missionary traveling back to France with a Thai delegation to the court of Louis XIV spends months at sea with a Buddhist monk and is able to ask him many questions. A Russian ship captain is held captive for three years in Japan and seeks to learn what he can from his jailers. An Italian merchant in the employ of a Mongol khan reports what he saw and heard in his travels. A Roman Catholic priest in China dresses like a Confucian gentleman and learns to disparage the Buddha. British army officers try to decipher the monuments, inscriptions, and statues they encounter in their surveys of India. An Italian missionary in Tibet lives in a Buddhist monastery to learn about the lawgiver of the Tibetans. An amateur scholar in England who never traveled to Asia reads the reports from such sources and concocts strange theories about the origins of religion.

Despite the long period of time covered in these pages, and the geographical diversity of both the origins of the authors and the places they visited, a number of shared images and themes can be found among many of the selections. This is due in part to the fact that many of the accounts of the Buddha reproduced here were drawn from previous European accounts. In some cases, entire passages would be copied, without attribution. In other cases, elements from a number of previous sources would be combined in creative ways. And in yet other cases, embellishments would be added to previous narratives.

Sometimes an element from a traditional biography of the Buddha would take on a life of its own in the European accounts. We might consider, for example, the birth of the Buddha. According to many Buddhist sources, the Buddha did not enter the world by passing through the birth canal but instead emerged from his mother's right side, without causing her the slightest discomfort or leaving a wound. It is also said that the Buddha's mother died seven days after his birth. When the reason for her death is given, it is said that another child may not enter the womb where the future Buddha has resided. In traditional sources, no causal connection is made between the Buddha's birth and his mother's death beyond this rather dubious explanation, an explanation of which early European writers were unaware. But these writers did know that the Buddha had emerged from his mother's side and that she had died shortly thereafter. Based on these two "facts," we find all manner of stories in European accounts of the Buddha's birth, one building on the other. And so the Buddha's mother died in childbirth. She not only died, but the infant Buddha killed her. How did he do so? He used his little teeth to gnaw his way through her womb and out through her right side. In later years, he was so burdened by the sin of matricide that he left the palace in which he lived as a prince and went off to do penance in the mountains, returning to teach idolatry to the world.

According to a Chinese legend, long ago the emperor had a dream of a golden flying man. When he told his ministers about the dream, he was informed that he had dreamed of a sage from the West called the Buddha. The emperor sent a delegation in search of this sage, and it returned with a statue of the Buddha and a book of his teachings. This story was known even to Marco Polo and was later learned by the early Jesuit missionaries to China. From this account, the Buddha was charged with introducing idolatry into China.

In some cases, it is difficult to trace these creative embellishments to their source. In other cases, the source is clear. Engelbert Kaempfer's account of Buddhism in Japan, published in 1727, made its way almost immediately into Bernard Picart's *Cérémonies et coutumes religieuses de tous les peuples du monde*, which in turn was an important source for Denis Diderot and Jean le Rond d'Alembert's *Encyclopédie, ou Dictionnaire raisonné des sciences, des artes et des métiers*, published in twenty-eight volumes beginning in 1751. To illustrate how elements of the biography of the Buddha—as told by Europeans—have evolved, I have included a number of selections in which repetitions and variations of a single incident occur. Readers will find various renditions of Prince Siddhārtha's decision to leave his palace and go out in search of enlightenment. They will find echoes of the Buddhist doctrine of *upāya*, that the Buddha taught different things to different people; for some, but not all, European writers, this is evidence of the Buddha's duplicity. And they will even find European versions of the famous statement "Thus did I hear," which traditionally begins Buddhist sutras, rendered as "He himself said," "It is thus I have learned," and "Thus it is in the book."

A number of important accounts of the life of the Buddha by Europeans remained unread for centuries. *The Temporal and Spiritual Conquest of Ceylon* by the Portuguese priest Fernaõ de Queyroz was completed in 1687 but not published until 1916. It contained not only Father Queyroz's account of the Buddha from Ceylon (which Queyroz never visited) but also the longest biography of the Buddha to be produced by a European writer during the seventeenth century, that of Queyroz's compatriot and fellow Jesuit Tomás Pereira, who served at the court of the Kangxi Emperor in Beijing. The most learned of European accounts of the Buddha from Tibetan sources was written by the Italian Jesuit Ippolito Desideri. However, because his works, like those of so many Jesuits, were placed on the Vatican's index of prohibited books, it would not come to light until the late nineteenth century.

This book is divided into five chapters chronologically, with the selections ordered by the publication date of the work in which they appear. For those selections whose publication followed their composition by an extended period of time, ordering is based on their estimated date of composition. The first chapter covers the long period from 200 to 1500 CE, that is, the period from what is regarded as the first reference to the Buddha in Western literature, that of Clement of Alexandria, to the first encounters of Christian missionaries and emissaries with Buddhism at the court of the Great Khan in China. From that point, the next three chapters deal with a single century, the sixteenth, seventeenth, and eighteenth. The final chapter begins in 1801 and ends with the publication of Eugène Burnouf's *Introduction à l'histoire du Buddhisme indien* in 1844. Each selection begins with a headnote that I have composed to provide basic information about the author as well as a brief comment on the selection. There is a great deal that could be said about each of the selections, but I have intentionally limited my comments in order to allow readers to form their own conclusions about these largely forgotten portraits of the Buddha.

Although I often signal the traditional referent for a garbled or fanciful episode in the Buddha's life, I have intentionally not provided here the standard Buddhist biography of the Buddha. There are several reasons for this. First, there is no single biography of the Buddha accepted across Asia and across the more than two millennia of Buddhist history. The many biographies of the Buddha share a great many elements, but they also differ, both over time and across the continent of Asia. Thus, the earliest biographical details occur piecemeal in various discourses of the Buddha, discourses that he may or may not have delivered; the teachings of the Buddha were not committed to writing until some four centuries after his death. The first biographies of the Buddha began to develop during the first centuries of the Common Era. Perhaps the most famous of the Sanskrit biographies, the *Buddhacarita*, or "Deeds of the Buddha," by Aśvaghoṣa, dates from the first half of the second century CE. The most famous of the Pāli biographies, the *Nidānakathā*, "Account of Origins," dates from the fifth century CE. Biographies of the Buddha became increasingly elaborate over time. And as Buddhism spread across Asia, local elements would sometimes be introduced, most often in the form of a visitation by the Buddha to that locale, where he left his footprints in stone.

A second reason not to include a standard Buddhist biography of the Buddha is to avoid the conclusion that there is a canonical norm in the Buddhist tradition, with the various European versions of his life seen simply as so many deviations, distortions, and perversions. Such deviations, distortions, and perversions—sometimes inadvertent, sometimes clearly willful—certainly occur in the chapters that follow. However, the readings herein provide an opportunity to ask whether there is a true Buddha of Asia and a false Buddha of Europe, or whether the Buddha, then and now, here and there, is the product of a more complex and interesting process of influence. Thus, a third reason for not providing a standard Buddhist biography is to allow the reader to examine the many biographies of the Buddha, and how they interact, one with the other. There are a host of questions and themes in these pages. I explored a small number of them in *From Stone to Flesh: A Short History of the Buddha*. In that study, however, I was able to consider only a few of the figures who are represented in this sourcebook. Students of Buddhism, European history, Asian history, and the history of Christianity will find much to ponder here.

As we consider the words of the European authors, at least two important factors should be kept in mind. The first is the level of their knowledge. Many travelers to Asia did not understand the languages they encountered and so had to rely on translators, themselves of varying levels of linguistic skill, even when we set aside the issue of translating the categories and concepts of one religion into another. Other travelers learned the languages of Asia to varying degrees, with some learning to speak the language but not to read the complicated scripts. Others read Buddhist texts with the help of native speakers (often Christian converts); still others relied on digests of those texts prepared by their informants. A vital change took place in the nineteenth century, when European philologists, many of whom had never traveled to Asia, gained the ability to read Buddhist texts, with general accuracy, on their own. It is important, however, not to assume that this development indicates a relentless march of scholarly progress. Even in the sixteenth century, Jesuit missionaries in Japan were reading the *Lotus Sūtra* in Chinese—the work would not be translated into a European language until Burnouf's French rendering of 1852. And yet other authors, many of whom are represented here, never attempted to learn a Buddhist language or read a Buddhist text, instead compiling their biographies of the Buddha from a variety of published sources in European languages.

The second factor to consider is that of motivation. Apart from two important Muslim works, the authors of the selections were all at least nominally Christian, and a significant number were ordained clergy, either Roman Catholic or Protestant (including Anglicans, Methodists, Presbyterians, and Dutch Reformed).

During most of the period covered in this volume, Europeans divided the world into four nations (in the sense of peoples): Christians, Jews, Mahometans, and Idolaters (also called Pagans and Heathens). For Christians, Jews and Muslims had had the opportunity to accept the True Faith and failed to do so. But idolaters generally had not. They were surely benighted, but their ignorance was not willful, and so they were also candidates for conversion. Hence, many of those who first came into contact with Buddhism were missionaries, who sought to understand Buddhism (a term that they did not use until the nineteenth century) in order to refute it. This is an obvious reason for the negative portrayals of the Buddha in so much of the writing from this period. The animosity of the missionaries, especially the Catholics, was deepened by what they regarded as the work of the Devil. When they visited Buddhist monasteries, they saw monks with shaven heads, chanting what sounded like prayers, carrying rosaries, and burning incense: a perverse mirror image of themselves. When they asked about the idol that these monks worshipped, they were told that he had descended from heaven to bring salvation to the world. Thus, what they encountered was not merely a human error that could be corrected through conversion; there was something demonic about it.

During this period, sometimes called the Age of Discovery, there was also a motivation among many to catalog as much information about the world and its peoples as possible. The religious practices of the peoples of far-off places (still regarded variously as idolaters, pagans, and heathens) were duly collected. A number of the selections in the pages that follow fall into this more ethnographic category. With the French Enlightenment and its aftermath came a particular fascination with Asia, especially with China as the site of the principled government of the mandarins, and with India as the site of the spirit. Buddhism did not fare particularly well at this time. The mandarins extolled by the French were Confucians who had little respect for Buddhism. And in India, Buddhism was long dead, with the Buddha only vaguely recalled as the ninth incarnation of the Hindu god Vishnu. By the late eighteenth century, the European enthusiasm for things Asian was both deepened and complicated by the newfound ability to read Asian texts in the original languages, including Chinese and Sanskrit.

It is at this point that our story ends, rather precisely, in the year 1844. The myriad idols coalesced into a single figure, who then became a historical figure, a founder of a religion, and a superstition became a philosophy. This new Buddha would be born largely from texts. The historical Buddha had been born in the fifth century BCE, in what is today southern Nepal. Buddhist monks carried texts and images to much of Asia over the next millennium and a half; but by the time that Vasco da Gama arrived in India in 1498, Buddhism had all but disappeared there. The reasons for this disappearance were complex (among many others: the invasion of northern India by Muslim armies), but its consequences were profound. During the colonial period, without Buddhists living in India to uphold their tradition, Buddhism, and especially what would come to be called "original Buddhism" or "primitive Buddhism"—that is, the teachings of the Buddha himself—could become the domain of European and, later, American and Japanese scholars. They would create a Buddha who was unknown in Asia, a Buddha who may never have existed there before the late nineteenth century. Just as European scholars went on a quest for the historical Jesus, there was a quest for the historical Buddha, and European orientalists felt they found him. This was the human and humane Buddha that Burnouf described in 1844, a Buddha who has remained largely unchanged in the Western imagination since then.

The authors represented in this book thus fall into a number of categories, including travelers, missionaries, compilers, traders (both private, like Marco Polo, and corporate, like the employees of the Dutch East India Company and the British East India Company), colonial officials, scholars, and eccentrics. These categories are not mutually exclusive. Missionaries, obviously, were also travelers. A number of the officers of the British East India Company were both scholars and colonial officials (although India did not formally become a British colony until 1858). Some travelers, such as François Valentijn, were missionaries early in life and compilers when they returned home. And any number of the writers might, at least by modern standards, be considered eccentric. Lieutenant (and later Captain) Francis Wilford of the East India Company detected names of Egyptian pharaohs in Hindu texts. The Flemish Jesuit Nicolas Trigault committed suicide when the Vatican rejected the term he had recommended as the official Chinese translation of *God*.

OVERVIEW OF THE CHAPTERS

The historical period covered by the first chapter, from 200 CE to 1500 CE, is the longest in the book. Clement of Alexandria never traveled to Asia, but drew his brief comments about the Buddha from the writings of Megasthenes (ca. 350–290 BCE), who had visited the Punjab and described Indian culture in his book *Indica*. References to the Buddha were quite rare in Western writings for centuries after Clement.

To provide some sense of how Muslims viewed the Buddha, selections from two Muslim works are provided here, including the one that served as the basis of perhaps the most influential Christian depiction of the Buddha during this period. It is the tale *Barlaam and Josaphat*, one of the most popular and widely translated saints' tales of the Middle Ages. The story of a prince who renounces the world against his father's wishes, it is clearly drawn from the life of the Buddha; the name of the prince, Josaphat, is derived from the Sanskrit word *bodhisattva*, a standard term for the Buddha in the years before his enlightenment. However, although Barlaam and Josaphat were each commemorated with a saint's day and their story was known across Europe, their connection to the life of the Buddha was not widely recognized until the middle of the nineteenth century.

At the end of the period that chapter 1 recounts, Europeans began to travel to Asia. Some, like Marco Polo, were traders. Others, like King Het'um of Armenia, went to seek peace with the Mongol khan. The earliest Roman Catholic missions to China also began then. They would increase in the following century.

Chapter 2 covers the period from 1501 to 1600. Perhaps the most significant event of this century was the visit of the Spanish Jesuit Francis Xavier to Japan. He arrived in 1549, having been led to believe by a Japanese convert to Roman Catholicism that the Japanese were monotheists. He thus arrived with high hopes for his mission. Those hopes were soon dashed, and so we find in the writings of this future saint disparaging comments about the Buddha, or Xaca, as he called him, setting a tone that would resonate within the Society of Jesus for centuries. Yet details about the Asian idol were few during this period, with the accounts of priests who visited China largely limited to descriptions of statues and temples. Also from this time, we find the works of the first compilers, those who did not travel to Asia but collected the accounts of others, often in creative ways. Chapter 2 includes selections from such Portuguese works as *Discurso de la navegación que los Portugueses hacen a los Reinos y Provincias de Oriente* by Bernardino de Escalante and *Historia de las cosas mas notables de la China* by Juan Gonzáles de Mendoza.

The period from 1601 to 1700, the scope of chapter 3, was something of a golden age for the Roman Catholic missions to Asia, best measured, perhaps, not by the number of converts but by all the things the missionaries said about the Buddha. They were not the only Europeans writing about the Buddha, however. Hence we find in this chapter a selection from Samuel Purchas, one of the most famous of the compilers. Unlike his Portuguese predecessors, he was not simply chronicling the travels of his countrymen. His intentions were grander. In 1613, he published his four-volume work, *Purchas his Pilgrimage; or, Relations of the World and the Religions Observed in All Ages and Places discovered, from the Creation unto this Present.*

There would be other works by other authors in this genre. Traders continued to travel to Asia, bringing back stories of the idol they encountered there. And so we have the account of the French diamond merchant Jean-Baptiste Tavernier. Robert Knox was shipwrecked off the coast of Sri Lanka and spent nineteen years in captivity there. His account, which contains several passages on the idol "Buddhu," was an inspiration for *Robinson Crusoe*. But the majority of the selections here are from Roman Catholic missionaries, especially Jesuits, in two places: China and Siam. These priests learned enough of the local languages to begin to compile stories—whether they were histories or legends is unclear—of the idol known by many names. For example, Matteo Ricci arrived in Macao in 1582. By 1603, his Chinese was good enough that he could publish a catechism in the language, entitled *The True Doctrine of the Lord of Heaven* (*Tianzhu shiyi*). Ricci disparaged the Buddha in this and other works.

Also included in this chapter is the most detailed European biography of the Buddha to date, one compiled by the Portuguese Jesuit Tomás Pereira, who served at the court of the Kangxi Emperor of China. It was written at the request of another Portuguese Jesuit, Fernaõ de Queyroz, who was based in Goa. Father Pereira dutifully recounts the events of the Buddha's life, but makes little attempt to conceal his contempt for the idol Fo. Father Queyroz included Pereira's account in his *The Temporal and Spiritual Conquest of Ceylon*, a work completed in 1687 but not published until 1916.

Louis XIV sent several delegations to Thailand. Chapter 3 contains accounts from those missions, by the diplomats who led them as well as the Jesuits who accompanied the embassies. We find in their accounts a strange and consistent fascination with the Buddha's evil cousin, Devadatta. In one case, the story of his life is longer than that given for the Buddha, whom the French call Sommonacodom. Devadatta attempted to assassinate the Buddha on three different occasions, and suffered a horrible fate for his sins—a fate that both the French and their Thai hosts regarded as uncannily similar to that of the God worshipped by the Europeans.

This chapter ends with the long and influential account of the Buddha found in the history of Japan by the German physician Engelbert Kaempfer, who spent 1690–92 in Japan in the employ of the Dutch East India Company. Kaempfer would postulate that the different idols known by different names were the same person, and proposed two views that would prove influential into the nineteenth century: the African hypothesis and the two-buddha theory.

Chapter 4, which covers the century from 1701 to 1800, begins with the work of the remarkable Jesuit missionary to Tibet, Ippolito Desideri. Although he and other members of the Society of Jesus appear in this chapter, the influence of the Jesuits was sharply curtailed during the eighteenth century. The society was officially suppressed by Pope Clement XIV in 1773, but its influence had waned considerably since Clement XI ruled against it in the Chinese Rites Controversy of 1715. Instead, we see the influence of the French Enlightenment on the European portrayal of the Buddha at this time. That portrayal is not immediately positive (with the notable exception of Voltaire), but for the first time it begins to appear with some consistency in works that are not single-mindedly Christian in their motivations. Especially important works in this regard are Picart's *Cérémonies et coutumes religieuses de tous les peuples du monde*, published in Amsterdam between 1723 and 1743 in nine volumes, and Diderot and d'Alembert's *Encyclopédie*, published in twenty-eight volumes beginning in 1751. We also have here the accounts of travelers, like Peter Simon Pallas, who explored Russia for Catherine the Great, and the French astronomer Guillaume le Gentil, who wrote about the Buddha while living in India, awaiting the return of Venus to the heavens.

In the last section of this chapter, the English begin to play a major role in the representation of the Buddha. They had been trading in India since the early seventeenth century, but it was not until 1757 that they had driven out the Dutch and the French, and defeated local rulers, bringing most of the subcontinent under their control. Their purposes were largely mercenary—Christian missions were not allowed until 1815—and the officers of the East India Company studied ancient Indian culture out of a combination of genuine interest and boredom. Buddhism had long since disappeared from India as an active religious presence, and so the British were left only with its remnants, in the form of statues, architectural monuments, and inscriptions. They learned from their Hindu interlocutors that the Buddha was the ninth incarnation of the Hindu god Vishnu, but they also found that the Brahmins sometimes spoke of the Buddha scornfully. This anomaly proved fascinating to a number of British officers, who proposed a range of theories to explain it.

The final chapter covers the period from 1801 to 1844. By this time, the Buddha had become a figure of particular fascination, especially among the various officers of the East India Company, whose range now extended beyond India. Learned journals, such as *Asiatick Researches*, had been established and were widely read in

Europe; essays debating the various theories about the identity of the Buddha also appeared in such publications as the *Edinburgh Review* and *Journal des Savants*. There were those who still held that the Buddha came from Africa or that he was in fact the Norse god Odin. Eccentrics like the Anglican cleric and biblical scholar George Stanley Faber continued to publish their theories, and clergymen like Robert Fellowes continued to condemn the Buddha. However, over the first decades of the nineteenth century, scholarly consensus began to congeal on three points: the various idols known by various names represented a single figure; that figure was not a myth but a historical personage; that historical personage had been born and died in India. European scholars could draw these conclusions with some confidence by this point, in part because they were gaining the ability to read Buddhist texts in the original languages. No longer were they relying on poorly understood conversations or a digest or paraphrase composed by a Christian convert.

FROM STONE TO FLESH

Yet as we move forward in time through the centuries, we do not discern a relentless linear march of scholarly progress from the past to the present. Nor do we see a blurry image of the Buddha, its defining lines unclear, coming slowly into focus. Indeed, the only thing that could be easily plotted would be the sheer bulk of verbiage about the Buddha, which clearly increases with the passage of time. But this is only the case if we assume that all the various gods and idols with so many names described by Europeans over the centuries referred to the same figure, the Buddha. This is an assumption that our authors did not make until quite late in our story.

As noted above, for most of the years covered in this book, the Buddha was an idol, and an idol known by many names. Travelers to the Kalmyk regions of Russia describe a god named Dschakshimuni. Travelers to China tell of the idol Fohi or Sciequia. A Jesuit in Tibet recounts the story of Sciacciá-Thubbá. The Japanese worship Xaca. The monks of Thailand pay obeisance to Sommona-Codom. In Sri Lanka, they make statues of Buddhu. There are hundreds of such names in the European literature of the period. But for the most part they are garbled variations of just four names and epithets: Buddha; Gotama; Śākyamuni, "the sage of the Śākya clan"; and Samaṇa Gotama, the ascetic Gotama. The Buddha is often referred to as Śākyamuni Buddha in Mahāyāna texts, and thus in the Buddhisms of China, Japan, Korea, Mongolia, and Tibet. He is often referred to as Gotama Buddha or Samaṇa Gotama in Theravāda Buddhism, and hence in Sri Lanka, Thailand, and Burma. With this information, the strange names are easily deciphered. Fo, Fohi, Fôe and so forth seem more difficult to decipher until we learn that in the Tang dynasty, the Chinese character that is today pronounced *fo* was pronounced *budh*.

The identity of these various figures was not clearly stated by a European author until the late seventeenth century. In *China Illustrata*, published in 1667, Athanasius Kircher wrote, "He was an imposter known all over the East. The Indians called him Rama, the Chinese Xe Kian, the Japanese Xaca, and the Turks Chiaga. This deadly monster was born in central India in the place which the Chinese call Tien Truc Gnoc."[2] About twenty years later, in *The Temporal and Spiritual Conquest of Ceylon*, Fernaõ de Queyroz wrote, "And as it has been observed that the Ganezes of Ceylon, the Talpoys of Arracan, Pegu, Siam and other neighbouring Realms, as well as the Lamazes of Tartary agree with the Bonzes of China and Japan in the essentials of their sect and profession, it is easy to understand that the Buddum of Ceylon, the Fô of China, the Xaka of Japan is the same as the Xekia of India, for the word Buddum is only an adapted name, and in Ceylon it means Saint by antonomasia."[3]

Engelbert Kaempfer was in Japan from 1690 to 1692. Before his arrival there, he visited Thailand. His *History of Japan* was published posthumously, in 1727. In his description of Thailand that appears there, we read:

> For *Wistnu* [Vishnu] by which they mean the Deity, having already many hundred thousands of years before assum'd different forms, and visited the World eight different times appear'd the ninth in the person of this Negro, whom for this reason they stile *Prahpuditsau*, that is to say, the Saint of high descent; *Sammana Khutama*, the Man without Passions: *Prah bin Tsjau*, the Saint who is the Lord; or plainly *Prah*, the Saint, or *Budha'* (or *Phutha'* in one syllable, according to their guttural pronunciation, like that of the Hottentots). The Ceylanese call him *Budhum*, the Chinese and Japanese *Sacka*, or *Siaka*, or plainly *Fotoge*, that is, the Idol, and with an honourable Epithet *Si Tsun*, the great Saint.[4]

Despite his correct identification of the various gods of Thailand, Ceylon, China, and Japan, Dr. Kaempfer's statement is not without its problems. We see here reference to "the African hypothesis," put forward by Kaempfer and repeated into the nineteenth century. Unlike the account of Father Queyroz, Kaempfer's book was widely read, and his conclusion about the identity of these various deities was soon repeated in other sources.

Thus, as we seek signs of progress among these sources, we could point to one:

rather late, around 1700, European authors, or at least some of them, came to the conclusion that the idols that their compatriots had seen across Asia over the past two hundred years all represented the same person. But even this claim requires a caveat. When Marco Polo was returning to Venice after his years of service to Kublai Khan, his ship stopped in Sri Lanka. In his account of the island, he says that on the peak of a tall mountain, there are footprints of Sagamoni Borcan. He uses this item of local geography as the occasion for one of the more detailed, and most sympathetic, accounts of the life of the Buddha to appear in European literature. But he does not call the local god Gotama or Gotama Buddha (or some garbled version of these), as the Buddha is known in Sri Lanka. He calls him Sagamoni Borcan, the Mongolian version of Śākyamuni Buddha. And so Marco Polo knew, sometime around 1290, that the idol worshipped in Sri Lanka was the same idol worshipped in Kublai Khan's pleasure dome in Xanadu (Shangdu, the Chinese emperor's summer capital)—something that Queyroz and Kaempfer would declare four centuries later.

Yet there is one significant change that occurred over the course of the long history covered in the pages of this book. It occurred in 1844, and it brings the book to a close.

The British army of the East India Company and the Gurkhas of Nepal had gone to war in 1814. Under the terms of the 1816 treaty, significant Nepalese territories were ceded to the British, and the British were granted the right to post a "resident" at the Nepalese court in Kathmandu. A member of that delegation and later holder of the position of British Resident was Brian Houghton Hodgson, who arrived in Kathmandu in 1821. With very little to do, Hodgson began to study the local culture; he would eventually make important contributions to Himalayan zoology, ornithology, botany, and linguistics. He learned that the Newar community in the Kathmandu Valley was Buddhist, and that they possessed Buddhist scriptures in Sanskrit. Up until this point, the Buddhist texts known to Europeans were in Chinese, Tibetan, Mongolian, and Pāli. Hodgson gathered many of the texts, had copies made, and offered them to various European learned societies. His offer arrived in the latter days of the Sanskrit craze in Paris; Hodgson would eventually send 147 Sanskrit Buddhist texts there, with the first dispatch of twenty-four arriving on or about April 20, 1837. They were reviewed by two scholars, one of whom was Eugène Burnouf, recently appointed to the chair of Sanskrit at the Collège de France.

Burnouf was immediately attracted to the *Lotus Sūtra*, and soon had the entire text translated into French. He concluded, however, that a European audience would not be able to understand the text without an introduction to Buddhist scholarship. Thus, in 1844, he published the modestly titled *Introduction à l'histoire du Buddhisme indien*. Despite its being 647 pages long, Burnouf envisioned the work as only the first volume of a multivolume study, a project never completed because of his untimely death. As the first European monograph devoted entirely to Buddhism, the *Introduction* was a highly influential work. The 1857 edition of *Chambers's Information for the People* describes it as "the beginning of anything like correct information on the subject among the western nations," noting—contrary to what appears in the pages of the present volume—that "until within the last fourteen years [since 1844], nothing was known in Europe respecting the nature and origin of this world-religion, beyond the vaguest notions and conjectures."[5]

But Burnouf was not the only European able to read Buddhist texts in their original languages. The German-Russian Isaak Jakob Schmidt (1779–1847) was born in Amsterdam, and served as a Moravian missionary in the Kalmyk region of Russia that Peter Simon Pallas described (see chapter 4). Schmidt learned both Tibetan and Mongolian, and in 1837 published a Tibetan-to-German rendering of the *Diamond Sūtra*—the first Buddhist text to be translated in full and with some accuracy into a European language. George Turnour, who appears in chapter 5, was born in Sri Lanka. The son of a British civil servant, after being educated in England, Turnour returned to his birthplace, where he spent most of his brief career studying Sinhala and Pāli literature and publishing important articles on the chronology of the life of the Buddha.

In searching for the home of the Magyar people, the itinerant Transylvanian scholar Alexander Csoma de Kőrös eventually reached Ladakh, where he studied Tibetan texts from 1827 to 1831 before proceeding to Calcutta (now spelled Kolkata). He provided the first detailed studies of the Tibetan Buddhist canon, including an essay from 1839 entitled "Notices on the Life of Shakya, Extracted from the Tibetan Authorities," a selection from which appears in chapter 5.

Prior to Burnouf's *Introduction*, the most substantial European study of Buddhism was the *Foe koue ki* by the great French Sinologist Jean-Pierre Abel-Rémusat. In 1814, at the age of twenty-six, he had been appointed to the new chair in Chinese at the Collège de France. Abel-Rémusat's translation of the *Record of Buddhist Kingdoms* (*Foguo ji*), the travel journal of the Chinese monk Faxian (ca. 337–ca. 422) excerpted in chapter 5, provides an invaluable description of Buddhism in India and Sri Lanka at the beginning of the fifth century. The Chinese text is relatively short, but Abel-Rémusat provided detailed notes, in which he sought to identify and explain the many Buddhist persons, places, and doctrines that occur in Faxian's work. Much of the life of the Buddha appears here, but out of chronological order, organized instead in connection with the places that Faxian visited. Abel-Rémusat died at the age of forty-three in the cholera epidemic of 1832, when his translation project was only half finished. Julius Heinrich Klaproth, who also appears in chapter 5, took over the project until his own death in 1835. It was completed by Ernest-Augustin Xavier Clerc de Landresse (1800–1862) and published in 1836.

And so, beginning in the 1830s, a new element was added to the European-language landscape of the Buddha: biographies that were direct translations (or in some cases straightforward paraphrases) of Buddhist texts, texts in Sanskrit, Pāli, Chinese, Tibetan, and Mongolian. Some forty percent of Burnouf's *Introduction to the History of Indian Buddhism*, for example, consists of his translations of a wide range of texts received from Brian Hodgson.

Compared with the many authors whose writings appear in the pages that follow, Burnouf differed in several ways. First, he never traveled to Asia, spending his entire life in France, with brief visits to Germany and England. Yet there are other authors here who never traveled to Asia; Samuel Purchas, for example. Second, Burnouf read Buddhist texts in the original. Again, this does not make him unique. The Jesuit missionary to the Qing court, Tomás Pereira, read a long biography of the Buddha in Chinese. Third, Burnouf was not a Christian missionary; he told his student Friedrich Max Müller that he hated the Jesuits. Again, other writers about Buddhism, such as the French astronomer Guillaume le Gentil, were not Christian missionaries either. Thus, although Burnouf was not unique in any of these three categories individually, he (and Abel-Rémusat) was unique in belonging to all three: Burnouf wrote about the Buddha, but he never left Europe, he could read Buddhist texts in the original, and he was not a missionary. These three factors are of varying significance taken alone. But taken together, they would prove crucial in the creation of the Buddha as we know him today.

Key terms for Burnouf are *human* and *humanity*. In his inaugural lecture at the Collège de France, he declared that Sanskrit literature in general was "a page from the origins of the world, of the primitive history of the human spirit,"[6] to be deciphered by European scholars. On the first page of the *Introduction to the History of Indian Buddhism*, he proclaims, "The present volume is dedicated in its entirety to put in relief the purely human character of Buddhism." For him, the most ancient Buddhism, the Buddhism of the Buddha, not the Buddha found in Asia in the nineteenth century, was a human Buddhism that consisted simply and almost entirely of rules of morality, embodied in the person of the Buddha. As he wrote, "He lived, he taught, and he died as a philosopher; and his humanity remained a fact so incontestably recognized by all that the compilers of legends to whom miracles cost so little did not even have the thought of making him a god after his death."[7] But, of course, the Buddha had been made into a god, and in the centuries before Burnouf's time, Europeans saw idols of this god being worshipped all over Asia. Burnouf thus saw his task as twofold: to return the Buddha to India and to return the Buddha to humanity.

However, although Burnouf declares that Buddhism is "a completely Indian fact," he also distinguishes the Buddha from other Indians, providing him with a humanity that transcends his place of origin. And in the process, Burnouf disparages the Buddha's followers: "This respect for human truth in Buddhism, which prevented the disciples of Śākya from transforming the man into God, is quite remarkable for a people like the Indians, among whom mythology has so easily taken the place of history."[8] This passage becomes more disquieting when he addresses the topic more openly in his private correspondence. On May 15, 1836, he wrote to thank Hodgson for the Sanskrit texts he had sent to Paris from Kathmandu: "It is necessary to remove from the apathy, from the superstition, from the avarice of the Orientals, the literary treasures they have saved from the shipwreck of time; it is necessary to transport them to Europe, where there is less fire, less upheaval, less religious hatred, where there are public repositories open to receive this precious debris as the property, I will not say of citizens of nations, but belonging to all of humanity."[9] For Burnouf, the Buddha was a figure of universal significance, a human figure belonging to all humanity—but a humanity whose custodians are Europeans. In the process, the Buddha turned from an idol worshipped by pagans into the founder of a religion respected around the world.

Ovid tells the story of Pygmalion, a sculptor so skilled that he falls in love with the statue of a beautiful woman he has carved. He prays to the goddess Venus, who brings the statue to life. Pygmalion and the statue marry and have a family.

The Buddha was also a statue. Europeans, their eyes trained to see beauty in Greek statues, statues like those carved by Pygmalion, found the statue of the Buddha to be not beautiful but monstrous. Then Burnouf, with the aid of the goddess Philology, turned the Buddha from a monster into a man. But the Buddha is always his image, ever his idol. We cannot imagine him without the things that made him freakish to European eyes centuries ago: the bump on his head, the tightly curled hair that never needs to be cut. Yet today, those same features look beautiful to us, not because the Buddha has turned from a demon into a god, but because Burnouf made him human. As he wrote, "It is enough to believe that the Buddha was a man who reached a degree of intelligence and of virtue that each must take as the exemplar for his life."[10] The Buddha was turned from stone into flesh.

CHAPTER ONE

FROM 200 TO 1500

♦ ST. CLEMENT OF ALEXANDRIA (D. 215 CE)

The earliest reference to the Buddha in European literature is found in the works of Clement of Alexandria, the Greek theologian and church father. Born circa 150 CE, he traveled from Greece to Alexandria around 180, where he would eventually become head of its catechetical school. His brief reference to the Buddha appears in his Stromateis (Miscellanies). *In this work, he argues that Jewish wisdom is superior to Greek philosophy, in part because philosophy came to Greece from barbarians, beginning with the Egyptians. He also mentions the Chaldeans in Assyria, the Druids in Gaul, the Magi in Persia, and the gymnosophists or "naked philosophers" in India.*

The precise identity of these Indian sarmanae *(also called* samanaeans*) remains a question. The term seems to derive from the Sanskrit term* śramaṇa, *often translated as "ascetic" or "mendicant," and appears in such ancient sources as the edicts of the emperor Aśoka in conjunction with the term* Brahmin *(*brāhmaṇa*). Taken together, the two terms refer to the priests and mendicants to be supported by a king, with* Brahmin *connoting those that we would today call Hindus, and* śramaṇa *connoting various non-Hindu ascetics, including Buddhist monks.*

We do not know the source of St. Clement's information. The "golden-mouthed" orator Dio Chrysostom, who died circa 120 CE, reports the presence of Indians in Alexandria, and Clement's own teacher Pantaenus is said to have traveled to India. However, the most likely source is Megasthenes, the fourth-century-BCE Greek scholar who served as ambassador to the court of the Indian emperor Candragupta Maurya (the grandfather of Aśoka) and provided a detailed account of the country in his Indica, a work that Clement cites verbatim in the passage below. It is noteworthy, however, that Megasthenes does not mention the Buddhists by name in his discussion of the religion of India.

All this makes this famous first reference in the passage below both intriguing and puzzling. The Buddhists were decidedly not "naked philosophers." In several Buddhist texts, those ascetics who go naked are mocked for their immodesty. It seems that Clement may be describing the Jains, whose "sky-clad" sect did go naked. Yet the name of the Buddha is clearly mentioned. Later in the text, Clement says that the gymnosophists "honor a kind of pyramid under which they believe the bones of some god are resting." This seems to be a Buddhist stupa, the reliquaries in which the cremated remains of the Buddha were enshrined.

––––––

The Indian gymnosophists are also in the number, and the other barbarian philosophers. And of these there are two classes, some of them called Sarmanae, and others Brahmins. And those of the Sarmanae who are called Hylobii "neither inhabit cities, nor have roofs over them, but are clothed in the bark of trees, feed on nuts, and drink water in their hands. Like those called Encratites in the present day, they know not marriage nor begetting of children." Some, too, of the Indians obey the precepts of Boutta; whom, on account of his extraordinary sanctity, they have raised to divine honours.[1]

◆   ST. JEROME (CA. 347–420)

St. Jerome, often depicted in Renaissance paintings with his pet lion, is best known for translating the Bible into Latin. In 393, in a work entitled Adversus Jovinianum (Against Jovinian), he condemned the heresies of Jovinian, a monk who came to reject asceticism. Jovinian had argued that married women and widows, once they had been baptized, were of equal merit to virgins; he also denied the perpetual virginity of Mary. This led Jerome into a long discourse on virginity, where the passage below appears (Adversus Jovinianum, I.42). Here, he alludes to the traditional story that the Buddha emerged from his mother's right side, rather than by the usual route in being born. Buddhist texts do not say, however, that the Buddha's mother, Queen Māyā, was a virgin.

Yet her supposed virginity was immortalized by Jerome in the passage below. It appears the Buddha's mother also found her way, via Jerome's work, into Geoffrey Chaucer's The Canterbury Tales, *although she is not mentioned by name there. In the prologue to the* Wife of Bath's Tale, *Chaucer explains that Jankyn, the young clerk who was the last husband of the Wife of Bath, enjoyed reading Jerome's* Against Jovinian *(or, in Chaucer's Middle English, "agayn jovinian"), the work in which the Buddha's mother is listed: "He hadde a book that gladly, nyght and day / For his desport he wolde rede always" (669–70). It was a book that extolled the virtues of virginity: "And every nyght and day was his custume / Whan he hadde leyser and vacacioun / From oother worldly occupacioun / To reden on this book of wikked wyves. / He knew of hem mo legendes and lyves / Than been of goode wyves in the bible" (682–87). This book, "bounden in o volume," included a variety of Latin works, including one by "A cardinal, that highte seint jerome, / That made a book agayn jovinian" (674–75).*

Here is the passage from Jerome.

———

To come to the Gymnosophists of India, the opinion is authoritatively handed down that Budda, the founder of their religion, had his birth through the side of a virgin. And we need not wonder at this in the case of Barbarians when cultured Greece supposed that Minerva at her birth sprang from the head of Jove, and Father Bacchus from his thigh.[2]

✦ SOCRATES OF CONSTANTINOPLE (B. CA. 380)

One of the chief rivals of Christianity in its early history was Manichaeism, the religion derived from the teachings of the Babylonian prophet Mani (ca. 216–276), who taught that light and darkness, good and evil, are in constant struggle. Mani described himself as a follower of Jesus, and according to some sources, claimed at different times to be the reincarnation of the Buddha, Krishna, and Zoroaster; he is said to have studied in Afghanistan, where Buddhism flourished during this period. He also claimed to be a reincarnation of Jesus, and was thus the target of the fathers of the church. In these polemics, one "Buddas" is sometimes mentioned, a name that may derive from Buddha.

In the fourth century, St. Cyril of Jerusalem provided an unflattering biography of Mani, explaining that there had been a Saracen (by which he likely meant a pagan from Arabia) named Scythianus, neither a Jew nor a Christian, who went to Alexan-

dria and imitated the life of Aristotle. He intended to go to Judea, but God smote him with a deadly disease. Scythianus had a disciple named Terebinthus who spread the errors of his teacher in Judea, but was driven out. Terebinthus then went to Persia, but fearing that word of his humiliation in Judea may have spread there, he changed his name to Buddas. He lived with a widow there until God cast him from a precipice. The widow inherited his money, which she used to buy a slave boy named Cubricus. When the widow died, the slave boy changed his name to Manes (Mani). By the fifth century, the story had been expanded to include references to reincarnation, a central doctrine of Buddhism, and one that was rejected by the church.

What follows is the biographical passage from the Historia Ecclesiastica *of Socrates of Constantinople.*

———

A Saracen named Scythian married a captive from the Upper Thebes. On her account he dwelt in Egypt, and having versed himself in the learning of the Egyptians, he subtly introduced the theory of Empedocles and Pythagoras among the doctrines of the Christian faith. Asserting that there were two natures, a good and an evil one, he termed, as Empedocles had done, the latter Discord, and the former Friendship. Of this Scythian, Buddas, who had been previously called Terebinthus, became a disciple; and he having proceeded to Babylon, which the Persians inhabit, made many extravagant statements respecting himself, declaring that he was born of a virgin, and brought up in the mountains. The same man afterwards composed four books, one he entitled *The Mysteries*, another *The Gospel*, a third *The Treasure*, and the fourth *Heads* [*Summaries*]; but pretending to perform some mystic rites, he was hurled down a precipice by a spirit, and so perished. A certain woman at whose house he had lodged buried him, and taking possession of his property, bought a boy about seven years old whose name was Cubricus: this lad she enfranchised, and having given him a liberal education, she soon after died, leaving him all that belonged to Terebinthus, including the books he had written on the principles inculcated by Scythian. Cubricus, the freedman, taking these things with him and having withdrawn into the regions of Persia, changed his name, calling himself Manes; and disseminated the books of Buddas or Terebinthus among his deluded followers as his own. Now the contents of these treatises apparently agree with Christianity in expression, but are pagan in sentiment: for Manichæus being an atheist, incited his disciples to acknowledge a plurality of gods, and taught them to worship the sun. He also introduced the doctrine of Fate, denying human free-will; and affirmed a transmutation of bodies, clearly following the opinions of Empedocles, Pythagoras, and the Egyptians.[3]

After late antiquity, the first version of the life of the Buddha to reach Europe came, like so many other important works, from the Islamic world. From Arabic sources, we learn that in Baghdad in the second century of the Hijra, that is, in the late eighth or early ninth century, a book called Kitāb Bilawhar wa Būdāsf, *the "Book of Bilawhar and Būdāsf," was translated from Middle Persian (Pehlevi) into Arabic. It tells the story of a king who is a persecutor of ascetics and wishes to save his son from asceticism. The Buddhist elements are clear to anyone who has read the famous story of Prince Siddhārtha's chariot rides outside the city, during which he encounters an old man, a sick man, a corpse, and an ascetic. The Buddhist provenance of the story is further confirmed by the fact that the Arabic name of the prince,* Būdāsf, *is derived from the Sanskrit* bodhisattva, *the term commonly used in Buddhist texts to describe the Buddha in the years before his enlightenment at the age of thirty-five.*

Bilawhar and Būdāsf does not mention the Prophet Muhammad, and there is only one brief reference to Islam. The narrator calls the ascetic religion persecuted by King Gunaysar and adopted by the king's son Būdāsf simply "the Religion." Both father and son claim to be followers of al-Budd (derived from Buddha*), and debate about how best to follow his teachings, with the prince receiving instruction from an ascetic named Bilawhar, who has come from the island of Sarandib (Sri Lanka). The various Arabic versions begin with the birth of Būdāsf, and their description of the prince's early life and his death is similar to the Buddhist accounts.*

The passage that follows shows the clear influence of Buddhist accounts of Prince Siddhārtha's departure from the palace, his enlightenment under the Bodhi tree, his teaching the dharma to his father, and his passage into nirvana. The passages in italics have been added from another version of the Arabic text.

——

Then God—blessed be His Name!—sent an angel to Būdāsf. The angel waited until he could find him alone, then revealed himself and spoke, standing before Būdāsf. "Happiness, health, and greetings, O you who are man among beasts, a captive among oppressors, virtuous among the corrupt, and wise among ignorant men. I bring you greetings and salvation from the God of creation. I have been sent to warn you and to announce good news, to reveal what is hidden from you about your life in this world and the next, and to show you the beginning, the middle and the end. Receive my counsel and my good news! Break with the world! Distance yourself from its pleasures! Renounce ephemeral royal succession and earthly power that does not endure and that ends in signs and regrets! Seek the royalty that never ends and the repose that never changes! Be truthful and virtuous! You will be this world's guide."

Būḏāsf rejoiced at the angel's words. He fell prostrate before him, confident in his words, and said: "I obey God's commandment. He is Powerful and Great, and I understand His will and am ready to follow it. Command me as you will. I praise you and I thank He who sent you to me. For He has been gracious and merciful to me, and He has not abandoned me among my enemies. I am ready for whatever you bring me."

The angel responded, "I will come to you in a few days and I will ask you to leave. Prepare for your departure, purify your heart and your soul! But do not let anyone learn about what you are doing."

Būḏāsf prepared then and did not tell anyone of the angel's prediction. He waited several days.

Finally the day of his departure arrived. The angel came in the middle of the night while people were sleeping. He said to Būḏāsf, "Get up and leave, do not tarry."

Būḏāsf left his bed. He did not reveal his secret to anyone except a faithful minister. He went toward the palace door, accompanied by the angel who had come to announce the good news. At the palace door, his squire was waiting on duty, and he told him to bring his horse. As he was about to mount, a young man came and prostrated himself before him saying, "Where are you going, fortunate, noble, and perfect son of the King? You leave us and you leave your kingdom and your country, whereas since your birth, we have not ceased to hope for the days of your reign!"

Būḏāsf said, to reassure him, "You should stay in your country, but I must go where I am sent and do what I have been ordered to do. If you help me, you will have a part in what I go to do."

He mounted his horse and went as far as he should, then he got off his horse and went on foot, leaving his minister to lead the horse. Then Būḏāsf said to him, "Take my horse back to my parents."

The minister began to weep and said, "With what face should I greet your parents? With what eyes should I look at them? By what tortures will they make me die? And you, how will you have the strength to walk and live in hardship, when you are not used to it? How will you endure the solitude, you who have never been alone, even for a single day? How will you bear the fatigue, the hunger, and the thirst? How will you have the strength to sleep in discomfort on the ground in the dust?"

But Būdāsf reassured and consoled him.

Then the horse stopped in front of him and began to kiss his feet. And having been given the power to speak by God, the Powerful and Great, the horse began to speak, "Do not abandon me, take me with you, do not leave me behind! I will never again have any happiness, and I will not allow any other to ride me. If you leave me and do not take me with you, I will go into the desert and live in the place of wild beasts."

To reassure him, Būdāsf said, "Expect only good for yourself! For I will have you taken back and I will send you to the king, recommending to him that he treat both of you, my minister and you, with honor and goodness. And you will not belong to any rider after me."

Then Būdāsf took off the royal vestments he wore and his jewels and gave them to his minister, saying: "Wear my clothes."

Then he gave him the ruby that he had worn on his head, and said to him, "Leave, and take my horse with you. When you arrive at my parents' home, prostrate yourself before them for me. Give the ruby to my father and give him and the Nobles many greetings on my behalf. Tell them that ever since I have understood the difference between the eternal and the ephemeral, and I have desired the eternal and renounced all that will perish. And when I saw clearly the difference between my allies and my enemies, I turned toward my allies."

Then he said to his minister, "When my father sees the ruby, he will rejoice, and when he sees you in my clothes, my cloak, my hat, and my jewels, he will recognize my love and affection for you, and that will prevent him from suspecting you or doing you any ill."

Then the minister turned away, leading his horse and weeping. He presented himself to Būdāsf's parents, and did what Būdāsf had ordered.

As for Būdāsf, he walked north and arrived at a great plain. Raising his eyes, he saw an immense tree beside a spring. It was the largest tree in existence, with the most beautiful branches, and the most savory sweet fruit. An incalculable number of birds were assembled in its branches. The sight of the tree cheered Būdāsf and filled him with happiness. He went toward the tree, and he began to explain the vision and interpret it for himself. He compared the tree to the Good News, the source of Wisdom and Knowledge, to which he would call men, and the birds were the men who would assemble and receive the Religion from him.

As he was standing there, four angels came to him. They walked before him and he followed their footsteps. Then they carried him up into the air. They showed him all things, and he saw them as one sees his face in a mirror. They gave him the

Wisdom and Knowledge necessary to know what to command and what to pro-hibit. Then they brought him back down to earth between the East and the North, and they gave him one of the angels as his companion. He dwelled in the country for some time and acquired considerable knowledge.

Then he returned to Sawilabatt. When his father learned of his arrival, he came to meet him, accompanied by all his Nobles. When they met him, they treated him with honor and respect. Then the people of his country assembled around him, as did his close relatives and his servants. They bowed before him and greeted him. Then he spoke to them and explained the Religion to them in these terms:

"Open your ears and make a place in your hearts to hear the Wisdom of God, which is the light of the soul. Strengthen yourselves with the Knowledge that shows the right path. Wake your intelligence and understand the difference between the true and the false, the right path and the lost way. Know that this religion is the Religion of God, that he sent to the tongues of his Messengers and Prophets—may they be blessed!—in the first centuries. Now God—may His Name be Praised and Exalted!—has chosen us in this time and place, through his gracious mercy, to save souls from the punishment of the tomb and the fire of Gehenna. Know that none will enter the Kingdom of Heaven unless he has wisdom and faith and has done good works. Strengthen your bodies to do good works and apply yourselves to this work, in order to win eternal rest and a never-ending life!

"Whoever among you has faith in the Religion, let not that faith be a hope for the life of the body, or hope for an earthly kingdom, a quest for the gifts of this world, but let his faith in the Religion be a hope in the Kingdom of Heaven, a hope for the deliverance of the soul, a quest for spiritual life, for salvation from the wrong path and from death, and for the prize of repose and joy in the future life! For earthly kingdom and earthly powers do not endure, and their pleasures end: whoever lets himself be seduced by them will be confounded when he stands before the Judge, who will judge him only according to what he merits, and for whoever gives himself to those pleasures, they will have consequences. Death comes to your bodies, but it watches your spirit: take care that it does not kill your spirit as it kills your body, if you live in the wrong! For your souls are at the mercy of death and in its power!

"Do good works and receive the Good News that I bring you! And know that just as the bird cannot live and save itself from its enemies except by the strength of its eyes, its wings, and its claws, so the soul cannot live and save itself except through knowledge, faith, and good and virtuous deeds. Consider then, O King, and you Nobles, too, what you hear, and hold to my words. Cross the sea while the ships are sailing; cross the desert while the guide is available! Prepare your provisions for the journey, and take to the road while the lamps are lit! Enrich your ears with the treasures of the ascetics, join them in the good and the beautiful, follow them as you should, be their disciples, join them in their deeds, so that you will live in the Kingdom of Heaven!"

They adopted the Religion he taught them and he made Wisdom thrive in the land of Sawilabatt, so that all lived according to his commandments and many became his disciples.

As for those among them who left the world, he said to them, "Live in this glorious poverty, observe your commandments, and prevent your souls from desiring the things of this world and from eating meat, drinking fermented beverages, and desiring women, and from all things that are base and detestable and dangerous for the body and soul. Avoid immoderation, anger, lies, and mutual wrongs. Whatever you would not have anyone do to you, do not do it to another. Let your hearts be pure and your intentions sincere, so that at your last hour, when you leave behind your body and it is taken from you, you will be rich in works of the soul! Abandon the life here below! Now I have shown you everything, I have shown you hidden secrets, and I have explained the commandments and the prohibitions. Now it is up to you to try to observe them perfectly!"

This reassurance consoled the king for his pain. He rejoiced in having ceded to Būdāsf and he remained in these thoughts, when the hour of his death finally arrived. Because he seemed perturbed, Būdāsf, who was seated at his bedside, said to him, "O King, do you not think that a man who has lived with worldly pleasures since the beginning of his existence until its end would be more worried, more corrupt, and less comforted, when he understands that he must leave the world, from the fact that he sees that he will lose a good that has for so long occupied his spirit, the pleasures that he has enjoyed for so long, a home that has become a homeland for him—than a man who has enjoyed the world only for a short moment of his existence, who has not profited from it, nor taken pleasure in it? By my life, the one who is most attached to the world is the one who merits mourning and disconsolate tears! What need have you to be sad about losing the world or to worry about what you have known of it? What do you wish to accomplish by such sadness? Is it because you want immortality in the world? That is not something that one can hope for. Is it because you wish to live in decrepitude, forgetfulness, trembling senility, and difficulty of movement? That is nothing to wish for. Is it because you want to expose yourself to leprosy or insanity or some other infirmity? These are not things that one can avoid. Is it in the hope of escaping dangers in this world? No one has ever been able to do that. Do you hope for a future time in this world, or a new life? There is nothing here but what you see of it in winter and summer, and in death and birth. Or is it to forget your ancestors and your friends, because you do not want to join them? That is not a gesture of generosity or concern for others. Or do you mistrust God and not want to meet Him? In that case, you invite His anger! You should console yourself, O King, for your death is certain and you must expect it."

"No," replied Gunaysar, "what disturbs me is the soul's natural repugnance for death; it is the thought of leaving the soft breeze and the peace of this happy state, for a place where we would be at ease, but without knowing if there is enough space or what awaits us there; it is the short time during which we have embraced this religion and the long existence living without it! For how can the little knowledge I have acquired so late compensate for all the damage that passion made me do during my youth?"

"Rejoice, O King," said Būḏāsf, "for you go to join a generous and merciful King, a lenient, indulgent, and compassionate adversary. You go toward the good and into the good. For compared to the place you will go, this light breath of air that you breathe and this space where you feel yourself at ease, are like the narrow and dark womb that holds the embryo, compared to a vast expanse swept by winds and breezes, or like the situation of a drowned man at the bottom of the sea that suffocates him, compared to the air found above the water!

"As for your fear to have lived for so long in error and for a short time in the truth, you are like the man who came to a river he wished to cross. He had with him one thousand sacks, each holding one thousand dinars, and he could not find a boat or a ford. He learned that he could gain a crossing only by distributing his money generously. He started to throw the sacks of money into the water so that it would be calmed and he could cross, or so that the sacks would form a bridge that he could cross. But even if he had possessed all the silver and gold in the world, he would never attain his goal this way. When he had only one sack of money left, a sailor arrived with a boat, and he gave him the dinars he had left and the sailor took him across the river easily. The sailor did not resent him for throwing the sacks of money into the water, and he did not reproach him for it. He only pitied him for having spent his money without gaining anything from it.

"So then, it is the same for you, O King. The few good deeds that you have done will multiply in God's eyes, because he is appreciative and generous, and all the evil you have done will count for little in His eyes, for He is indulgent and good."

Gunaysar rejoiced then and his sadness lifted. He said, "May God reward you with all the good you can wish for! I put my wives, my subjects, and my body into your care. I advise you to be virtuous, pious, and to do good."

Then he breathed his last breath, and his soul departed. Būḏāsf buried him according to the customs of the ascetics.

Then he assembled his clan and the princes of blood. He called them to the Religion of God, and they embraced it. He put an end to idols and transformed their temples into places of worship where the commandments of God were spoken and followed. He taught the truth to all men by his gentleness, his mercy, and the clarity of his expositions, and he converted all the inhabitants in the land of Sawilabatt to the Religion of God. He did not cease until he had recruited thirty thousand ascetics from among them, both men and women, who withdrew from the world, in addition to the Faithful, who remained there. Then he chose as his successor in the land of Sawilabatt his uncle Samta, who was the wisest and most pious of them all.

Then he left and led an itinerant life, passing through the cities of India and calling to the Religion of God *and the Indians claim that four angels accompanied his departure, supporting him with their friendship, and he was raised into heaven, they say, where he saw the Invisible and heard the revelation of the Supreme Cohort, and was then brought back to earth, and he was among the Messengers of God in the first centuries, and he led an itinerant life in the land of the Indians* and he did not enter a city without recruiting disciples and without converting its inhabitants, who could not resist his wisdom.

He arrived finally in Kasmir, and there his story ends. His time came, and he left the world. He made his last recommendations to one of his servants, called Ababīd, who took care of him and watched over him, and who was perfect in all ways. He gave his last instructions to him and the people of Kasmir who were there, saying to them:

"I have taught, protected, and raised up the Church, I have put there the lamps of those who came before me, I have reassembled the dispersed flock of Islam to which I was sent. Now the moment comes when I will be raised out of this world and my spirit will be freed from its body. Observe your commandments, do not stray from the truth, adopt the ascetic life! Let Ababīd be your leader!"

Then he ordered Ababīd to level a spot for him on the ground. He stretched out his legs, lay down on his side, pointing his head toward the North and his face toward the East. Then he died.

His uncle Samta remained to succeed him in the country of Sawilabatt, and he had a good and virtuous reign. At his death, Samil, Būḏāsf's son, ruled the land according to his father's religion. He had many descendants, who transmitted the kingdom as their inheritance, and they were attached to the path and the lessons of the True Path.[4]

◆ ST. EUTHYMIUS OF MOUNT ATHOS (CA. 955–1028)

In Jerusalem, sometime between 800 and 900 CE, the Arabic tale of conflict between life in the world and the life of the ascetic was translated into Georgian. However, it was not a simple translation; the story was transformed into a Christian tale. The king became a persecutor of Christians, doing everything he could to protect his son from the evils of Christianity. The ascetic who came from the island of Sarandip (Sri Lanka) to convert the prince (whose name was changed from Būḏāsf to Iodasaph) became a Christian monk (whose name was changed from Bilawhar to Balahvar). Then in the tenth century, the story was translated, perhaps by St. Euthymius of Mount Athos, from his native Georgian into Greek, resulting in the heroes becoming Barlaam and Josaphat. The story found its way into the collected works of St. John of Damascus (although he did not write it) and from there was rendered into Latin and then a host of European languages, becoming one of the most popular saints' tales of the Middle Ages. European scholars would not recognize its connection to the life of the Buddha until the nineteenth century.

Here is a passage about the prince's famous excursions beyond the palace walls and his confrontation with illness and old age.

———

And immediately he ordered that choice steeds, and an escort fit for a king, be made ready, and gave him license to go abroad whensoever he would, charging his companions to suffer nothing unpleasant to come in his way, but to show him all that was beautiful and gladsome. He bade them muster in the way troops of folk intuning melodies in every mode, and presenting divers mimic shows, that these might occupy and delight his mind.

So thus it came to pass that the king's son often went abroad. One day, through the negligence of his attendants, he descried two men, the one maimed, and the other blind. In abhorrence of the sight, he cried to his esquires, "Who are these, and what is this distressing spectacle?" They, unable to conceal what he had with his own eyes seen, answered, "These be human sufferings, which spring from corrupt matter, and from a body full of evil humours." The young prince asked, "Are these the fortune of all men?" They answered, "Not of all, but of those in whom the principle of health is turned away by the badness of the humours." Again the youth asked, "If then this is wont to happen not to all, but only to some, can they be known on whom this terrible calamity shall fall? or is it undefined and unforeseeable?" "What man," said they, "can discern the future, and accurately ascertain it? This is beyond human nature, and is reserved for the immortal gods alone." The young prince ceased from his questioning, but his heart was grieved at the sight that he had witnessed, and the form of his visage was changed by the strangeness of the matter.

Not many days after, as he was again taking his walks abroad, he happened upon an old man, well stricken in years, shrivelled in countenance, feeble-kneed, bent double, grey-haired, toothless, and with broken utterance. The prince was seized with astonishment, and, calling the old man near, desired to know the meaning of this strange sight. His companions answered, "This man is now well advanced in years, and his gradual decrease of strength, with increase of weakness, hath brought him to the misery that thou seest." "And," said he, "what will be his end?" They answered, "Naught but death will relieve him." "But," said he, "is this the appointed doom of all mankind? Or doth it happen only to some?" They answered, "Unless death come before hand to remove him, no dweller on earth, but, as life advanceth, must make trial of this lot." Then the young prince asked in how many years this overtook a man, and whether the doom of death was without reprieve, and whether there was no way to escape it, and avoid coming to such misery. They answered him, "In eighty or an hundred years men arrive at this old age, and then they die, since there is none other way; for death is a debt due to nature, laid on man from the beginning, and its approach is inexorable."

When our wise and sagacious young prince saw and heard all this, he sighed from the bottom of his heart. "Bitter is this life," cried he, "and fulfilled of all pain and anguish. If this be so, how can a body be careless in the expectation of an unknown death, whose approach (ye say) is as uncertain as it is inexorable?" So he went away, restlessly turning over all these things in his mind, pondering without end, and ever calling up remembrances of death. Wherefore trouble and despondency were his companions, and his grief knew no ease; for he said to himself, "And is it true that death shall one day overtake me? And who is he that shall make mention of me after death, when time delivereth all things to forgetfulness? When dead, shall I dissolve into nothingness? Or is there life beyond, and another world?" Ever fretting over these and the like considerations, he waxed pale and wasted away, but in the presence of his father, whenever he chanced to meet him, he made as though he were cheerful and without trouble, unwilling that his cares should come to his father's knowledge. But he longed with an unrestrainable yearning, to meet with the man that might accomplish his heart's desire, and fill his ears with the sound of good tidings.[5]

◆   KING HET'UM I OF ARMENIA (1215–1270)

During the first half of the thirteenth century, Europe lived in fear of the westward-advancing Mongol armies, who dealt Christian armies devastating defeats in Russia and eastern Europe. Their advance miraculously stopped in 1242, sparing western Europe. The Mongol leader Ögedei Khan, son of Genghis, had died on December 11, 1241. When word reached the armies in Europe, the Mongol commanders, many of them royal princes, returned to Mongolia for the election of the new khan.

Fearing the armies' return, a number of European princes and potentates sent embassies to the Mongol capital at Karakorum. Pope Innocent IV dispatched a Franciscan mission to the Mongols in 1254. The Mongol empire was cosmopolitan, and included Buddhists, Daoists, Muslims, and Nestorian Christians, together with Mongol shamans. Some of the first direct European contact with Buddhism occurred during this period, with the Franciscans being particularly active; the missionary William of Rubruck arrived in Karakorum in 1254. Also present at the capital was King Het'um I of Armenia, who visited the Mongol khan Möngke, the grandson of Genghis Khan and brother of Kublai Khan, there from 1253 to 1255.

In King Het'um's description of his time in Karakorum, we find references to two idols: Šakmonia, that is, Śākyamuni Buddha, and Matrin, that is, Maitreya, the buddha of the future, who according to Buddhist doctrine will appear when the teachings of Śākyamuni have disappeared from the world. The word toyin *in the penultimate paragraph is presumably taken from the Chinese* daoren (literally, "person of the way"), *a general term for a religious adherent applied also to those on the Buddhist path.*

————

There is also a country with many idolators who worship very large clay idols called Šakmonia; and they say [this is] a god three thousand and forty years old. And there are also another thirty-five *tumans* of years, one *tuman* being ten thousand, and then he will be deprived of his divinity by another god called Matrin, of whom they have made clay images of immense size, in a beautiful temple.

And the whole nation, including the women and children, are priests and are called *toyins*. They shave both the hair of the head and the beard; they wear yellow cloaks like Christians, but they wear them from the breast and not from the shoulders. And they are temperate in their food and in their marriages. They take a wife at twenty, and up to thirty approach her three times a week, and up to forty three times a month, and up to fifty, three times a year; and when they have passed fifty, they no longer go near her.

The learned king related many other things regarding the barbarous nations which we have omitted lest they might appear superfluous.[6]

◆   MARCO POLO (CA. 1254–1324)

By far the most famous European to visit the Mongol court was Marco Polo, who departed for China with his father and uncle from their native Venice in 1271, returning in 1295. In 1298, he was taken prisoner by the Genoese at the Battle of Curzola. While in prison, he is said to have dictated his account of his travels to his cellmate, the writer Rustichello da Pisa.

The passage below comes from the part of the story dealing with Marco Polo's return voyage to Venice, when his ship stopped in Sri Lanka (or Seilan, as he calls it), probably in 1292. He begins by mentioning the mountain there that is known as Adam's Peak, derived from the Muslim belief that the footprints found there mark the spot where Adam departed from the Garden of Eden. Marco Polo gives a different version, explaining that "the Saracens" believe it is the tomb of Adam. However, "the idolaters" say it is the tomb of Sagamoni Borcan; here he uses the Mongol version of the Buddha's name: Śākyamuni Buddha.

Marco Polo uses this as an occasion to provide one of the most detailed, and certainly the most sympathetic, descriptions of the life of the Buddha to appear in Europe for centuries to come. His reference to the Buddha being "the first in whose name idols were made" refers to a story discussed in the next chapter, in the selection from Matteo Ricci.

―――

CHAPTER XV

*The Same continued. The History of Sagamoni Borcan and
the beginning of Idolatry*

Furthermore you must know that in the Island of Seilan there is an exceeding high mountain; it rises right up so steep and precipitous that no one could ascend it, were it not that they have taken and fixed to it several great and massive iron chains, so disposed that by help of these men are able to mount to the top. And I tell you they say that on this mountain is the sepulchre of Adam our first parent; at least that is what the Saracens say. But the Idolaters say that it is the sepulchre of SAGAMONI BORCAN, before whose time there were no idols. They hold him to have been the best of men, a great saint in fact, according to their fashion, and the first in whose name idols were made.

He was the son, as their story goes, of a great and wealthy king. And he was of such an holy temper that he would never listen to any worldly talk, nor would he consent to be king. And when the father saw that his son would not be king, nor yet take any part in affairs, he took it sorely to heart. And first he tried to tempt him with great promises, offering to crown him king, and to surrender all authority into his hands. The son, however, would [have] none of his offers; so the father was in great trouble, and all the more that he had no other son but him, to whom he might bequeath the kingdom at his own death. So, after taking thought on the matter, the King caused a great palace to be built, and placed his son therein, and caused him to be waited on there by a number of maidens, the most beautiful that could anywhere be found. And he ordered them to divert themselves with the prince, night and day, and to sing and dance before him, so as to draw his heart towards worldly enjoyments. But 'twas all of no avail, for none of those maidens could ever tempt the king's son to any wantonness, and he only abode the firmer in his chastity, leading a most holy life, after their manner thereof. And I assure that he was so staid a youth that he had never gone out of the palace, and thus he had never seen a dead man, nor any one who was not hale and sound; for the father never allowed any man that was aged or infirm to come into his presence. It came to pass however one day that the young gentleman took a ride, and by the roadside he beheld a dead man. The sight dismayed him greatly, as he never had seen such a sight before. Incontinently he demanded of those who were with him what thing that was? and then they told him it was a dead man. "How, then," quoth the king's son, "do all men die?" "Yea, forsooth," said they. Whereupon the young gentleman never said a word, but rode on right pensively. And after he had ridden a good way he fell in with a very aged man who could no longer walk, and had not a tooth in his head, having lost all because of his great age. And when the king's son beheld this old man he asked what that might mean, and wherefore the man could not walk? Those who were with him replied that it was through old age the man could no longer walk, and had lost all his teeth. And so when the king's son had thus learned about the dead man and about the aged man, he turned back to the palace and said to himself that he would abide no longer in this evil world, but would go in search of Him Who dieth not, and Who had created him.

So what did he one night but take his departure from the palace privily, and betake himself to certain lofty and pathless mountains. And there he did abide, leading a life of great hardship and sanctity, and keeping great abstinence, just as if he had been a Christian. Indeed, and he had but been so, he would have been a great saint of Our Lord Jesus Christ, so good and pure was the life he led. And when he died they found his body and brought it to his father. And when the father saw dead before him that son whom he loved better than himself, he was near going distraught with sorrow. And he caused an image in the similitude of his son to be wrought in gold and precious stones, and caused all his people to adore it. And they all declared him to be a god; and so they still say.

They tell moreover that he hath died fourscore and four times. The first time he died as a man, and came to life again as an ox; and then he died as an ox and came to life again as a horse, and so on until he had died fourscore and four times; and every time he became some kind of animal. But when he died the eighty-fourth time they say he became a god. And they do hold him for the greatest of all their gods. And they tell that the aforesaid image of him was the first idol that the Idolaters ever had; and from that have originated all the other idols. And this befel in the Island of Seilan in India.[7]

◆   RASHĪD AL-DĪN (1247–1318)

One of the most detailed biographies of the Buddha in Muslim sources is found in the famous Compendium of Chronicles *(Jāmiʿ al-tavārīkh) by the Persian scholar of Jewish descent Rashīd al-Dīn. In 1300, he was commissioned by the Mongol prince Ghazan (who had converted from Buddhism to Islam in 1295) to compose a history of the Turkish and Mongol tribes from Genghis Khan down to Ghazan himself. After Ghazan's death, his brother and new khan Uljaytu instructed Rashīd al-Dīn to write a second volume, this one a history of the world or "a detailed history of every nation of the inhabited quarter of the earth," which for the author meant the Persians, Arabs, Greeks, Chinese, Indians, and Franks. This later work is the* Compendium of Chronicles. *It is in the chapter about India that we find a lengthy life of the Buddha, composed in 1305.*

By the time the account was written, the Mongols had had extensive contact with Buddhists in Tibet and China. Rashīd al-Dīn states that he is drawing the story of the Buddha from information provided by a Kashmiri Buddhist named Kamalaśrī. As a result, we find much more detail and specific textual references here than in the Christian accounts of the day, and of the days that would follow. Nonetheless, the biography has a markedly Muslim tone, with the Buddha declared to be the last of the six prophets of India, teaching a book (for all prophets have a book) called Abhidharma *and proclaiming that Allah is the creator of the universe. When the Buddha is attacked under the Bodhi tree prior to his enlightenment, his antagonist is not Māra but Iblis, the Muslim devil. Apart from these elements, the story is largely familiar, with some notable twists. Thus, after the prince sees a sick man, an old man, a corpse, and a hermit and then informs his father of his wish to renounce the world, his father has his son put into a well-guarded prison, where he spends several years.*

In traditional accounts of the life of the Buddha, his final days are typically recounted in great detail. However, in Rashīd al-Dīn's Compendium of Chronicles, *the account is quite succinct.*

———

In Hindustan there is a town named *Qūsh.n.q.r* (*Kuśinagara*), whose inhabitants are renowned for their courage and intrepidity. They heard that Shākamūnī intended to come to their town. But the way there was barred by a high and vast mountain. So they decided, in order to save him from having to cross it, to remove this mountain with hammers and pickaxes. And they set out to destroy the mountain. But Shākamūnī descended miraculously into the town from the sky without crossing the mountain. When they heard of his arrival, they departed from the mountain and hastened to him. Then spake Shākamūnī unto them: "What have I to do with your toil and efforts? For me the celestial journey has the same significance as for you the terrestrial."

After some time the end of his life approached and the ship of his existence sank in the storm-swept waves.

And in the town there arose all at once a dome-shaped edifice made of pure solid crystal. Shākamūnī entered this domed building and slept there like a lion. And from outside the people saw him in there owing to the transparency of the crystal. Yet there was no entrance and the gates which had first been open were now closed. And suddenly there could be seen a shining light in the form of a pillar rising up from the top of the dome.

Three days after this there came a stranger to be taught through Shākamūnī's words. When he heard of his death, he mourned exceedingly and committed suicide, for the former occurrence was worse for him than his own death. Suddenly he cast up his eyes and saw Shākamūnī in Heaven. And all people saw him, being again sound in body. But Shākamūnī spake from Heaven to this man: "Grieve not, neither mourn, for me there is neither birth nor death, no beginning and no end, no past and no future."

And when the man heard Shākamūnī's words, he became joyful and of good cheer.

And the words and useful sayings of Shākamūnī have been collected and put together in a volume, which is called *K.shūr (Kanjur)*.[8]

✦ ODORIC OF PORDENONE (1286?–1331)

In 1289, Pope Nicholas IV dispatched the Franciscan friar Giovanni da Montecorvino (known better to history as John of Montecorvino) as papal legate to the Great Khan. He arrived in Calambec (Beijing) in 1294, where he received permission to build two churches, establishing the first Roman Catholic presence in China. He remained in Beijing until his death in 1328. Some years earlier, perhaps in 1324, his fellow Franciscan Odoric of Pordenone arrived in the city. His account of his travels through China would prove to be one of the most popular travel narratives of the period, especially in the version heavily embellished in The Travels of Sir John Mandeville, *one of the best sellers of the fourteenth century.*

The story below does not involve the Buddha himself but rather relates Odoric's visit to a Buddhist temple and the wondrous events that he observed there. It is provided here as an example of conflation. This story may result from his visit to two different sites in Hangzhou, one where a monk fed the apes who lived on a nearby hill and another where various animals who had been saved from the butcher lived out their lives. A traditional form of merit making in Buddhism is "animal liberation," saving animals from slaughter. In China, this practice required that those who liberated animals provide for their welfare by feeding and sheltering them for the rest of their lives (hence the preference for liberating birds into the air and fish into the sea). The fantastic menagerie described here may be based on such a sanctuary.

OF A MONASTERY WHERE MANY STRANGE
BEASTS OF DIVERS KINDS DO
LIVE UPON AN HILL

In the foresaid city [Canasia] four of our friars had converted a mighty and rich man unto the faith of Christ, at whose house I continually abode, for so long time as I remained in the city. Who upon a certain time said unto me: Ara, that is to say, father, will you go and behold the city. And I said, Yea. Then embarqued we ourselves, and directed our course unto a certain great monastery; where being arrived, he called a religious person with whom he was acquainted, saying unto him concerning me: this Raban Francus, that is to say, this religious Frenchman, cometh from the western parts of the world, and is now going to the city of Cambaleth to pray for the life of the great Can, and therefore you must show him some rare thing, that when he returns into his own country, he may say, this strange sight or novelty have I seen in the city of Canasia. Then the said religious man took two great baskets full of broken relics which remained of the table, and led me unto a little walled park, the door whereof he unlocked with his key, and there appeared unto us a pleasant fair green plot, into the which we entered. In the said green stands a little mount in the form of a steeple, replenished with fragrant herbs, and fine shady trees. And while we stood there, he took a cymbal or bell and rang therewith, as they use to ring to dinner or bevoir in the cloisters, at the sound whereof many creatures of divers kinds came down from the mount, some like apes, some like cats, some like monkeys: and some having faces like men. And while I stood beholding of them, they gathered themselves together about him, to the number of 4200 of those creatures, putting themselves in good order, before whom he set a platter, and gave them the said fragments to eat. And when they had eaten he rang upon his cymbal the second time, and they all returned unto their former places. Then, wondering greatly at the matter, I demanded what kind of creatures those might be. They are (quoth he) the souls of noble men which we do here feed, for the love of God who governeth the world; and as a man was honourable or noble in this life, so his soul after death, entereth into the body of some excellent beast or other, but the souls of simple and rustical people do possess the bodies of the more vile and brutish creatures. Then I began to refute that foul error: howbeit my speech did nothing at all to prevail with him: for he could not be persuaded that any soul might remain without a body.[9]

CHAPTER TWO

FROM 1501 TO 1600

✦   ANJIRŌ (1511–1550?)

In December 1547, the Spanish Jesuit (and later saint) Francis Xavier was in Malacca on the Malay Peninsula when he met Anjirō (often appearing in other works as Yajiro), an unlettered Japanese who had fled there from his native country aboard a Portuguese ship to escape a murder charge. He spoke some Portuguese, and described Japan to the priest. Anjirō was sent to the Jesuit headquarters in Goa on the southwest coast of India, where he was baptized as Paulo de Santa Fe. While in Goa, he provided a detailed report about Japan and its religion, which was recorded by the Italian priest Nicolò Lancilotto.

The following passage contains Anjirō's account of the life of the Buddha (called Sciacca in the original and Shaka in the translation here).

———

All adore one single God whom they call in their language *Deny-chy* [that is, Dainichi, the Buddha Vairocana] and he says that they sometimes paint Denychy with only one body and three heads. They then call him Cogy. But this man said that he did not know the meaning of those three heads; but he knew that all were one, Denychy and Cogy, as with us God and Trinity.

This man also told the history of a man who is regarded among them as a saint and who is called *Shaka* by them, and the account runs as follows:

He says that there is a land on the other side of China towards the west called Chencigo. In it there was a king who was called Jombondaiuo [Jōbon Dai Ō in Japanese], and he was married to a woman by the name of Maiabonym [Maya Bunin in Japanese]. This king, when he was once sleeping during the day, dreamed that a boy appeared to him who said that he must enter into the body of his wife; and this boy appeared to him three times on the same day and each time spoke the same words to him. And this king immediately told his wife what had happened to him. Since they were so frightened by the dream, they no longer had any marital relations with each other; and in the same month she discovered that she was pregnant without having had any relations with anyone. At the end of nine months she bore a son whom they called Shaka; and, immediately after the child's birth, its mother died and its father had Shaka brought up by a sister of the mother of the boy.

He says that when this Shaka was born, two large snakes with wings miraculously appeared. They came in the air over the boy, and they spewed water out of their mouths upon the said boy. And he says that this boy got on his feet at the end of three months and took three steps and lifted a hand to heaven and pointed the other to the earth and said, "I am one alone above in heaven, and one alone on earth." This Shaka grew until he reached the age of nineteen and his father ordered him to marry against his will. And when he reflected upon the misery of mankind, he did not wish to unite himself with his wife and fled at night and came to a very high and barren mountain, where he remained for six years and practiced great penance. After this he went forth and began to preach to those inhabitants, who were still pagans, with great eloquence and enthusiasm. Through this he gained such a reputation for the greatest sanctity and virtue that he renewed all the laws and gave to that people a law and a new kind of divine worship. And he says that he won over eight thousand disciples who led the same life of perfection as he. Some of his disciples came to China, where they preached their laws and their kind of divine worship and thus converted the whole of China and had all the idols and pagodas that were in China destroyed. And they came from China to Japan and did the same. And he says that in all of China and Japan are found pieces of old statues as in Rome. This Shaka taught all these peoples to worship one single God, the Creator of all things; and he ordered that he be painted, as has been said above, with one single body and three heads. . . .

This Shaka, who gave laws to these people of China and Japan, ended his life as follows. He called all of his disciples and the people in general together and preached to them and said at the end that he would soon die. And he stepped into a marble tomb which he had ordered to be built and died before the eyes of all.

His disciples then burned his body, and as they were placing his ashes in the same tomb, Shaka himself, in the presence of all, appeared in the air above a white cloud with a cheerful countenance and a marvelous aspect and thus went up to heaven and was seen no more. He was ninety years old.[1]

✦ ST. FRANCIS XAVIER (1506–1552)

On July 27, 1549, Francis Xavier arrived in Japan, accompanied by Anjirō and three Jesuit priests. The Japanese assumed that the European priests were Buddhist monks from India, and they were welcomed as such. Based on Anjirō's account, Francis Xavier believed that Dainichi (literally, "Great Sun" in Japanese, and the name of the important buddha Vairocana) was another name for God, and in his early sermons he encouraged the Japanese to pray to Dainichi. This attracted the interest of Japanese monks of the Shingon school, for whom Dainichi is the central buddha. But Francis Xavier soon came to understand that contrary to what Anjirō had led him to believe, the Japanese did not worship the one true God, and that the Buddha (whom he calls Xaca, that is, Shaka) was not a smasher of idols but in fact a demon.

———

All the Japanese, both the bonzes and the common people, recite prayers with the help of rosaries that have more than one hundred and eighty beads. While they are reciting them, they continuously repeat at each bead the name of the founder of their sect. Some are devoted to frequently reciting their beads, but others less so. All of these sects, as I have said above, have two main founders, namely, Xaca and Ameda. The male and female bonzes who wear grey habits are all attached to Ameda, and the majority of the people of Japan worship Ameda. Many of the male and female bonzes who wear black habits, though they worship Ameda, have Xaca as their main object of worship, and many others.

I tried to learn if these two, Ameda and Xaca, had been men dedicated to philosophy. I asked the Christians to make an accurate translation of their lives. I discovered from what was written in their books that they were not men, since it was written that they had lived for a thousand and two thousand years, and that Xaca will be born eight thousand times, and many other absurdities. They were thus not men, but pure inventions of the demons.

For the love and service of our Lord, I entreat all those who will read this letter to ask God to give us victory over these two demons, Xaca and Ameda, and over all the others as well, for in the city of Yamaguchi, through the goodness of God, they are already losing the credit which they used to have.[2]

◆ GUILLAUME POSTEL (1510–1581)

As we will see elsewhere in this chapter and in the chapters that follow, for Catholic priests of the sixteenth and seventeenth centuries, the Buddha was an idol. But for a brief moment, the Buddha was a smasher of idols, as we saw in a previous selection. And for one European scholar of the sixteenth century, the Buddha was Christ himself. His name was Guillaume Postel.

Father Postel subscribed to the theory of divine simplicity, according to which God created a single human race to be united in a single faith, a universal religion based on the worship of the one true God. Diversity, including the diversity of languages and the diversity of religions, was the work of man. For Postel, Hebrew was the original language, spoken by Adam and Eve. He thus devoted much of his life to the study of the Hebrew Bible and of Kabbalah. He believed that if the Bible could be translated into other languages, the entire world would naturally convert to Christianity.

A friend of Ignatius Loyola, he joined the Society of Jesus in Rome in 1544, only to leave the order (although he remained a priest) the following year. In 1547, he went to Venice, where he served at a small hospital. There he became the confessor of a pious woman who had founded the hospital, Madre Zuana or Mother Johanna. Postel eventually became convinced that she was a prophet, calling her the "Virgin of Venice," the "Mother of the World," the "Female Pope," and the "New Eve." She revealed to him that it was the will of God that all of humanity be united into a single flock. In 1555, Postel was declared dangerous and delirious by the Inquisition and condemned to life imprisonment. However, he escaped after four years and returned to his native France to continue his mission. He was eventually confined to the monastery of Saint Martin des Champs, where he contributed anonymously to the famous Polyglot Bible, published in Antwerp in eight volumes between 1568 and 1573.

Father Lancilotto's report on the religion of Japan was sent back to Europe, where it found its way to Postel. He published it, with his own interlinear commentary, as Des merveilles du monde *(Wonders of the World) in 1553. In it, he describes the religion of Japan as "the most marvelous religion in the world, which remains without knowing its author, who is Jesus Christ, his name unknown." This is because its priests "slowly converted the truth of Jesus into the fable of Schiaca." The signs are unmistakable. He was born in a country beyond China called Cegnico (that is, Tenjiku, the Japanese name for India), which Postel identifies with Judea. His father was Jambon Daino (Jōbon Dai Ō in Japanese) and his mother was Magabonin (Maya Bunin in Japanese); for Postel they are clearly Joseph and Mary. He reports that Xaca destroyed idols, whose remnants can still be seen in Japan. And because there have been only two destroyers of idols in history (it is unclear why the Hebraist Postel does not mention Moses)—Jesus and Muhammad—one who did so with his goodness and one with his sword, and because Xaca apparently destroyed idols peacefully, it follows that Xaca is Jesus. Postel ends the passage given below by condemning the Muslims (descendants of Ishmael, son of Abraham and the slave Hagar, hence "bastards and half-Jews") for their rejection of Jesus.*

Postel's comments on the Jesuit report appear in italics in his text.

———

To this king *to Joseph or to all of the Judaic or Abrahamic Church* [came] in a dream *this is the Gospel, speaking of Joseph*, I know not what small child *According to ancient sources, the angel was the cherubim, that is to say, they were like small children, announcing and speaking in the name of God, who sent them* appeared in a dream or in a vision saying, I want to be born and will be born from your wife *For this is what the virgin was called* and this vision came to him three times. He was most astonished and after he told the Queen he decided not to touch her for that month *or ever again*, and in this way, without the deed of a man, she found herself pregnant. *This is the divine incarnation known by the astronomy of the Magi, who were neighbors of that place, as from here to Jerusalem.* And after she gave birth she died *in this way the false is joined to the true as we see in the Old Testament where holy things are told through fables.* When the father saw this he sent the child to be brought up by his sister. He was called Schiaca, and as soon as he was born two serpents of extraordinary size came to him and bathed him in water. *This is confused with the memory of baptism, of which all are baptized, in the survival of this fable, and the serpents are from the memory of Satan, who appeared first in a serpent and was condemned under the name of serpent.* And his legs and limbs grew so that he could stand up in his third month *which signifies his divine nature.* Holding one hand to Heaven and the other to the earth he said, I was the sole emperor of Heaven and earth *these are the very words where he said: the complete power of Heaven and earth is given to me.* He was nineteen years old when his father wanted to force him to marry, but when he considered human misery, he did not want to obey his father or know a woman. In the night he fled to a mountain. *For most of the life and the teaching of the Savior took place in the mountains.* There he spent six years in penance. After he left the mountain, he began to preach with such marvelous devotion that the people who were idolaters benefitted so much that they admired him immediately and he changed their laws, teaching them all the way to worship God. He assembled eight thousand disciples who followed his way of living *a number that is certainly uncertain* and from among whom a certain number went into the land of the Chinese *who are the ancient Sines or their neighbors* where they preached his holy laws so that they converted them all to their teaching and doctrine *and their words went out to the ends of the earth* and broke their idols and destroyed their temples and the places where they were worshipped, they did not hesitate to ruin them *by this we see with certainty that the fable of Schiaca, or if we read the letter x in the Spanish way, Xaca, is nothing other than a thick fog drawn from the Gospel story. For there have never been but two destroyers of idols and their temples, one without sword and force, but only the goodness of his life and the truth of his teaching, the other by the sword and a most evil and vicious life. The first is Jesus Christ, the second is Mohammed, of whom it is most certain that such a fable could not be composed, for he has in all the Orient a world of devotees who know his story through the Coran. But in the Orient, before books or doctrine confirmed by councils could be joined to the good and miraculous life, tyrants and the false priests of idols and heretics destroyed the good principles, and so Jesus appeared as the omnipotent conservator of order and of life, even though they had no knowledge of the doctrine of the Gospels as such.* Having arrived in Giapan, they did the same, so that even up to our time, you can see bits and pieces of statues and idols on that aforementioned island. This Xaca taught that there is one God, creator of all things, and he had him painted with one body and three heads. *This shows us clearly, not simply by the image but by doctrine and signification that he was Jesus Christ, who alone revealed the doctrine of God Three in One, against which principally the bastards and half-Jews, the Ismaelites, have, through their Muhamed, raised themselves as much as they are able.*[3]

◆ MARTÍN DE RADA (1533–1578)

The Spaniard Martín de Rada joined the Order of Hermits of St. Augustine (Ordo Eremitarum sancti Augustini, or OESA*) in 1554. Six years later he was sent to Mexico, where he distinguished himself in mathematics and in the local languages. He was also so highly regarded as a theologian that he was considered for service in England had the Spanish Armada been successful. From Mexico, he was transferred to the Philippines, arriving in 1565 and eventually becoming regional superior in 1572. He is remembered there for evangelizing the island of Cebu and for defending the Filipino people against the unjust collection of tribute by Spanish officials. He died at sea while returning to Manila from Borneo in 1578.*

In 1575, Father de Rada was part of a delegation that made a brief visit to China, arriving on July 5 and returning to Manila on October 28. It spent two months and nine days in China.

The following passages from de Rada's report describe a ritual performed by Buddhist monks in which food is offered to a statue of the Buddha Śākyamuni, Shijia-mouni in Chinese, whom de Rada calls Siquag.

They also keep as a very great feast the fifteenth day of their seventh month. We saw this feast in Hocchiu [Fuzhou] because they keep it in all the houses of the community, and so they celebrated it likewise in the inn where we were lodged. It is the feast of the dead in honor of Siquag, who was the founder of such religious orders as there are in China. They erected in one of the halls an image of Siquag with many other images which were on their knees around him. There was also a large altar with seven or eight separate tables all loaded with food. At nightfall three men began to sing from their book, one of them being a priest and the other two cantors. Sometimes they sang after the manner of psalms, and at other times like hymns, always playing on some small handbells and a tambourine. From time to time, the priest took a little dish of food from the tables, said a prayer, and placed it on the altar. This continued until all the dishes were finished, which was nearly midnight. . . .

The founder of these orders is called Siquag, whom they revere as a saint. He was a foreigner, and said to be from the region of Tiantey [India], although one of the friars told us he was from Syria.

The Chinese believe souls are immortal, and that the good and the holy go to Heaven. As regards the others, a Huexio [*heshang*, or monk] told us that they become demons. Their friars are held in scant respect and regard; only the captains and the mandarins are respected on account of the punishments they can inflict. Finally, the land is very fruitful, abundant and populous, although with people who are heathen and thus suffer from the evils which afflict those who do not know God, to whom be honour and glory for evermore, and may He convert and bring them to the knowledge of Himself. Amen.[4]

✦ BERNARDINO DE ESCALANTE (CA. 1537 TO AFTER 1605)

After the account of Marco Polo, one of the first European works on China to be widely read (although not achieving the fame of Juan Gonzáles de Mendoza's His-

toria de las cosas mas notables de la China [The History of the Great and Mighty Kingdom of China], *described below) was* Discurso de la navegación que los Portugueses hacen a los Reinos y Provincias de Oriente (Discourse on the Navigation that the Portuguese Made to the Kingdoms and Provinces of the Orient) *by Bernardino de Escalante, a Spanish seaman, soldier, and later priest who would serve as an inquisitor. It was published in 1577. Like Gonzáles, he never traveled to China, drawing his work from two Portuguese works,* Tratado das cousas da China (Treatise on the Things of China) *(1569) by the Dominican priest Gaspar da Cruz and* Décadas da Ásia (Decades of Asia) *by João de Barros (1496–1570), whose section on China was published in 1563.*

The Discourse *was translated into English in 1579. The passage below, from that translation, is found in chapter 15, on "the religion, lawes, and ceremonies which they have and use." The "Diuell" (devil) that the Chinese worship is presumably the Buddha; the claim that he has the power to turn the good into devils and the wicked into cattle is likely a garbled reference to the doctrine of rebirth. Escalante goes on to describe the two types of Chinese priests, referring to Buddhist monks and Confucian scholars.*

———

They worship the Moone, the Sunne, and Starres, and all other Images which they make without respect, and some figures or shapes of Lawyers, and of the priestes of their Idolles which they were most affectioned to, in some principal seruice they had done. And likewise they worship any maner of stones that they sette vpon theyr Aultars, where they doe make their Sacrifices, and also the Diuell which they paint after the same shape and manner as we doe among vs. The common sort of people doe say that they worship him, for bycause the good people, hee maketh Diuels, and the euill people he conuerteth into Kine [cattle], and other kind of beastes. The men of most knowledge and that be most pollitique, they say they worship him & regarde him, bycause he should do them no hurt. They haue in al cities and places of habitation, and also in the fieldes, a great number of sumptuous Temples, and of goodly buildings, which are of great Maiestie. There are two sortes of Priestes, and they are contrarie the one to the other in maners: the one sort goeth all shauen, and appareled in white, and with certaine high cappes made of felt somewhat piked before. These sort liue in common together, and haue their chambers and lodgings after the maner of our Friers. The others doe weare their haire long, and deuided in the higest parte of their head with a strike verie curiously varnished with blacke, after the fashion of a hand closed togither. They apparell themselues with silke or blacke Serge as all the rest of them do vse: they dwell euery one of them by themselues: they assist in the seruice of the Temples, and in the festiuall dayes and burying. The one and the other are not maried, but they are euill liuers, and therefore they are not esteemed among the people, and they are punished with stripes amongst the Iudges for a small occasion.[5]

◆ JUAN GONZÁLES DE MENDOZA (CA. 1540–1617)

After serving in the Spanish army, Juan Gonzáles de Mendoza joined the Order of Hermits of St. Augustine (Ordo Eremitarum sancti Augustini, or OESA). He served in the Aeolian Islands, in Mexico, and in Colombia. At the request of Pope Gregory XIII, he published Historia de las cosas mas notables de la China *in Rome in 1585. Father Gonzáles never traveled to China himself, instead drawing information from the account of Miguel de Luarca, a member of the same diplomatic mission to China from the Philippines in which Martín de Rada served. He also drew heavily from* Décadas da Ásia (Decades of Asia), *by the Portuguese João de Barros (1496–1570), which chronicles Portuguese travels, as well as the work cited above,* Discurso de la navegación que los Portugueses hacen a los Reinos y Provincias de Oriente (Discourse on the Navigation that the Portuguese Made to the Kingdoms and Provinces of the Orient) *by Bernardino de Escalante.*

Three years later, the book was translated into English by Robert Parke as The historie of the great and mightie kingdome of China, *from which the following is taken.*

———

They likewise doo sacrifice unto the divell, not as though they were ignorant that he is evill, or condemned, but that he shoulde doo them no harme, neither on their bodies nor goods. They have manie strange gods, of so great a number, that alonely for to name them, is requisite a large hystorie, and not to be briefe as is pretended in this booke: And therefore I will make mention but of their principals, whom (besides those which I have named) they have in great reverence.

The first of these they doo call Sichia, who came from the kingdome of Tranthlyco which is towards the west: this was the first inventer of such religious people, as they have in their countrie both men and women, and generally doth live without marrying in perpetuall closenesse. And all such as doo immitate this profession do weare no haire, which number is great, as hereafter you shall understand: and they greatly observe that order left unto them.[6]

✦ WILLIAM ADAMS (1564–1620)

The English mariner William Adams landed in Japan in 1600 and spent the rest of his life there, becoming a favorite of the Tokugawa shogun Ieyasu, who made him a samurai with the name of Miura Anjin. Six of his letters, composed between 1611 and 1617, were published in 1850 by the Hakluyt Society as Memorials of the Empire of Japon: In the XVI and XVII Centuries. *The letters were prefaced by a document entitled "The Kingdome of Japonia," taken from a work entitled "The Firste Booke of Relations of Moderne States." The author of this work and the date of its composition are not provided, but elsewhere in the book it is stated that the monarch of England is Elizabeth, who reigned from 1558 to 1603.*

The following passage is drawn from this document. The author explains here that the gods of Japan—among whom he includes both Śākyamuni and Amitābha—were once Japanese lords who had been immortalized for both their exploits in battle and their skills as rulers.

He [the emperor] trusteth through these greate buyldinges, famous expeditions, and through much amplenesse of dominions, and ioyninge together of kingedomes under one crowne, that he shall obtayne an immortall name, and be accounted for a god: which thinge all they have done, that have obteyned the opinion of gods amonge the Japonians: for Amida [Amitābha], Xaca [Shaka], Camis [Kami], and Fatoques [Hotoke, or Buddha], to whom they attribute divine honour, were nothing els but lordes of Japonia, whoe by the glory of war, or skill in tyme of peace, obtained the opinion of divinitie among the Japonians: no otherwise then did Hercules and Bacchus in Grece, Saturnus and Janus in Italie, and there be no lesse fabulous and tryffelynge tales spreade abroade of those then of these.[7]

✦ CESAR FREDERICKE

In 1563, the Italian merchant Cesar Fredericke set sail from Venice on a long journey that took him to Babylonia, India, Sri Lanka, Malacca, Siam, and Pegu (in modern Burma) before returning home, stopping in Jerusalem along the way. Here, he expresses his admiration of the gilded idols (likely Buddha images) of the king of Pegu.

The king of Pegu has no naval force; but for extent of dominion, number of people, and treasure of gold and silver, he far exceeds the Grand Turk in power and riches. He has various magazines full of treasure in gold and silver, which is daily increased, and is never diminished. He is also lord of the mines of rubies, sapphires, and spinels. Near the royal palace there is an inestimable treasure, of which he seems to make no account, as it stands open to universal inspection. It is contained in a large court surrounded by a stone wall, in which are two gates that stand continually open. Within this court there are four gilded houses covered with lead, in each of which houses are certain heathen idols of very great value. The first house contains an image of a man of vast size all of gold, having a crown of gold on his head enriched with most rare rubies and sapphires, and round about him are the images of four little children, all likewise of gold. In the second house is the statue of a man in massy silver, which seems to sit on heaps of money. This enormous idol, though sitting, is as lofty as the roof of a house. I measured his feet, which I found exceeded that of my own stature; and the head of this statue bears a crown similar to that of the former golden image. The third house has a brazen image of equal size, having a similar crown on its head. In the fourth house is another statue as large as the others, made of *gansa*, or mixed metal of copper and lead, of which the current money of the country is composed, and this idol has a crown on its head as rich and splendid as the others. All this valuable treasure is freely seen by all who please to go in and look at it, as the gates are always open, and the keepers do not refuse admission to any one.[8]

CHAPTER THREE

FROM 1601 TO 1700

✦ MATTEO RICCI (1552–1610)

The most famous of the many Jesuit missionaries to China was Matteo Ricci, who arrived in Macao in 1582. At the suggestion of a Chinese official, Ricci and his fellow priests adopted the appearance of Buddhist monks in order to be more immediately accepted. The Jesuits cropped their hair and shaved their beards and donned monks' robes. They also described themselves as monks from the West; in China, the West often denoted India. However, in 1595, at the urging of his Chinese scholar friends and with the permission of his superior, Ricci and the Jesuits abandoned the dress of Buddhist monks—who, he reports, the Chinese held as "vile and lowly"—for the long beard and silk robes of the Chinese literatus. From that point onward, Ricci's slogan would become qin ru pai fo, *"Draw close to Confucianism and repudiate Buddhism."*

Ricci criticized the Buddha and Buddhism in two works. The first was his catechism of 1603 written in Chinese, The True Doctrine of the Lord of Heaven *(Tianzhu shiyi). The second was his history of Christianity in China, published posthumously (considered in a subsequent selection).*

The first passage below is Ricci's ingenious reading of the famous Chinese story of how Buddhism first came to China. The emperor Ming (28–75 CE) of the Eastern Han dynasty is said to have had a dream of a golden flying man. One of his advisors explained that this was the sage of the West, called Buddha. The emperor sent a delegation to retrieve the teachings of this man (and, according to a later version of the story, a statue of him). Matteo Ricci argues that it was a case of mistaken identity.

The second passage is drawn from Ricci's attempt to refute the Buddhist doctrine of rebirth, which, as other Christian missionaries would do, he traces back to Pythagoras. Ricci devotes a long section to the refutation. He begins here by dismissing the doctrine—which he said the Buddha had taken from Pythagoras—because it comes from the insignificant and uncivilized land of India.

———

When His [Jesus'] work of preaching was complete He ascended to Heaven in broad daylight at a time forecast by Himself. Four saints recorded the deeds he had performed whilst on earth, as well as His teachings. These were transmitted to many countries, and large numbers of people from all quarters believed in Him, keeping His commandments from one generation to another. From this time onwards many nations in the West took great strides along the road to civilization.

When we examine Chinese history we find that Emperor Ming of the Han dynasty heard of these events and sent ambassadors on a mission to the West to search for canonical writings. Midway these ambassadors mistakenly took India to be their goal, and returned to China with Buddhist scriptures which were then circulated throughout the nation. From then until now the people of your esteemed country have been deceived and misled. That they have not heard the correct Way is truly a great tragedy for the field of learning. Was it not a disaster?[1]

After the death of Pythagoras few of his disciples continued to hold his teaching [of reincarnation]. But just then the teaching leaked out and found its way to other countries. This was at the time when Śākyamuni happened to be planning to establish a new religion in India. He accepted this theory of reincarnation and added to it the teaching concerning the Six Directions [that is, the six places of rebirth: gods, demigods, humans, animals, ghosts, hell beings], together with a hundred other lies, editing it all to form books which he called canonical writings. Many years later some Chinese went to India and transmitted the Buddhist religion to China. There is no genuine record of the history of this religion in which one put one's faith, or any real principle upon which one can rely. India is a small place, and is not considered to be a nation of the highest standing. It lacks the arts of civilization and has no standards of moral conduct to bequeath to posterity. The histories of many countries are totally ignorant of its existence. Could such a country adequately serve as a model for the whole world?[2]

✦ SAMUEL PURCHAS (1577?–1626)

By the early seventeenth century, there were sufficient accounts of world travelers, and sufficient interest in those accounts, for the writings to begin to be compiled. One of the most popular of such compilations in English was that of Samuel Purchas; his work Purchas his Pilgrimage *was first published in four volumes in 1613. The purpose and contents of the first volume, from which the passage below is drawn, may be discerned from its full title:* Purchas his Pilgrimage. Or Relations of the World and the Religions Observed in All Ages and Places discovered, from the Creation unto this Present. In foure Parts, This First Containeth a Theologicall and Geographical Historie of Asia, Africa, and America, with the Islands Adiacent. Declaring the Ancient Religions before the Floud, the Heathnish, Jewish, and Saracenicall in all Ages since, in those parts professed, with their several Opinions, Idols, Oracles, Temples, Priestes, Fasts, Feasts, Sacrifices, and Rites Religious: Their beginnings, Proceedings, Alterations, Sects, Orders and Successions. With briefe Descriptions of the Countries, Nations, States, Discoveries, Private and Publike Customes, and the most Remarkable Rarities of Nature, or Humane Industrie, in the same.

Purchas was an Anglican cleric who never left England, basing his work on his conversations with sailors who had returned from abroad, on various published sources, and especially on the manuscripts of Richard Hakluyt (ca. 1552–1616). Purchas would publish Hakluyt's manuscripts in four volumes as Hakluytus Posthumus *in 1625.*

The passage below, however, comes from the first volume of Purchas his Pilgrimage, *from 1613. Here, the description is of the religion of Pegu (in modern-day Burma) as described by the Italian Jesuit scholar and diplomat Giovanni Botero (ca. 1544–1617), who also never visited Asia. It comes from Botero's* Relationi Universali (Universal Reports), *published in 1595, which includes a section entitled "Delle idolatrie de' Peguini" ("Of Idolatry of the Peguans," part 3, book 2).*

In this passage, we find reference to the five buddhas of the Theravāda tradition of Southeast Asia. Śākyamuni Buddha is the fourth, and Maitreya, the future buddha, will be the fifth. According to Buddhist doctrine, at the end of the current eon, the world will indeed be destroyed by fire. Purchas describes three postmortem destinations—a reference to the Buddhist doctrine of rebirth—heaven, hell, and Niba, *that is, nirvana, noting correctly that beings continue to be reborn until they enter nirvana. The "Divell" mentioned below is likely the Buddha.*

———

Boterus [Giovanni Botero] saith, that they hold an innumerable multitude of worlds successively one after another, and also innumerable number of Gods: but not all at once. They imagine that five have governed this present world, whereof foure are passed above two hundred yeares agoe. Now they are without a God, and expect the fift many ages hereafter: after whose death, they conceive that the world shall perish by fire, and then another world shall follow, and other Gods to rule it. They reckon likewise in the number of their Gods certaine men, which yet have first passed into fishes, beasts, and birds of all sorts. After death they beleeve three places, one of pleasure; (like the Mahumetane Paradise) another of torment; the third, of annihilation, which they call *Niba*. The soules after their phantasie abide in the two former places, whence they returne so often into this life till at last they be holden worthy that *Niba*. He addeth, that they have Covents, or Colledges of Priests, which live three hundred together, or more in one place, have no use of women, are harbourers of strangers and live some of almes, some of rents. They have like Nunneries also for the women. There is supposed to be in one Idol-sanctuarie (whereof they have many) 120000 Idols. . . .

The Divell is highly worshipped of these Peguians, to whom they erect a stately Altar, and adorne it with varietie of flowers, and meates of all sorts, so to see and feede him that he should not hurt them. This is principally done when they are sicke: for then they make vowes, and build Altars, which they cover with clothes and flowers.[3]

◆   NICOLAS TRIGAULT (1577–1628)

Nicolas Trigault was a Flemish Jesuit who arrived in Peking in 1611, shortly after Matteo Ricci's death. However, he was quickly recalled to Europe to serve as procurator for the Jesuits' China mission. On the voyage home, he began the task of translating Ricci's unfinished history of Christianity in China, composed in Italian, into Latin. Father Trigault translated, edited, and expanded it into a book he called De Christiana expeditione apud sinas suscepta ab Societate Jesu *(The Christian Expedition among the Chinese undertaken by the Society of Jesus). First published in Latin in 1616,* De Christiana expeditione apud sinas *proved to be immensely popular, being translated into French, German, Spanish, Italian, and English by 1625.*

Trigault returned to China in 1619 and would spend the rest of his days there, before apparently committing suicide over a dispute about how to translate God *into Chinese. He favored the traditional Chinese term* Shangdi, *"High Sovereign."*

Because of Trigault's contributions to the text, the authorship of De Christiana expeditione apud sinas *is sometimes referred to as Ricci-Trigault. But the passage below, concerning Buddhism, derives from Matteo Ricci. He sees in Buddhism various Christian elements, but in sinister and distorted forms.*

———

The second important sect among the Chinese is known as Sciequia [Shijia, that is, Śākya] or Omitose [Amituo, that is, Amitābha]. The Japanese call it Sciacca [Shaka] and Amidabu [Amidabutsu], the sect being quite similar in character in both countries. The Japanese also call it the Lex Totoqui [that is, Hotoke, or Buddha]. This code of law was brought to China from the West, in the year sixty-five of the Christian era. It was imported from the region of Thiencio [Tianzhu, the Chinese name for India], also called Shinto, which was formerly two kingdoms but today is known by the single title of Hindustan, lying between the rivers Indus and Ganges. A written record is extant that the King of China sent legates to this country, after being enlightened in a dream to do so. These messengers brought back the books of the laws and also interpreters to translate them into Chinese. The founders of the sect had died before the doctrine found its way into China. From this it would appear quite evident that this doctrine passed from the Chinese to the Japanese, and it is not at all clear why the Japanese followers of this creed assert that the Sciacca or the Amidabu was introduced into Japan from the kingdom of Siam, where they say it had its origin. It is made quite evident in the books of the followers of this doctrine that Siam was too well known to the Chinese to be mistaken from the far-distant Thiencio in a matter of this kind.

It is historically clear that this doctrine was brought into China at the identical period in which the Apostles were preaching the doctrine of Christ. Bartholomew was preaching in upper India, namely in Hindustan and the surrounding countries, when Thomas was spreading the Gospel in lower India, to the South. It is not beyond the realm of possibility, therefore, that the Chinese, moved and interested by reports of the truths contained in the Christian Gospel, sought to contact it and to learn it from the West. Instead, however, either through error on the part of their legates, or perhaps through ill-will toward the Gospel on the part of the people they visited, the Chinese received a false importation in place of the truth they were seeking.

It would seem that the original authors of the teachings of this second sect had drawn certain of their ideas from our philosophers of the West. For example, they recognize only four elements, to which the Chinese, rather foolishly, add a fifth. According to the latter, the entire material world—men, beasts, plants, and mixed bodies—is composed of the elements of fire, water, earth, metal, and wood. With Democritus and his school, they believe in a multiplicity of worlds. Their doctrine of the transmigration of souls sounds like that of Pythagoras, except that they have added much commentary and produced something still more hazy and obscure. This philosophy seems not only to have borrowed from the West but to have actually caught a glimpse of light from the Christian Gospels. The doctrine of this second sect mentions a certain trinity in which three different gods are fused into one deity, and it teaches reward for the good in heaven and punishment for the wicked in hell. They make so much of celibacy that they seem to reject marriage entirely and it is a common custom with them to abandon their homes and families and to go on pilgrimage to beg alms. In some respects their profane rites resemble our own ecclesiastical ceremonies, as for instance their recitation in chant which hardly differs from our Gregorian. There are statues in their temples and the vestments worn by those offering a sacrifice are not unlike our copes. In reciting prayers they frequently repeat a certain name, which they pronounce Tolome but which they themselves do not understand. Again, it might possibly be that in doing this they wish to honor their cult with the authority of the Apostle Bartholomew.

Whatever ray of truth there may be in their doctrine is, however, unfortunately obscured by clouds of noisome mendacity. Heaven and earth are quite confused in their ideas, as are also a place of reward and one of punishment, in neither of which do they look for an eternity for souls departed. These souls are supposed to be reborn after a certain number of years in some one of the many worlds which they postulate. There they may do penance for their crimes if they wish to make amends for them. This is only one of the many nonsensical doctrines with which they have afflicted the unfortunate country.[4]

◆ ROBERTO DE NOBILI (1577–1656)

The Jesuits established a significant presence in India in the seventeenth century, with a headquarters at Goa. Among the most remarkable missionaries of this period was the wellborn Tuscan Roberto de Nobili, who arrived in Goa in 1605. Preaching in South India, Father de Nobili learned Sanskrit, Tamil, and Telegu. Just as Matteo

Ricci and his fellow Jesuits in China first dressed as Buddhist monks and then as Confucian scholars, so de Nobili dressed as a Brahmin saṃnyāsin, *an ascetic who has renounced family life; he shaved his head, abstained from meat, and wore the sacred thread across his shoulder. He also allowed his converts to wear the sacred thread and shave their head, save for a topknot. Some of de Nobili's Jesuit brethren criticized his garb and lifestyle, but after an investigation Pope Gregory XV ruled in his favor. This policy of "accommodation" would be rejected as a result of the Malabar Rites Controversy after de Nobili's death.*

Buddhism was long dead in India by the time of de Nobili's arrival there, but was known among the Brahmins from philosophical works that described the various heterodox Indian schools, that is, those schools that rejected the authority of the Vedas. In the passage below, de Nobili, drawing from these texts, describes Buddhism and raises a question that would engage European scholars into the nineteenth century: which came first, Buddhism or Hinduism?

––––––

The first school is that of the Buddhists, who pose as atheists. Their system is very subtle or, rather, bristling with fallacies, as we shall explain in the next chapter. Their conception of theology consists in this, that they jumble together all things divine and human alike. They have produced books on the subject, keep many on hand, and are certainly remarkable for erudition. As we shall see later, no academy in India has discoursed more subtly and more copiously on natural philosophy and on the other liberal faculties. . . .

Now we come to the second proposition I have undertaken to prove, i.e., that of all the sects established in India the sect of Buddhists boasts the remotest antiquity. My first proof is gathered from an historical work, entitled the *Jina Puranam*, in which it is recorded that not only the brahmins of this realm, but the entire region together with its ruler (who bore the common and hereditary name of Devapandya) were at one time Buddhists or atheists; that subsequently, after a long period of time, there arrived from some northern region a company of men who brought with them that body of laws now current among the brahmins of the idol-worshipping class and preserved by the proponents of *maya* (as I will show later on); and that, by healing the king from a fever which he happened to contract and by doing certain other notable deeds that seemed miraculous, these men converted the king and a large portion of his subjects from the teaching of the Buddhists to the worship of idols that is now commonly practiced.

A second obvious proof in support of the antiquity of the sect of Buddhists is the fact that there is not a single book of the sacred sciences used by the other brahmin sects which fails to attack this particular sect, the Buddhists and their doctrine; strictly speaking, they could not possibly do this unless the Buddhist sect was older than their own. For how could they attack or even conjecture sects that were non-existent in their day, cropping up only after their time? Finally, because the academy of Buddhists dates so far back, the Buddhists are said to be related to the sun or born along with the sun; this is as much as to say that the appearance of the sun in the world did not precede, but was contemporaneous with, the birth of the Buddhist sect.[5]

◆ RICHARD COCKS (1566–1624)

The shogun banned Christianity in Japan in 1614, although he allowed the presence of Dutch and British traders, who had expressed no interest in converting the Japanese. Accordingly, the accounts of Buddhism by the English during this period vary considerably from those of the Jesuits in China, for example, in that they reveal very little interest in doctrine but considerable skill at the detailed description of the idols they encountered.

Richard Cocks was head of the East India Company trading post in Hirado from 1613 until it went bankrupt ten years later. In the passage below, he depicts some of the sights of Kyoto, including temples of "Dibottes"—that is, daibutsu, *or "great Buddha." The second paragraph contains his detailed description of the famous temple of Sanjusangendo. And in the final paragraph, Cocks describes Toyokuni, the shrine and tomb of the renowned general Toyotomi Hideyoshi (1537–1598), and the nearby Mimizuka, or "Ear Mound," said to contain the ears and noses of the thirty-eight thousand killed during Hideyoshi's invasions of Korea between 1592 and 1598.*

———

I went to se the monumentes of the towne, viz., the temple of *Dibottes*, w'th the hudge collosso or bras imadg (or rather idoll) in it, it being of a wonderfull bignes, the head of it reaching to the top of the temple, allthough he sat croselegged, it being all gilded over w'th gould, & a great wall or plate behind the back of it the lyke, whereon was carved the pickture of the son. The temple of it selfe is the hvgest peec. of building that eaver I saw, it not haveing any other thing in it but the idoll, w'ch standeth in a cercle or chappell just in the midell thereof, w'th 4 rowes of pillars of wood, 2 on eather side, frõ the on end of the temple to the other, each one reaching to the top if it; the compose of each pillar being 3 fathom & all dyed over w'th red occar, as all the temple w'thin is the lyke. And a littell from the North end of the temple is a tower w'th a bell hanging in it, the biggest that ever I saw. And from the Easter dore of the temple stand two rowes of ston pillars, of som dozen in a rowe, a pretty distance on from the other, going downe to a mightie hvge gate-howse, on eather side of w'ch w'thin stands a mightie gilded lyon, & w'thout the gate on lack saide (as portars) a hvdge giant, mad after a furious fation. The truth is, all of it is to be admired.

And not far from this temple is an other, of very neare 10 skore yardes in lenghe, I say ten skore; but it is narow. And in the midest thereof is placed greate bras *Dibotes* (or idoll), but nothing neare the greatenes of the former. & out of the sids of it proceed many armes w'th hands, & in each hand on thing or other, as speares, sword, dagges, spades, arrowes, knyves, frutes, fyshes, fowles, beastes, corne, & many other matter & formes; & out of the head procead many littell heades, & over the great head proceadeth a glory of long bras rayes made lyke to the son beames, as the papostes paynt over the saints. & on both sids, to the end of the howse, are set 3333 other bras images, standing on foote vpon steps, on behind an others back, all apart on from an other, w'th glories over their heades, armed out of their sids, and littell heades out of the great, as the *Dibotes* had. I enquired what those handes, & heads did signefie; and it was answered that they signefied the good and charetable deeds that those saintes (or holy men) had donne while they were living. And it is to be noted that both the *Dibotes* & all the other 3333 idols were made after an excellent forme neare to the life, & clothed w'th a gowne (or loose garment) over them, and all gilded over w'th pure gould, very fresh and glorious to behould. And just before the *Dibotes* below were sent [*sic*] 3 or 4 roes of other idolls, most of them made after a furious forme, rather lyke divells then men; & behind them all stood two deformed ons, one carring a sack of wynd on his shoulders, & the other a cerkled wreath or hoope w'th many knotes in it, the one resembling the wyndes, & the other the thvnder. In fyne this temple is the most admerablest thing that ever I saw, & may well be reconed before any of the noted 7 wonders of the world.

And som distance Westward frõ these 2 temples stands the sepulcre of ticus Samme, *allis* Quambecon Dono, a thinge to be wondred at, & rather by me admired then to be discribed, it is a hudge big howse, of an admerable workmanshipp both w'thin and w'thout far excelling either of the other temples, an w'thin it many pillars covered w'th bras enameled & gilded ou[e]r w'th gould, & the flowre of plankes very black, shynyng lyke ebony. But we could not be sufferd to enter, but only to look in a wyndos or grates. And to the place where the corps (or ashes) are set, yow must assend vp 8 or 9 steps or degrees, very lardg, made p'rte of gilded bras & p'rte of black wood or ebony. & by the corps borneth a contynewall lampe, watched by a *boz*, or pagon prist. And for the workmanshipp about that place, it exceedeth my memory to discribe it; only all I can say, it may well befitt the entering of so famouse an Emperour. And I had forgot to note downe that before the east gate of the temple of *Dibotes* stands a rownd hill of an endifferant biggnes, on the top whereof standeth a ston pillar, lyke the crosses in papistes churchyardes; w'ch hill, as I was tould, was made of the eares & noses of the Coreans w'ch were slayne when Ticus Samme did conquer that cuntrey som 24 or 25 years past. In fine, we saw divers other monumentes & pagods, very sumptuous, w'th cloisters rownd about them lyke papistes monestaries, wherin the *bozes* or pagon pristes live in great pomp, lyke our frairs & monkes in Christendom, frõ whence it seemeth they had their origenall; for the pagon religion is of more antiquetie, & as many sectes or orders as the Xxrtians.[6]

✦ CRISTOFORO BORRI (1583–1632)

Cristoforo Borri was a Milanese who joined the Society of Jesus in 1601. He distinguished himself in mathematics and astronomy, so much so that he was appointed to teach at the Jesuit Collegio di Brera in Milan. He was an advocate of the theories of Copernicus, Kepler, and Galileo, rejecting the Ptolemaic system supported by the church. Father Borri also developed his own theory of three heavens—the air, the planets and stars, and the empyrean—all of which were liquid. As a result, he ran afoul of Claudius Acquaviva (1543–1615), General of the Society of Jesus, who demanded Borri's public penance and removed him from his teaching post. Seeking to devise a new method to determine latitude with magnets, Borri requested permission to go to India. In 1615, he departed for Asia, arriving two years later in what is today Vietnam. There, along with his missionary duties, he continued his work as an astronomer, recording comets and eclipses of the sun and the moon. He left Vietnam in 1622 and returned to Europe in 1624.

In 1631, Borri published an account of Cochin China (southern Vietnam) that included a biography of the Buddha, here called Xaca. The work, from which an excerpt is given below, is significant in several ways. First, unlike so many Christian accounts before and after Borri, it is remarkably sympathetic, even comparing the Buddha to Aristotle. Second, Borri accounts for the spread of Buddhism across Asia not through the importation of idols but through the Buddha's own preaching; he believed that the Buddha was born in Siam, traveled to China, and then arrived in Japan, where he died. Third, Borri ascribed to the Buddha "the doctrine of nothing," that is, the central Mahāyāna doctrine of śūnyatā, or emptiness; reflecting his interest

in astronomy, Borri imagines that the Buddha derived this theory while contemplat-
ing the night sky. This doctrine, which Borri likely read about in Jesuit reports of
conversations with Zen monks in Japan, would profoundly affect the representation
of Buddhist philosophy in Europe in subsequent centuries. Borri's discussion here,
couched in Aristotelian terms, mentions the analogy of the rope, which occurs in
Buddhist sources. And finally, Borri explains that the Buddha changed his teachings
over the course of his life, based on the responses of his audiences; when the Chinese
objected to the radical view of nothing, the Buddha instead taught a more conven-
tional view of morality (perhaps not unlike Borri's experience with his superiors re-
garding the movement of heavenly orbs). This adaptation is reminiscent of the Bud-
dhist doctrine of upāya, *or skillful methods. Here, Borri's presentation is benign; later*
European accounts would portray it as a more sinister deathbed recantation.

———

The end of all sects is either the god they adore, or the glory and happiness they
expect; some believing the immortality of the soul, others concluding that all ends
when the body dies. Upon these two principles the eastern nations build all their
sects; all which took their origin from a great metaphysician of the kingdom of
Siam, whose name was Xaca, much more ancient than Aristotle, and nothing inferior to him in capacity, and the knowledge of natural things. The acuteness of this
man's wit exciting him to consider the nature and fabric of the world, reflecting on
the beginning and end of all things, and particularly of human nature, the chief
lady of this worldly palace; he once went up to the top of a mountain, and there
attentively observing the moon, which rising in the darkness of the night, gently
raised itself above the horizon to be hid again the next day in the same darkness,
and the sun rising in the morning to set again at night, he concluded that moral as
well as physical and natural things were nothing, came of nothing, and ended in
nothing. Therefore returning home, he wrote several books and large volumes on
the subject, entitling them, "Of Nothing"; wherein he taught that the things of this
world, by reason of the duration and measure of time, are nothing; for though they
had existence, said he, yet they would be nothing, nothing at present, and nothing
in time to come, for the present being but a moment, was the same as nothing.

His second argument he grounded on the composition of things; let us instance, said he, a rope, which not being naturally distinguished from its parts,
inasmuch as they give its being and composition, so it appears that the rope as a
rope is nothing; for as a rope it is no distinct thing from the threads it is composed
of, and the hemp has no other being but the elements whereof its substance consists; so that resolving all things after this manner into the elements, and those to

a sort of *materia prima* and mere *potentia*, which is therefore actually nothing, he at last proved, that the heavenly things, as well as those under the heavens, were truly nothing!

In the same manner did he argue as to moral things; that the natural happiness of man did not consist in a positive concurrence of all that is good, which he looked upon as impossible, but rather in being free from all that is evil, and therefore said, it was no other thing but to have no disease, pain, trouble, or the like; and for a man to have such power over his passions as not to be sensible of affection or aversion, to honor or disgrace, want or plenty, riches or poverty, life or death, and that herein consisted true beatitude: whence he inferred, that all these things being nothing, they took their origin as it were from a cause not efficient but material, from a principle which in truth was nothing but an eternal, infinite, immutable, almighty, and to conclude, a God that was nothing, and the origin of this nothing! . . .

Having established this doctrine of nothing, he gathered some scholars, by whose means he spread it throughout all the east. But the Chinese, who knew that a sect which reduced all things to nothing was hurtful to the government, would not hearken to it, nor allow there was no punishment for wicked men, or that the happiness of the good should be reduced only to being free from sufferings in this world, and the authority of the Chinese being so great, others following their example rejected his doctrine. Xaca dissatisfied that he was disappointed of followers, changed his mind, and retiring wrote several other great books, teaching that there was a real origin of all things, a lord of heaven, hell, immortality, and transmigration of souls from one body to another, better or worse, according to the merits or demerits of the person; though they do not forget to assign a sort of heaven and hell for the souls of departed, expressing the whole metaphorically under the names of things corporeal, and of the joys and sufferings of this world. . . .

The Japanese and others making so great account of this opinion of nothing, was the cause that when Xaca the author of it approached his death, calling together his disciples, he protested to them on the word of a dying man, that during the many years he had lived and studied, he had found nothing so true, nor any opinion so well grounded as was the sect of nothing; and though his second doctrine seemed to differ from it, yet they must look upon it as no contradiction or recantation, but rather a proof and confirmation of the first, though not in plain terms, yet by way of metaphors and parables, which might all be applied to the opinion of nothing, as would plainly appear by his books.[7]

The Portuguese Álvaro Semedo joined the Society of Jesus in 1602, departing for Goa six years later. In 1613, he arrived in Nanjing. In 1616, he and his fellow Jesuits were imprisoned during an anti-Christian persecution and exiled to Macao, returning to the mainland in 1621. In 1625, he visited the ancient Tang capital of Xian, where he became the first European to study the famous Nestorian Christian stele erected in 781.

In 1636, Father Semedo was ordered to return to Europe to raise funds and find recruits for the China mission. Motivated in part by these aims, he wrote a description of China that was published in his native Portuguese in Lisbon in 1642 as Relação da propagação da fé no reyno da China e outros adjacentes *(Report on the Propagation of the Faith in the Kingdom of China and other adjacent [lands]). Quickly translated into Spanish, it was edited by Manoel Faria y Souza (Manoel Freyre, whom we shall meet in chapter 4) and published as* Imperio de la China. *After that edition enjoyed considerable success, it was translated into English and published in 1655 as* The history of that great and renowned monarchy of China.

In the passage that follows, Semedo describes the Buddha as having renounced the world out of guilt over his mother's death (according to traditional accounts, his mother died seven days after his birth, but he did not cause it), then teaching the doctrine for forty-nine years (according to the tradition, forty-five), after which his followers "collected his papers." Semedo elaborates on the idea found in Father Borri's account that the Buddha had two doctrines: an exterior doctrine for the common people, in which rebirth occurs as a result of one's deeds, and an interior doctrine meant for the wise, in which all things are but transformations of a first principle.

―――――

The third *Sect* is of the *Pagods*, from *India*, from the part of *Indostan*; which Sect they call *Xaca*, from the Authour of it: concerning whom, they fable; that he was conceived by his Mother *Maia*, only upon the sight of a white Elephant, which she saw in her sleep; and for the more puritie she brought him forth at one of her flancks, and then presently died, being but nineteen yeares of age. And that, considering the death of his Mother, the cause whereof he was by his Birth, he resolved to leave the world, and to do pennance; the which he did in a Mountain called the Snowy Mountaine, where he had fower Masters, with whom he studied twelve yeares; so that by that time he was thirty yeares of age, he was accomplished in the Science of the first principle. He took the name of *Xekia*, or *Xaca*: he taught his doctrine for the space of 49 yeares; he had many Scholars, who, after his death collected his papers, and spread his doctrine through the greater part of Asia.

This *Sect* entered into *China* in the year of our Redemption 63. The Emperor *Hanmin*; being commanded in a dream, (as their books report) to send for it in. The *Bonzi*, who were the preachers of that *Sect*, were well received of him, and at the beginning, were very powerfull, much esteemed, and in so great number, that they say, they were three *millions*. But at this day they are very few in respect of that number: whether it were that they trusting in their multitude, or in the Kings favour, committed some notable disorder; or (what is more likely) by reason of the misfortune that befell many Kings, since their coming in: and by this meanes they are so declined, that unlesse it be in the offices and Acts of their divine worship, there is but little account made of them among the *Chinesses* . . . .

The end of all these *Sects* of the *Bonzi* is to do penance in this life, to be better provided in the next. They believe the Transmigration of *Pythagoras*, and that the soules departed go to hell; which, they hold, doth containe nine severall places; and after they have passed through them all, those of the best sort, are borne men againe, others of a middle sort, are turned into living creatures, like unto men. But they are in the worst condition, that go into birds, who may not so much as hope in the next Transmigration to become men; but at soonest in another after, having first gone into some other living creature. This is the generall beliefe, not only of the common people (in whom, these errours are radicated beyond imagination) but also in people of better account.

But their wisest men, or to speak more truly, they that are most given to Atheisme, forsaking this way, which they call the Exteriour, do follow another, more *interiour* or secret; the knowledge whereof they preserve, with great care among themselves; placing their whole intent on the understanding of the *first principle*, (which is properly the doctrine of *Xaca*) whom they believe to be the same, in all things; and all things to be the same with him; without any essentiall difference; operating according to the *extrinsick* Qualities of the subject; as wax is formed into severall figures, the which being dissolved by liquefaction, remaine in substance the selfe same waxe.[8]

◆ ATHANASIUS KIRCHER (1602–1680)

One of the most famous scholars of the seventeenth century was the great Jesuit savant Athanasius Kircher, described as "the last man who knew everything." He wrote some forty works on a remarkable range of topics, including biblical studies, geol-

ogy, biology, and engineering. The most famous of these was his Oedipus Aegyptia-
cus *(Egyptian Oedipus), a three-volume study of Egypt published between 1652 and
1654, so named because Father Kircher believed—incorrectly, as it turned out—that
he had solved the riddle of Egyptian hieroglyphics. He thought that Egypt was the
source of human civilization; Adam and Eve, he argued, spoke Egyptian.*

Another of Kircher's famous works was China Illustrata, *published in Latin in
1667. He wrote it without leaving Rome, drawing from the (by that time) considerable
corpus of reports and letters sent by his fellow Jesuits from India, China, and Japan.
From these, Kircher discerned a direct connection between Egypt and China. After
the flood, Noah's son Ham (Cham) went to Egypt and then to Persia, eventually establishing colonies in Bactria. From there, his progeny spread to China, which was
the last region of the earth to be colonized. The Chinese were thus descendants of the
Egyptians, and derived their writing system from hieroglyphics. They also received
their religion from Egypt, many centuries later. Drawing from Herodotus, Kircher
notes that in 525 BCE, the Persian king Cambyses II, son of Cyrus the Great, defeated
the Egyptians at the Battle of Pelusium and proceeded to Memphis, where he captured the pharaoh, killed the sacred cow, and slaughtered thousands of Egyptians,
including hundreds of priests.*

Kircher also explains in China Illustrata *that the Egyptian priests who survived
the slaughter escaped by sea to India, where they discovered ancient monuments to
Hermes, Bacchus, and Osiris, and revived the worship of these gods. From there,
Egyptian religion, with its gods and goddesses and its doctrine of the transmigration
of souls, spread to Indochina, China, and Japan. This is specifically the case with
Buddhism in China, which Father Kircher calls the sect of Siequa (that is, Śākyamuni Buddha) or Omyto (Amitābha), and whose idols and temples resembled Egyptian shrines. The figure responsible for spreading Egyptian superstition across Asia
was the Buddha. Based on reports from the China mission, and his own research on
the religions of India, Kircher provides this unflattering portrait in the passage that
follows.*

———

The first creator and architect of the superstition was a very sinful brahmin im-
bued with Pythagoreanism. He was not content just to spread the doctrine, but
even added to it so much that there is scarcely any one who is able to describe the
doctrine or to write about it. He was an imposter known all over the East. The
Indians called him Rama, the Chinese Xe Kian, the Japanese Xaca, and the Turks
Chiaga. This deadly monster was born in central India in the place which the Chinese call Tien Truc Gnoc. His birth was portentous. They say his mother had a

dream and saw a white elephant come first from her mouth and then from her left side. Hence the white elephant was held in great esteem by the kings of Siam, Laos, Tonchin, and China. These kings value white elephants more than their kingdoms. They think themselves blessed if one of these beasts is given them by a gift of the gods. We will discuss the apotheosis of this elephant later. So Xaca was born and he was the first who is said to have killed his mother. Then he pointed one hand toward heaven and the other down to the earth and said that except for him, there was none holy, not in heaven nor in earth. Then he betook himself to the mountain recesses and there he instituted this abominable idolatry with Satan's help. Afterwards he infected the whole Orient with his pestilent dogmas. The Chinese Annals say that when he emerged from his solitary hermitage, a divine, (or more likely, a satanic) spirit filled him. He gathered together about 80,000 disciples. He selected 500 of these, and then 100 from these. Finally, he selected ten as being the best suited for teaching his horrible doctrines. He had chosen them as intimate counselors and associates in his crimes. Lest his doctrines be called in question by anyone, when dying, he decreed that the Pythagorean epithet be placed in his books. This phrase is, "He himself said," or, "So our books teach us." This means that it is evil to question the truth or the infallibility of these absurd fables, which are horrible and execrable. These are not tenets, but crimes. They are not doctrines, but abominations. They are not histories, but fables.[9]

◆   JEAN-BAPTISTE TAVERNIER (1605–1689)

The French diamond merchant Jean-Baptiste Tavernier is best known for acquiring the huge uncut Tavernier Blue on one of his journeys to India. He then sold it to Louis XIV for a large sum. The diamond would eventually be cut to become the Hope Diamond, currently on display at the Smithsonian Institution.

Over the course of his life, Tavernier traveled extensively throughout Europe and the Middle East. His voyages also took him to Asia, sailing as far as Java. He visited India at least five times between 1640 and 1667. In 1676, he published Les Six Voyages de Jean-Baptiste Tavernier, *which was widely read, followed in 1679 by* Recueil de Plusieurs Relations *(Collection of Several Reports). This supplement included accounts by his brother Daniel, whose travels took him to Tonkin (spelled Tunquin) in what is today Vietnam.*

The following description is from a chapter in that supplement entitled "Of the Religion and Superstition of the Tunquineses." Here, the Buddha is called Chacabout, and a version of "ten non-virtues" of Buddhism—killing, stealing, sexual mis-

conduct, lying, divisive speech, harsh speech, senseless speech, covetousness, harmful intent, and wrong view—is provided. We also find an early use of the term medita-tion *to describe one of the activities of Buddhist monks, although it likely carries an earlier connotation of study or contemplation rather than the formal seated practice it connotes today.*

The *Tunquineses* as to matters of Religion are divided into three Sects: The first takes its original from an ancient Philosopher called *Confucius*, whose Memory is very famous over all *China*, and the neighbouring Countries. Their Doctrine asserts that Man is compos'd of two parts, the one fine and subtil, the other mate-rial and gross; and that when Man dies, the subtiler part goes into the Air, and the grossest part stays in the Earth. This Sect maintains the use of Sacrifices, and adores the seven Planets. But among all their Gods and Idols they have four in particular venerations; the Names of these Gods are *Rauma*, *Betolo*, *Ramonu*, and *Brama*. They have a Goddess also, whose Name is *Satisbana*, which is she whom the Women adore; but for the King and the *Mandarins*, especially the more stu-dious sort, they adore the Heavens. The second Sect had for its Founder a certain Hermite called *Chacabout*, and is followed by the most part of the meaner people. He has taught them the Transmigration of Souls, and has enjoyn'd his Followers to observe 10 Commandments.

The first is, That they shall not kill. 2. That they shall not steal. 3. That they shall not defile their Bodies. 4. That they shall not lye. 5. That they shall not be un-faithful in their words. 6. That they shall restrain their inordinate Desires. 7. That they shall do injury to no man. 8. That they shall not be great Talkers. 9. That they shall not give way to their Anger. 10. That they shall labour to their utmost to get Knowledge.

As for them that design to live a Religious Life, they must renounce the Delights of this Life, be charitable to the poor, overcome their Passions, and give themselves up to Meditations. He taught moreover, that after this Life there were ten distinct places of Joy and Torment: and that the Contemners of this Law should feel Tor-ments proportionable to their Offences, without any end of their Torments. That they that endeavour'd to fulfill his Law, and had fail'd in any point, they should wander in divers Bodies for 3000 years before they entered into happiness. But that they who had perfectly obeyed his Law, should be rewarded without suffering any change of Body. And that he himself had been born ten time, before he en-joyed the Bliss which he possessed, not having in his first Youth been illuminated with that Knowledge which he afterwards attained. This *Chacabout* was one of the greatest Impostors that ever was in *Asia*, having spread his Opinions over all the Kingdom of *Siam*, over a great part of the Provinces of *Japan*, and from thence into *Tunquin*, where he died.[10]

◆   ROBERT KNOX (1641–1720)

In 1659, a young Englishman named Robert Knox was among a crew of sailors taken prisoner by Rājasiṃha II, the king of Sri Lanka, after their ship lost its mast in a storm. Knox spent more than nineteen years there, eventually escaping from his Buddhist captors to a Dutch settlement on the island. From there, he sailed to England. On his long voyage home, he drafted a volume entitled An Historical Relation of the Island Ceylon in the East-Indies. *It was published in 1681 and read widely, serving as one of Daniel Defoe's inspirations for* Robinson Crusoe.*

Here, Knox describes the making and consecration of images of the Buddha.*

───

And these are their *Anniversary Feasts* to the honour of those Gods, whose power extends to help them in this Life; now follows the manner of their Service to the *Buddou*, who it is, they say, that must save their Souls, and the *Festival* in honour of him.

To represent the memorial of him to their eye, they do make small Images of Silver, Brass, and Clay, and Stone, which they do honour with Sacrifices and Worship, showing all the signs of outward reverence which possibly they can. In most places where there are hollow Rocks and Caves, they do set up Images in memorial of this God. Unto which they that are devoutly bent, at *New* and *Full* Moons do carry Victuals, and worship.

His great *Festival* is in the Month of *March* at their New-years Tide. The Places where he is commemorated are two, not Temples, but the one a *Mountain* and the other a *Tree*; either to the one or the other, they at this time go with Wives and Children, for Dignity and Merit one being esteemed equal with the other.

The *Mountain* is at the *South* end of the Countrey, called *Hammalella*, but by Christian People, *Adam's Peak*, the highest in the whole Island; where, as has been said before, is the Print of the *Buddou's* foot, which he left on the top of that Mountain in a Rock, from whence he ascended to Heaven. Unto this *footstep* they give worship, light up Lamps, and offer Sacrifices, laying them upon it, as upon an Altar. The benefit of the Sacrifices that are offered here do belong unto the *Moors Pilgrims*, who come from the other Coast to beg, this having been given them heretofore by a former King. So that at the season there are great numbers of them always waiting there to receive their accustomed Fees.

The *Tree* is at the *North* end of the King's Dominions at *Annarodgburro*. This *Tree*, they say, came flying over from the other Coast, and there planted it self, as it now stands, under which the *Buddou-God* at his being on earth used, as they say, often to sit. This is now become a place of solemn worship. The due performance whereof they reckon not to be a little meritorious: insomuch that, as they report, Ninety Kings have since reigned there successively, where by the ruins that still remain, it appears they spared not for pains and labour to build Temples and high Monuments to the honour of this God, as if they had been born only to hew Rocks, and great Stones, and lay them up in heaps. These Kings are now happy Spirits, having merited it by these their labours.

Those whose Ability or Necessity serve them not to go to these Places, may go to some private *Vihars* nearer.

For this God above all other, they seem to have an high respect and Devotion: as will appear by this that follows. Ladies and Gentlewomen of good Quality, will sometimes in a Fit of Devotion to the *Buddou*, go a begging for him. The greatest Ladies of all do not indeed go themselves, but send their Maids dressed up finely in their stead. These Women taking the Image along with them, carry it upon the palms of their hand covered with a piece of white Cloth; and so go to mens houses, and will say, *We come a begging of your Charity for the Buddou towards his Sacrifice.* And the People are very liberal. They give only of three things to him, either *Oyl* for his lamps, or *Rice* for his sacrifice, or *Money* or *Cotton yarn* for his use.

Poor men will often go about begging Sustenance for themselves by this means: They will get a Book of Religion, or a *Buddou*'s Image in a Case, wrapping both in a white Cloth, which they carry with great reverence. And then they beg in the name of the Book or the God. And the People bow down to them, and give their Charity, either Corn, or Money, or Cotton Yarn. Sometimes they will tell the Beggar, *What have I to give?* And he will reply, *as the saying is, as much as you can take up between your two fingers is Charity.* After he has received a gift from any, he pronounceth a great deal of blessing upon him, *Let the blessing of the Gods and the* Buddou *go along with you; let your corn ripen, let your Cattle increase, let your Life be long, &c.*

Some being devoutly disposed, will make the Image of this God at their own charge. For the making whereof they must bountifully reward the Founder. Before the *Eyes* are made, it is not accounted a God, but a lump of ordinary Metal, and thrown about the Shop with no more regard than anything else. But when the *Eyes* are to be made, the Artificer is to have a good gratification, besides the first agreed upon reward. The *Eyes* being formed, it is thenceforeward a *God*. And then, being brought with honour from the Workman's Shop, it is dedicated by Solemnities and Sacrifices, and carried with great state into its shrine or little house, which is before built and prepared for it.

Sometimes a man will order the *Smith* to make this Idol, and then after it is made will go about with it to well-disposed People to contribute toward the Wages the Smith is to have for making it. And men will freely give towards the charge. And this is looked upon in the man that appointed the Image to be made, as a notable piece of Devotion.[11]

♦ ABBÉ DE CHOISY (1644–1724)

François Timoléon, Abbé de Choisy, was a well-known diarist and transvestite of seventeenth-century France. Although appointed an abbé *as a young boy, his mother, a frequent presence at the court of Louis XIV, dressed him as a girl until he was eighteen, and he would regularly dress as a woman later in life. A serious illness seems to have briefly increased his interest in the religious life, and in 1684 he coauthored a work on the immortality of the soul.*

The Abbé also expressed an interest in the foreign missions, and when Louis XIV decided to send a delegation to the court of Siam, he volunteered to lead it. The Chevalier de Chaumont (see the following entry) was chosen instead, with the Abbé made second in command. They set sail in 1685. After his return, the Abbé was elected to the French Academy and wrote books on the French monarchy and on the history of the church. Although these were popular works, the Abbé de Choisy is remembered primarily for his memoirs of scandalous life at the French court and his account of his life as a woman, both published posthumously.

Unlike other Roman Catholic clerics who visited Buddhist lands, in his account of the journey, the Abbé expresses little interest in religious matters, but seems particularly interested in gold. This passage is from his journal entry of October 30, 1685.

———

Then, after having walked a lot, we arrived at the King's pagoda. When I went in I thought I was in a church. The nave is supported by tall thick columns, without architectural decoration. The columns, walls, vault, everything is gilded. The choir is closed off by a kind of heavily decorated rood-screen. Above the screen are three idols or pagodas (you know that "pagoda" can be both the name of a temple and of an idol) of solid gold, as high as a man, and seated in the fashion of the country. They have diamonds on their forehead, fingers, and navel. The image on the left on entering is the most esteemed. It is the image of their God, who lived 2,000 years ago in the island of Ceylon: it was moved to several countries and finally was taken by a King of Siam. The monks say this image sometimes goes for excursions outside the palace, but the desire to do so only comes when one can see nothing. The choir is small and very dark; there are at least fifty lamps continually lit there. But what will surprise you is that at the end of the choir is an image in solid gold, that is to say gold poured into a mould. It may be forty-two feet high by thirteen or fourteen feet wide, and three inches in thickness. It is said there is 12,400,000 *livres* of gold here. We also saw in other parts of the pagoda seventeen or eighteen figures in solid gold, as high as a man, most having diamonds on their fingers, emeralds and some rubies on their foreheads and their navels. These images are without doubt of gold; we touched and handled them, and although we only got to within five or six feet of the big statue, without touching it, I think it is made of gold like the others; to the eye it seemed the same metal. In addition to these there were more than thirty idols with golden vestments. I have not mentioned the three idols twenty-five feet high, nor the 150 or more of ordinary height, for they only had two or three layers of gold. I only saw two made of silver, and a few in copper. There were also some two feet high, made of a mixture of gold and copper, more brilliant than gold, which were called *tambac*. I do not find this as beautiful as they make out; it is perhaps the *electrum* of Solomon. I also noticed several trees, whose trunks and leaves were of gold; the work is very delicate, and is the tribute which most kings dependent on the King of Siam send. After having seen so much gold, we admired a cannon so prodigiously big that the balls from its bore must weigh more than 300 pounds, according to the estimates of the experts; the mouth was fourteen inches across.[12]

✦ ALEXANDRE, CHEVALIER DE CHAUMONT (1640–1710)

Alexandre, Chevalier de Chaumont, a distinguished naval officer, was appointed by Louis XIV to lead a diplomatic mission to Siam in 1685. His purpose was twofold: to establish trade relations and to convert the king to Christianity. Toward the latter end, four Roman Catholic missionaries were sent as members of the delegation, along with six Jesuits, who went officially as scientific observers (they were astronomers and mathematicians) rather than missionaries. One of these Jesuits was Guy Tachard, who appears later in the chapter.

In the chevalier's account of Buddhism, the Buddha is Nacadon and Buddhist monks are Talapoins. The Buddha's brother, who he has crucified, is in fact his evil cousin, Devadatta, whose story we soon will encounter in greater detail.

———

Their Religion to speak properly, is onely a parcel of Fabulous Tales which serve onely to bring respect and profit to the *Talapoins*; who recommend not so much any Vertue to them, as that of giving them Money: They have Laws, which they strictly observe, especially outwardly. Their end in all their good works is the hope of a happy Transmigration after their death, into the body of a rich Man, of a King, or great Lord, or of a tame animal, as Cows or Sheep, for these People are so far *Pythagoreans*; they for this reason do much esteem these Animals, and dare not, as I have noted, kill any of them, as knowing not but they may kill their Father or Mother, or some other of their Relations. They believe a Hell, where great enormities are severely punished, onely for a time; and also a Paradise, wherein men of vertues are rewarded, where having become Angles for some time, they afterwards return into the Body of some man or other animal.

The *Talapoins* chief business is, to read, sleep, eat, sing and beg; they go every morning to the Houses or barges of persons they know, and stand there for a while with great reservedness, holding their Fan so that they cover half their Faces; if they see any one disposed to given them any thing, they tarry till they have received it; they eat whatsoever is given them, whether Pullets or any other flesh, but they never drink Wine, at least before people; they perform no office nor prayers to any Divinity. The *Siamoises* believe there have been three great *Talapoins*, who by their most sublime merits in several thousand Transmigrations, have become Gods, and having been so, have moreover acquired such great merits, that they have been wholly annihilated; which is the term of the greatest merit, and the greatest recompence attainable, being no longer fired by their frequent changes of bodies: The last of these three *Talapoins* is the greatest God called Nacodon, because he has been in five thousand bodies; in one of these Transmigrations, of *Talapoin* he became a Cow, his brother would have killed him several times; but there needs a great book to describe the miracles, which they say, Nature, and not God wrought for his preservation. In short, his Brother was thrown into Hell for his great sins, where Nacodon caused him to be crucified; and for this foolish reason they abominate the Image of Christ on the Cross, saying we adore the image of this Brother of their God, who was crucified for his Crimes.

This *Nacodon* being annihilated, they have no God at present, yet his Law remains, but onely among the *Talapoins* who affirm that after some years, there will be an Angel who will become *Talapoin*, and afterwards an absolute Divinity, who by his great merits may come to be annihilated. These are the principles of their Creed; for 'tis not to be imagined they adore the Idols, which are in their *Pagodes* as Divinities, but honour them onely as men of great deserts, whose Souls are at present in some King, Cow or *Talapoin*. And herein consists their Religion, which to speak properly acknowledges no God. Vice, say they, carries with it its own punishment, making the Soul pass into the body of some vile Fellow, or Hog, or Crow, or Tyger, or such like animal. They admit of Angels, which they believe to have been the souls of just men and good *Talapoins*; as to Demons, they say, they have been the souls of wicked persons.[13]

✦ FERNAÕ DE QUEYROZ (1617–1688)

The Portuguese Jesuit Fernaõ de Queyroz lived in India from 1635 until the year of his death. In 1687, he completed The Temporal and Spiritual Conquest of Ceylon; *he intended its title as a prophecy. Pedro de Basto, a Portuguese lay brother of the Society of Jesus, had died in Cochin in India in 1645. Although uneducated, he was respected for his deep piety and for his visions of Jesus in which he received prophecies. He predicted, for example, that as punishment for their sins, the Portuguese would lose Ceylon to the Dutch, which in fact occurred in 1656. However, Brother Pedro also predicted that the Portuguese would regain the island from the Dutch. In preparation for this, Father Queyroz wrote a book about Ceylon that could be used by his compatriots in their temporal and spiritual conquest of the island.*

The prophecy never came to pass, and Queyroz's book would not be published in Portuguese until 1916 (with an English translation following in 1930). The book contains two descriptions of the life of the Buddha. The first is by Queyroz himself, and details the life of the Buddha as he understood it was known in Sri Lanka. The second biography, one commissioned by Queyroz from a fellow Jesuit in China, follows in the next section.

Here, Queyroz begins by describing "the Sect of Ganezes"; in Singhalese, ganinse, *literally "master," is a term for a Buddhist monk.*

———

It behoves now to give some account of the Sect of the Ganezes. It is absolutely necessary not to confuse this Sect with that of the Veddaõs [followers of the Vedas] or of the Bramanes [Brahmins], a mistake into which some have fallen, because both are received in Ceylon and in all India beyond the Ganges, in Tartary and Japan. The short account we give here, because we could not find a more complete one, will also serve to compare what the Chingalas [Singhalese] say with what the Bonzes of China affirm, in order to see what the Chinese have added, as Father Thomas Pereyra, who communicated to us a short summary of the writings of the Bonzes of China, conjectures with good reason.

It is recorded in the Chingala scriptures that there was a King in Vdelî (at first the court of the Great Mogul, after he conquered the Kingdom of the Patânas whither the present King again transferred his Court after residing a long time in Agra) the lord of many provinces. There was born to him a very handsome son; and assembling many Astrologers, he ordered them to cast his nativity. This being done, they told the King in amazement that his son would not only despise his Kingdom and Lordship, but also all the things of this life, and that he would go travelling about the world teaching a new Law and doctrine. The King, becoming a prey to fresh anxiety, tried to avert the inclination of the son, and when the years of infancy were past, he ordered him to be kept in a Palace, newly built, very sumptuous and gay, and so taken care of, that he should neither speak nor deal with any one save with those deputed for the purpose, [so that he should] neither see nor hear anything which could give him pain or sorrow; and so he kept him making much of him and giving him pleasure up to the age of 18 years; wherein owing to the constant prayers and importunities he made to his Father and Mother, because he saw himself like a prisoner, they finally gave him Permission to sally from the Palace and cloister in which he had been brought up and to see and converse with whomever he liked. He went out, accompanied by many who guided him and followed him, some on the orders of the Father, and meeting a cripple on crutches, he asked in surprise why he walked on wooden feet. They answered that it was a common thing to meet with people who were lame, blind, or subject to other natural or accidental defects. He went on his way confused till he met a decrepit old man leaning on a staff; and as it was a thing never seen by him, he inquired how it was caused. They satisfied him by saying that it was a defect of old age. Being now more sad, on this or on another occasion he came upon a dead man whom they were carrying for burial amidst the wailing of children, kinsmen and friends. Struck by what he saw, he inquired the cause, and they replied that they were going to bury the corpse, because it would soon be corrupted. And seeking to know what manner of thing death was which caused so many evils, he understood from them that it proceeded from a want of natural heat which sustains life, and that without that the body is bereft of all sensibility and that all living things infallibly must die. "Then, have I also to die?" asked the Prince. They assured him that it was so. He asked "When"? They said in reply that they did not know, because it was reserved to God. He became very sad, and going about with this thought, he met a pilgrim or Yogi and telling him of the sadness and affliction which surrounded him in consequence of what he had seen and heard, he begged him counsel about determining [a way of] life. He advised him to quit the world and lead a solitary life. Determining to do so, he escaped one night without being noticed and went wandering about the world. He gathered 10,000 disciples and of them he picked out 500 and finally kept only 10, and in the year 896 before our Redemption, when Joas was the High Priest in Jerusalem, he came to Ceylon, accompanied by many disciples, and went to live in the country of Deorâta on the skirts of the Peak of Adam, leading a penitential life in the yellow garb, which the Ganezes adopted from him and which is used also by the Bramanes who chose that life.

Some say he taught the worship of one only God, penance and mercy, about which they relate of him impossible instances; but it is false that he gave them the ten precepts of the commandments adding two, not to drink wine nor kill any living thing, that he denied the immortality of the soul and attributed all the successes and human events to fate and to the Planets; whereby they deny the first cause, attributing everything to chance, a principle most in keeping with ingratitude. Others would have it that he taught them the law of Moses, but this is because they confuse this Sect with that of the Veddaõs, about which we shall speak presently. He taught the transmigration of souls, a Dogma common to all Asiatic heathendom, adopted by Pythagoras in Italy and by Plato in Greece. Before crossing the sea on his way to the coast of Arracan and Pegu, he left some disciples to establish his doctrine, and they say he impressed on the Peak of Adam the footprint of which we have already treated. Lomba only tells us that he had many other errors and that his penances served as a bark to Hell. For he who considers the extensive regions which venerate him, at least will doubt whether he leads more to perdition than shameful Mahomet, whom he preceded by more than 1400 years. The worship they pay him is to prostrate themselves on the ground three times repeating the words *Buddum Sarnaõ Gachaõ*, as if to say: Buddum, be Mindful of me.[14]

✦ TOMÁS PEREIRA (1645–1708)

The Temporal and Spiritual Conquest of Ceylon contains the most detailed biography of the Buddha to be produced by a European in the seventeenth century. It was written not by the author of the book, Fernaõ de Queyroz, in India, but by another Portuguese Jesuit, Tomás Pereira, in China. Father Pereira was one of the most fa-

mous of the Padres da Corte, the Jesuits who served the emperor in Beijing. He was a skilled musician, writing a book entitled "The Elements of Music" in Chinese, performing on both the clavichord and the organ (he built a large organ in a church in Beijing), and instructing the children of the Kangxi Emperor in European music. Upon his death in Beijing in 1708, the emperor ordered special honors at his funeral.

At the request of his compatriot in Sri Lanka, Father Queyroz, Pereira procured a three-volume biography of the Buddha with the assistance of a recent Chinese convert, himself a former Buddhist monk, or as Queyroz describes him, "a Bonze converted to our Holy Faith, who had been a Prelate among them."[15] From this, and likely with the help of that monk, Pereira produced a summary some eight thousand words in length, at the time the most extensive biography of the Buddha in a European language—but it would not be read until the twentieth century. Queyroz included the biography in his account of Sri Lanka, under the heading "Account which the Missionaries of China give of the Idol Buddu."

Although faithfully following a Chinese Buddhist source, Pereira intersperses his paraphrase of the text with all manner of rude remarks about the Buddha and Buddhism.

———

CHAPTER 17

Account which the Missionaries of China
give of the Idol Buddu

As I [Father Queyroz] came to know that it was the general opinion of the Missionaries that the Buddū of Ceylon is the same as the Fô (or Föe as others write it) of China, I wrote on the subject to Father Thomas Pereyra of our Society, Missionary resident at the Court of Pekin, the Metropolis of that vast Monarchy. And he making a summary of the books of a Bonze converted to our Holy Faith, who had been a Prelate among them, wherein are contained the Scriptures which are fully believed in by them, sent me the following account, though greatly abridged from what is contained in the original. He said as follows:—

In order to satisfy the desire of Your Reverence without being irksome, I took no small pains on account of the awkwardness of the Chinese style, so contrary to ours, to put things as far as I could in our own way, for their style would certainly cause great confusion, although as a political nation they do not fail to observe the substantial and common rules of historical composition. For this purpose I thought it best and more to the purpose to give a full account of what the bonzes here believe of their Fô, the principal Pagode [deity] out of many others, drawn from the writings, the most authoritative among them, although in everything they are blind and deceived by the Devil. I took this resolution, because I thought that by comparing the fables, many of them invented by those people, with the notices which Your Reverence will find there, any of them would be found to be conflicting, and you would be able by comparision [*sic*] to discover the falsity of the—for them—infallible Scriptures. It is really unworthy of so cultured a people to deviate so widely from the truth, but when the light of the true Faith does not shine, the saying of St. Paul—*Tradidit illos Deus in reprobum sensum* [Rom. 1:28: God delivered them up to a reprobate sense] I very clearly verified.

I must point out, however, that what they give at length in three tomes I have here summarised in short chapters, taking what is to the purpose, and leaving out what is useless, with all fidelity. I have also omitted some chapters, fruitless to our purpose, inverting the order of others by placing them where they are more to the purpose, pointing out however on the margin the number of the Chinese chapter which contains the statement and giving it almost always in their very words, so that in this way all things may be clearer and better arranged.

Summary of the First Part

OF THE BIRTH AND LIFE OF FÔ UP TO THE
THIRTIETH YEAR OF AGE

After the text of the first chapter [which reads] ("The marks and signs of Xekia (or Fô) began from his own essence; the essence descends to take form; the essence and form were joined into one"), it continues in obscure language ("If he wished to remain without being born, who would convert the world? Who would guide the age unless he became man?") and other expressions which may, without violence, be applied to the first cause or according to their Philosophy to some *materia prima* incapable of any intrinsic change, which ever remains the same being, though it varies with the variety of extrinsic changes, deceiving the ignorant by this confusion and obscurity. There are many discussions over these words. But the common enemy could not better pervert what we believe of our Redeemer, many centuries before the Incarnation of Christ, as will be seen later, unless it is a false addition due to the malice of the Chinese, after they came to know of our Holy Faith, which was brought thither some 900 years ago.

In Chapters 2, 3, 4, 5, 6 and 7 this Scripture gives the transmigration of Pythagoras, giving to Fô many previous ages. At one time he is the son of a King, at another a Hermit or a Pagode in Heaven, again a servant boy on earth, but always mindful of a last incarnation to help men, ever speaking on this point with Angels and other inhabitants of Heaven whom this Sect supposes to have been men, converted into good and evil spirits according to their deeds, keeping ever before his eyes the family of King Tsimfan as the most virtuous and best fitted for his birth, and because it is in the middle of the world adapted for the promulgation of his Law throughout the whole of it.

When the time of his Incarnation had arrived, he, being then a Pagode, descended from Heaven and entered through the right side of the Princess Moye, his Mother, who at the same time, as if in a dream, saw him descending from heaven, riding upon a white elephant with six tusks, and it appearing to her likewise that she saw him in her womb as if in a vase of glass; at sight of which she felt supreme delight and was filled with a resplendence, considering in her heart this mystery, and thenceforth her food came to her from Heaven. When the time of birth arrived, which according to their and our computation was 1027 years before the true Incarnation of the Word of God, in the reign of King Cheo in China, on the eighth day of the fourth moon in the twenty-fourth year of his reign, was born in India in the Kingdom of Gûci, Gûcilô, his Father being Tsimfan (who must have been his suppositious father, if they wish to be consistent, a matter to which they pay little attention) and when he was expelled from the Kingdom, his son, though he was the first born, did not accept the Crown, though the people gathered round him and acclaimed him. The Father coming to know of this said: my son Xekia knows how to be dutiful. Hence it is that in China the Bonzes are generally called Xekia, just as we say Dominicans or Franciscans. At that hour the Mother accompanied by many Dames went into a garden in which was a tree called Pelôlo (as the Chinese language has no R in it may even be Perôro) and catching hold of a branch of it with the right hand she gave birth to the son through the armpit, according to their pictures, though the text does not mention it.

As soon as he was born, he stood up and turned without help! to the four quarters, and took seven steps in each of the four directions; and from his footprints there sprang at once water lilies sacred in China, and towards each side of the world he uttered these words: "In Heaven and on earth I am the only Superior, wherefore let the Angels and Saints and men of the earth serve and venerate me" (the same is repeated in chapter 25 of the second chapter of his life), which words made such an impression on the world, that the rivers of China and the Royal Palaces quaked. And in this way they relate other hyperbolical prodigies, as for instance, that there were then prophecies in China about his birth.—A Heathen's fancy is greater than a poet's and [reminds one] of the "*Grœcia mendax audet in Historia*" [from Juvenal: "The lies Greece had the audacity to tell in its history"]—but their annals, which omit nothing, make no mention of these prodigies. They add here that he sent forth such resplendence that he illumined the whole world; and the whole world will say they lie.

The Father, hearing of the birth, hastened to the garden, and as he was in suspense considering how to take the child to the Palace, there appeared many heavenly spirits of the one and the other sex (what an idea they have of spirits!) and accompanied the carriage with various perfumes paying him court. The Father called the soothsayers, a superstition greatly practised in China, and they said everything exactly. He granted a general pardon and gave large alms. After seven days the Mother died of weakness, and the son being offered to God in the Temple, all its statues rising from their seats inclined the head as he entered and reverenced him and welcomed him with poesy in the Chinese fashion.

In his eighth year of age they gave him a Teacher, to whom the boy forthwith put such questions, that the Teacher acknowledging his superiority owned himself a pupil. The same happened with the Master of the soldiers and liberal arts. Could the devil counterfeit any better so many centuries in advance the mysteries of the infancy of Christ our Redeemer?

After he was sworn in as Prince of the Kingdom, when he went to take his ease in a garden and considered the troubles of the gardeners and farmers, there came to him the thought of quitting the world (previously they supposed him to be eternal) and the Father coming to know of this was exceedingly grieved. The same thing happened to him, when he went out to the suburbs of the city. And in spite of all this detachment from the world, immediately in the 16th chapter he is praised as so excellent a bowman, that to exercise that art he brought down with one arrow five unclean animals, made of iron, opening a deep well where it fell, with other similar fantasies.

On the order of his Father he married three wives, though he lived as if he were not married (for which purpose one was more than enough) and the King was very uneasy lest he should run away to the wilderness. At the same time a Heavenly spirit by dint of miracles tried to move him to become a Religious, which is inconsistent with what is said in Chapters 2, 3 and 4, for which purpose he caused his Father to have marvellous dreams, the same spirit transforming itself in the form of a Bragmane to interpret the dream, because no one could be found to do so. And afterwards he came to meet Fô himself in a pleasure garden in the shape of an old man, in a miserable and pitiful state, expressive of all human misery, and the Prince resolved to quit the world. This was strengthened by another apparition which he showed him on the road whereby he passed, at one time feigning to be at the gates of death, at another time a dead body; all this merely to convert him. Another Heavenly spirit undertook the same task appearing to him in the shape of a Bonze, though there was none yet, giving him many reasons for quitting the world. This is little coherent with the eternal desires of saving it.

At this time the Princess, wife of Fô, was taken with great pains of labour (unless they wish to give another Father to this son they must needs admit that he was wanting in the continence which they supposed in chapter 1). But though well married, Fô was not able to resist any longer, and determined to ask permission from his Father to quit the world, representing to him these four motives which led him to it, namely, Fô alleged (1) I desire not to grow old. (2) I like to remain young (this is the same as the first). (3) I do not relish to have diseases. (4) I wish to be immortal (fine notions indeed for a novice!). The Father did not grant it, and the Angels seeing this made the guards fall asleep, and he mounted a horse, the earth shook, and he fled through the air, which happened to him on many other occasions, the four legs of the horse being sustained by 4 Angels (then the horse is useless), up to a certain copse where the novice cut his ear with his own hand, and the Angels gathered it and took it to Heaven to be adored (they seem to suppose that he was a Chinese as regards hair, though they said that he was born in Hindustan. The text does not say where the equerry was, but as it says that he was with him at the copse, and that he sent by him messages to the Princess and the other ladies giving them hopes of a speedy return, which he never fulfilled, he must have clung to the mane while the Prince flew through the air).

In this wilderness he noticed the various and severe penances which many Hermits practiced in order to be reborn in Heaven and he told them "You will have to be born again on earth and will not evade the troubles of this life, to which I will put a stop, and I shall not be reborn again." For this reason they say that the Glory of Heaven as well as the pains of Hell have a limit, except in the case of those who take upon themselves the life or state of Pagodes. For this purpose he asked a Hermit: "What was the root of death." He replied pointing out various maxims of perfection, but Fô made no account of them, and opposing him with various thrusts and arguments to the contrary, he concluded saying: "If you undo your own being, putting aside all cares and thoughts of this life, you will eat the root of death." He did not speak in the moral meaning, nor do his followers so understand him, but physically, and all their meditations consist in suspending the advertence of the mind and occupying themselves solely in counting the number of respirations, in order not to think of anything else, spending many years in meditating on nothing, pretending to be in an ecstasy and out of the senses, and more accurately beside themselves, a doctrine which Fô taught them in chapter 34 as the highest perfection for them. And yet they do not achieve the object of becoming immortal, for they die like the rest, deceiving however the ignorant people so long as they live, and they find people who give credit to this delirium, though among the wise they gain no credit.

Fô spent six years in penance without eating anything save a grain of *gergilim* and another larger one of wheat each day; and by this mortification he made satisfaction for the sins he had committed in past ages: all this in order to save the dwellers in Heaven and earth, though they suppose him to have been a god in all past ages. Calvin will find this theology a great help.

At last he felt hungry, whereupon an Angel, to whom they also give a name, moved some shepherdesses to recruit his strength with Milk, and with this refreshment he became glad and strong.

He began Redemption with the fishes (even in these their theology must have found sin) and obtained it by washing the body—it is a common mistake of all Eastern heathendom that sins are got rid of by Ablutions—whereupon the fishes straightway went to be reborn in Heaven. Then, when he wished to sit under a tree, the Angles [*sic*], spirits of the wind, swept the place for him by blowing hard, and for a seat they placed a cushion of straw whereon he sat in the shade. This tree without doubt is the one which in India is called [the tree] of the Pagode, which for that reason is found in all Pagodes. And under it, they pretend, is acquired perfection and the rank of Pagode, though there is no (tree) more attached to the earth, because the fresh roots which the branches throw on the ground form so many trunks, that sometimes one cannot know which is the principal one.

Then appeared the King of the Dragons (which, though they do not deny them to be animals, they esteem as supernatural beings) with his wife and daughters applauding his intention of saving living beings; and there were found under that tree 48,000 Pagodes exercising themselves in virtue. But at this time the chief of the Demons, moved by some dreams he had, (dreams and spirits scarcely go together) mustered his troop to frustrate the plan of Redemption, though they also were to be redeemed; and the principal son of the Demon did many things to dissuade him from it, but failed completely with Fô. Seeing this, the captain of the gang determined to make war on him by means of female Devils, assailing him with Lascivious things, but he behaved as if he were not of flesh, and it must have been no small feat to resist many women Devils, if all this had not been a fable.

I omit many answers of Fô, all based on the transmigration of souls, a common error of the Oriental Heathen, which he teaches to be the lot also of Angels and Demons, which error infects nearly all the Chapters of this Scripture. He imagines also Heavenly Angels in Heaven, on earth earthly Angels, in the mountains mountainous ones, reborn like men in all these places, and becoming, according to their merits, sometimes men, at other times Demons and Angels, imagining prodigies and nonsensical things, of which the chapters 45, 49, 52, 53, 55, 59 and many others of the second part are full, everything leading to the conclusion and main business of honouring Fô, and of gaining large alms for his Bonzes.

After this resistance, he became confirmed as a Pagode under the name of Fô, for up to this time he was called Xekia; and being free from all that to which human nature is subject, incapable of change, with a general and abstract nature which is invariable, and realising this privilege, he made a kind of litany of his praises and good deeds of past ages by means of which he had obtained his present state.

CHAPTER 18

Summary of the Second Part

OF THE LIFE OF FÔ, FROM THE THIRTIETH
YEAR TILL HE BECAME OLD

The first chapter begins with the congratulations which all kinds of spirits and Heavenly Kings gave him, offering him scents and perfumes for being confirmed as a Pagode and as a conqueror, with divers poems which the text gives in full, in return for which he communicated to them various doctrines beginning with his own praises and comparing himself to the Sun which illumines the just and the unjust, high and low, without any acceptation of persons, hills and dales, wherein he imitates the luminary illumining by his doctrine all kinds of living beings in order to save all. He sat down in the Palace of the Dragons, which they considered a great happiness, and their King received the law of Fô, and the text says that he was the first Dragon to be saved. Afterwards one of the Emperors of Heaven alleged this service, saying that when he was a shepherd, he had given him milk. He must have been fond of this, for this offer is found in many places, and even in Heaven, when he went to see his mother, she let fall from her breast a quantity of it as is related in Chapter 105 of the second part. This Emperor begged him for a favour, and Fô granted it, and also ordered him to become a Bonze and to observe his precepts, to which he submitted, being the first of that family.

As he was already sanctified, he began to distribute his relics, giving hairs and nails to some merchants on the following occasion. When some merchants were passing by the place where Fô was with 500 loaded wagons, the [draught] cattle stood motionless till they offered him something to eat; and when he gave them these relics in recompense, they promised to build a beautiful tower wherein they were to be worshipped. Then there came down a Heavenly King, with a further troop from the 33 Heavens (they imagine as many) begging Fô to preach his precepts to them, who replied to them: "When I wished to prove the Law which in itself is very profound, it is difficult to see and believe what it contains, neither by discussion nor even by thought can it be properly declared; and only those who become Fô can do it" (then he was not one yet) "wherefore it is better for me to be silent." In proof that this reply is also taken from the Koran, in that very Chapter this crowd of spirits recommends the Kingdom of Meca to Fô, begging him to go there to preach, because it was troubled and confused by many and perverse Sects, and in it, they say, was his longest stay calling it Mekia, because of the incapacity [to write it properly] with their letters. Fô resolved to preach therein, but only five were converted, whom he taught to make acts of Faith, questioning them whether Fô existed in all things; for thus they explain the being of God, saying in Chapter 35 that all things partake of his nature whether they be Angels or Kings, or men or women, and that he exists in all as their universal cause.

It is here in this ninth chapter that they place the ten commandments of their Law. 1. Not to kill any kind of thing; 2. Not to steal; 3. Not to fornicate; 4. Not to bear false witness; 5. Not to drink wine; 6. Not to murder; 7. Not to praise oneself at another's cost; 8. Not to be avaricious; 9. Not to be wrath; 10. Not to speak ill of Fô and his precepts. He gave no precept to obey one's Father and Mother, although that is the first duty of men, rather he allowed his Father to prostrate himself at his feet and to adore him as a Pagode, acknowledging him as Lord of the 3,000 worlds, for they imagine so many.

Soon there gathered round him various disciples, one of whom he constituted his successor in the chair, because he was an excellent Preacher. A boatman pretended to ignore all this, and would not let Fô cross a river without first paying for it. He crossed it through the air, and not forgetting the injury, he complained to the King, who obliged the boatman to let henceforth all Bonzes pass free, like the Fakirs of the Moors and the Yogis of the Heathens who in all use of boats have this privilege. Fô gave other favours similar to these which are narrated in chapter 58. Not the smallest prodigy was to divide the waters of a river, as happened in the Jordan, to cross it without payment with an army of disciples who followed him;

and malice had no shame to imagine and write such things. Very solicitous for the conversion of a man of name, he went to him, and as he was lying down at night in a small house of rock, a Dragon tried to prevent him by fire, but he made little account of it, and put the Dragon under the bowl in which he used to receive alms. It must have been a small Dragon or the bowl must have been a big one, but a big bowl was unnecessary for a grain of *gergilim* and another of wheat, which they said was all his fare, and besides it would seem that the friendship with the Dragons had already ceased. He preached some apposite moral precepts, without ever promising an eternal reward or punishment for their good or bad actions, placing before them as their end the *materia prima*, incapable of glory or pain, which they consider to be independent and immutable, though it can be united with various forms.

In the Kingdom of Teulôkivãchã, which name seems to have been invented or adulterated, he converted a famous Bragmane by name Kiaiye, who profited so well by his doctrine, that he was the Preacher of the Panegyric at the funeral of Fô, and was much esteemed by the Angels on that account. Some false sectaries persuaded a woman in labour to impute it to Fô, but a principal spirit with his Angels hastened to prove the falseness of the charge; and of such prodigies many are related.

To one of his brothers, who also became a Bonze along with a servant whom he had ill treated and despised, Fô gave a fraternal warning, saying that Religion is like an Ocean into which flow great Rivers and small, but none is distinguished from another in the Ocean, and that though that man was his servant that distinction should not have place in Religion, but he, however, wished to be worshipped by the nations. He showed no small contempt of the world in a matter of great delicacy, for though it was 12 years since Fô parted from the company of his wife, and when it was only seven years, she had a child, he received him for his own in order not to stain his wife, just as it happens with Guzarate Banianes [Gujarati traders] who, if their wives conceive in their absence, say that it was because the wives called them to mind.

He did not lack Apostates from his Sect, and one was his own Brother, for whose salvation it was necessary to take him body and soul to Heaven, where at the sight of many women, who flattered him [by saying] that he would be future emperor, if he persevered, and other fictions, he resolved to become a Bonze, and attained consummate perfection within 37 days. Not less was necessary to make his son become a virtuous Bonze. Such was the devotion caused by the zeal with which he preached, that there was one who gave him so much silver to build a large monastery, as was sufficient to cover the whole space of the ground. At this time it happened that the fishermen caught a fish of such size, that a thousand men were needed to drag it to the shore, where they counted in it a hundred heads; and Fô compelled it to own that it was in former times a Bragmane of acute ingenuity, and because in the school he despised the others, calling them blockheads and brutes out of pride, he paid for his fault in that form. There arose against him a persecution of six principal sectarian Patriarchs of the Law who disputed with him, and various spirits taking the side of Fô, the text says, they placed bombs of fire on the top of mortars and fired them above the heads of the sectaries, who fled in such terror, that they could not see their way. And this is the first time I see a law defended by pounding with mortars, a course for which there was great need.

He wished to introduce the veneration of his image and did it by [means of] a prodigious transfiguration, changing his real being and appearing full of admirable resplendence, which issuing from his head spread throughout the whole world, his face becoming like a mountain of precious pearls; and forthwith there appeared a hundred-thousand images of him, and there bloomed before it a water-lily with a thousand petals, each petal with a thousand resplendences, and in each resplendence a thousand Pagodes. By this transfiguration he introduced his adoration after death, concluding it with large promises and with the eternal gift which is granted only to Pagodes.

In chapter 116 he greatly praises a King for the good example of making a statue of him, canonising him among the Saints for it, and promising him many good things. Here they imagine that one of the greatest Angels came to offer his congratulations to this King, because he heard Fô speak in Heaven in great praise of him at a time when he was still on earth. Thus he prepared the way for making statues of scented wood, and cast in silver and gold with great pomp, promising his benefactors many temporal goods, honours and long life, exhorting all to celebrate his birth, to wash his image, alleging his great merits and good deeds of past ages, whereby he had merited to be the son of a King; (they had said that this was his own choice) making mention also of the prodigies of his birth, and of those seven paces towards the four quarters of the world granting more than plenary indulgences to those who invoke his name, and set up his statue.

There were not wanting those who envied him so great dignities, and therefore they induced King Nacànâlô to make drunk 500 elephants, so that they might attack Fô and his followers. But he, holding up the five fingers of his hand, produced five Lions, whose roaring made the 500 elephants fall on their knees without daring to raise their heads. In chapter 53 the same is imagined with regard to birds, and the same also with ragard [*sic*] to oxen in chapter 54, imagining that they talked and begged pardon of Fô for their audacity and sins, besides other similar fables which human invention can imagine, which I omit to be short.

A daughter of a King was so ugly, that she did not dare to show herself, and commending herself to Fô became good looking, and the door was opened to more shameful invocations, for there are monasteries of Lamazes (who have already penetrated hither) with such Pagodes, that they persuade the barren women that they will be fruitful, if they touch their genital parts with them. The Tartars forbid it, because of other shameful consequences; but even then these Pagodes are opened sometimes during the year.

It will be irksome to recount the prayers they have invented. One of his disciples dreamt that he saw the Demon in various terrible and monstrous figures, and that it told him he would die in three days and would be reborn among famished devils. He had recourse to the Master, who taught him a certain prayer, and making use of it and offering moreover some dishes to the numberless famished devils, the Demons were for once satiated and he became free from the tribulation. This same prayer saved him on many other occasions, especially in a furious temptation of the flesh, when he made use of it, and they say it has the power to save one from hell.

One of the disciples wishing to free his Mother from a ravenous appetite, Fô gave him this prescription: On the fifteenth of the seventh Moon get together all kinds of viands, the best in the world, with good wine (though it is against his fifth commandment) and invite the Bonzes, and your parents who have gone before you for the last seven centuries will have a hundred years of life, and they will be free from all torments, and will be reborn in better condition, free from all hunger. Here is disclosed the intention of providing the Bonzes with food.

A devil who lived on human flesh seized a boy of six years, to eat him. Fô rescued him promising the devil the necessary sustenance by recommending his Bonzes to take care of him, a diligence whereby he saved the boy and reduced the devil to the observance of his doctrine and commandments.

A female Demon who had a family of 500 little devils was also feeding on human flesh. Fô seized the youngest of them whom she loved very much, and hid him under the bowl from which he ate. The mother searched him all over the world and not finding him, asked Fô for him, who said to her: "You have 500 devil sons and are still so importunate, because of the loss of one, without minding that each day you eat those of others, even the only sons of their mothers, only in order to feed yourself." She realised her fault, promised amendment, and received his law and precepts.

In chapter 80 they add that all kinds of Angels, Demons and Dragons assembled and listened very devoutly to his doctrine, [preached] in parables and figures all directed to his Pythagorean end, reducing everything to a confusion of effects put together and kept as in a sack, from which they come out into the world or into which they enter, as it falls to each one's lot. And in order to make illustrious the holiness of his doctrine, it is said in chapter 99 that he had recourse to very powerful Kings, because his disciples without this authority would not be able to achieve it.

He sought to practice something of what he preached, and being absent and at a distance, he was found present at the death of his Father, and he wanted to carry the bier on his own back. Four Heavenly Kings prevented this act of humility, begging Fô to leave the matter to them, which he at once conceded, but he followed them to the place of cremation, as is the custom of the heathen of further Asia, when with his own hands he piled up the wood and set fire to the dead body, making an exhortation to all, declaring all the greatness of the world to be little worth, even praising himself into the bargain and saying that to be a Pagode is a permanent thing. Nor did he show less pride in setting himself up as Master of death, giving to an aunt, who asked him for it, permission to die, because her heart would not suffer her to live after the death of Fô, and he also gave this permission to 500 other devout women who wished to accompany him, encouraging them to bear that trial with a brave heart.

CHAPTER 19

Summary of the Third Part

THE OLD AGE AND DEATH OF FÔ AND WHAT

HAPPENED AFTER HIS DEATH

As it seemed to the Devil that the life of Fô was already sufficiently long, the very chief of the Demons (Lucifer as we should say) came, and with great reverence and courtesy proposed to him that it was now a convenient [time] for his passage (thus making out in this text that the Demon was the author of death and life); and though in former times, because his doctrine was not yet promulgated, he had rejected this proposal, yet this time, as this reason did not now hold, because his doctrine had then taken root and a multitude of disciples had been confirmed in it, he agreed to the arrangement, saying that three months thence he would pass to another life. This answer greatly delighted the Ambassador, who communicated the news to his companions, who received it with equal pleasure and joy. If he were going to Heaven, Hell would not have rejoiced so much! Onan [Ānanda] alone of his disciples was grieved by this reply, and running up to Fô he said: "Lord, Master, Thou hast told me that thou wouldest not leave us and the four spirits so soon" (it would seem that he meant the four senses, for they do not admit [the sense] of touch; or the four powers of the soul, for they add one and judge the head to be an element, which powers, plus the elements, make up the man), "and that in this way we can live a long life; and would it not be good to live a century doing thy will with joy, since thou hast taught that the ignorant and the wise, the good and the bad, the noble and the plebian, all come to the same thing and will be the same." This is also affirmed in chapter 92 of the second part, and in many other places they disclose this veiled atheism. But Fô, being compelled not by his will, but by his old age, answered Onan in that way, though he had greatly desired to remain young, as was mentioned in his motives for embracing Religion. Onan became very sad and wept copiously at this news.

After this embassy also there occurred an opportunity of showing his power, for appearing in the figure of a Bonze with his two fingers and a breath he reduced to powder a rock which thirty-thousand men could not move.

Feeling that he was growing old and feeble, he went to a River to wash himself, warning Onân to notice carefully the 32 beauties or marks of his body. Here the disciple asked him what he should do with his relics after his death, and the reply was that his body would be divided into portions as small as the seeds of mustard and these should be divided into three parts and one given to the Angels, another to the Dragons and the other to the Demons, who would adore his relics, as if the body were present, and excite desires of their perfection with his presence. What remains over would be taken by a King who would build 84,000 towers wherein to adore them, and his example would be followed by 60 thousand Kinglets who would build towers of their own and would adore the same relics with sweet scents, flowers, roses, lights and sweet songs and with humility, for which he granted a plenary indulgence to those who receive his habit with devotion. In conclusion [he said]: "And as my eternal essence is united to my material body, their merits will be infinite." From all this one can see how the Devil counterfeited the mysteries of the Incarnation.

He wished also to advise the Heavenly Spirits to acknowledge him as their Superior and to protect his Sect, for which purpose he ascended to the third Heaven, where the Supreme Spirit gave him the first place, and prayed in this wise with humble submission. "I shall not live very long, wherefore I recommend to thee the protection of my Law." The hearers broke out into tears, bewailing his absence, (then it was not to Heaven he was going!) saying: "Reverend Master wherefore art thou going to another life so soon? Will thy bodily eyes be closed for ever? We will do with great pleasure and with all our power whatever thou recommendest us." The Supreme Angel added: "I have helped thee so much as I was able, so long as thy last hour had not arrived, but to deliver thee from death my power is not equal, nor does my might extend so far."

He made the same recommendation of his doctrine to all the Kings of the Dragons, whom they imagine to be supernatural Spirits, in spite of which the text goes on to say that they replied: "We Kings or the Dragons are ignorant and brutal, and are therefore numbered among animals, and when we leave, we do not know what our lot will be in the next world." (Under such a name and shape did the Devil get himself adored).

Many people gathered on the eve of his death, begging him not to die, (though it had been said that this was not within his power, and that not even the Angels could help him) and as he did not say anything in reply, they all began to weep and lament. The same lamentations are said to have been made by those in Hell, when they heard that Fô was going to die (they must have thought that he was going into imaginary space, since his absence was lamented both in Heaven and Hell!). But Fô consoled them saying that one must needs die, if he is born, which is little in keeping with the themes of his conversations. There came then the chief of the Demons with many Heavenly Spirits, men and women, offering many dishes to Fô to revive him, saying a certain prayer which they had composed for his approval, which he did at once, giving permission to publish it. One of his devotees also asked him not to die; and when his request was not granted, as his heart was not able to bear the death of Fô, he asked to die before him, which he granted, and his obsequies were performed with great solemnity.

There came on that same day all kinds of Spirits to offer him their regrets at his death, and because one of them failed in this duty, the others resented it so much, that they killed him by curses. At this time there was born to him a Spirit from one of his arms, while he was saying a prayer, and it promised great things to those who would have recourse to him. Then he named Onân as his successor, giving him wholesome advice and declaring that he had authorized his doctrine by his deeds. Finally he consoled his disciples, saying that death must needs come, that he had fulfilled his duty, and other suitable sentences, among which is found one of that Spiritual Master in chapter 65 of the second part, for when some novices were disputing which was the greatest temporal evil, and each one had settled it according to his fancy, Fô defined it [saying] that the body was the greatest evil, that it follows us, even when we do not want it, in spite of us, and that we have to carry that worthless thing about us and are unable to get rid of it. The Bonzes venerate his last sermon as a token of that hour, just as we [venerate] that final [pledge of] love which Our Redeemer gave us at the last Supper.

His last command consisted in saying to Onân: "Take my body, and when thou hast dressed it properly and embalmed and burnt and venerated it with all royal pomp, gather the ashes in seven precious vessels, and in the city, in the four principal streets, erect seven towers with four gates to each, and place my relics there to be venerated by all spirits, and see that there is equity in the distribution; (he who invented this falsifies and contradicts, for he had already said that his body should be divided without burning it)." Hearing this, the Angels and men and those who were present broke into lamentations, but he consoled them saying: "Do not grieve, for though I go away, I shall be with you for ever by means of my relics; and whoever sees them sees me."

The last hour approached with pains all over the body, and on these he began to meditate, not by applying the senses, but by suspending them, (as was already said, they suspend the senses little by little till it ends in the quietude and confusion of effects and of indistinct causes [which is] their imaginary happiness, which they place in a certain quietude without glory, but with the negation of pain, imagining that there is an intelligible centre free from all manner of life or death. To try to understand, not what they say, but what they mean to say, makes one's head turn giddy, though it is not worth the while).

Thus while he was in this devout occupation in the city of Kiŭxinãkiã, under the polo tree (or in the Poro tree, for there is no R in Chinese) with many people and surrounded by eight orders of Dragons (fine guardian Angels indeed!) on the fifteenth of the second Moon, in his royal bed, reclining on his right side, with the head towards the North and the feet towards the South and his face to the West and his back to the East with two polo trees in each of these directions, at dead of night, he died. As soon as he was dead, the branches of the eight trees bent down and joined one with the other covering the royal couch, [and] changing their green colour into white (which is the Chinese style of mourning), they little by little withered up. There was forthwith an earthquake throughout the whole word, the sea was agitated and the fountains and rivers ran dry. I do not know how they dared to publish such falsehoods in China, where one can convict them from the very Chronicles of the Realm wherein all notable events and among them the deluge of Noe are found [recorded]. There was also darkness throughout the whole world, for the Sun and the Moon did not give light, and unless they had a revelation about what took place in the Antipodes, this miracle of the Sun takes place whenever one dies at night. Such moreover were the shouts uttered by the Angels at his death, that they were heard throughout the world, and the whole world testifies that all this is false and was perhaps added by the Chinese after they had noticed the death of Christ. At the very instant of his death, his defunct Mother had horrible dreams in Heaven which led her to suspect that her son had died. (The dead person then did not go there.) A Bonze arrived in haste with the news, (he passed many thousand leagues in a short time) whereupon she knew it for certain and complained greatly that death came on him too soon, though he had the news three months before. There was great lamentation and much evil was said of death, and she ended by saying: "From all eternity we have ever been together, Mother and Son, but now we shall not see each other again." (The beginnings are here quite inconsistent with the end.) The Mother at once came down from Heaven with many damsels to wail for the departed, but she was consoled on seeing the staff and bowl of her son, which appeared before her with Pagodes [who were] his creatures to give her due thanks for coming from so far. The second apparition was to one of his disciples who came from Meca (it could only be through the air) along with 500 others to venerate his body, which, though already enclosed in a coffin, stretched out the feet, which the disciples saw and touched.

They placed the coffin in a large and splendid theatre to be burnt, and though they applied lighted torches once and again several times, it could not be set on fire. Seeing this the Spirits of the sea applied their own torches, but in vain. Thereupon Fô, pitying their labors, sent forth fire from his own breast (too much they saw, unless the lid was of glass) and the body taking fire slowly was consumed in seven days. Then there came down four Heavenly Kings with much water to quench the fire and to take possession of the relics, but they did not succeed. There followed those of the sea with a great deal more [water], but it did not suffice. Then a disciple came forward and chid them for their covetousness, and they repented and desisted from their purpose.

Seeing however that the eight Kings present each with his soldiers (which addition also within so short a time is supposed to be miraculous) attempted to take away that treasure by force, the Spirits pretended to be men in order not to be defrauded, but a person of authority settled everything by dividing the ashes into three portions and giving one to the Spirits, another to the Dragons, and the third to those eight Kings, keeping for himself three measures. Of what was left of the earth [sanctified] by contact and out of reverence they took 40 *picos* (which is a Chinese measure) and erecting as many towers, they placed these *picos* in them with much music, where they are venerated (but I know not in which place), while Fô emits such light, that the nights become day.

When this division had been made, one of his disciples who had come with 500 pupils demanded attention and said: "Go over the whole world and preach to all." And the preaching having begun, there was found to be present 84,000 listeners assembled, to whom Onân, the successor of Fô, made a sermon. A devout King erected innumerable towers and placed some relics therein. And here end his testament and his commands which in intelligent men cause laughter, in the pious pity, and in the ignorant wonderment.

This is the substance of their Scripture, printed with great authority and engraven in the Palace in large-sized letters, figures and engravings, which illustrate what is related in each chapter. They say that this translation was made with great authority by Bonzes from India and by learned Chinese, who held conferences and settled the foregoing. But to my mind there is no doubt that the greater part of it is fiction, first of the Devil, and secondly of Chinese cunning, because there are many things which are peculiar to China and are unused in India, which have been adapted to their taste, as for instance the rhymes which are imagined at every step in praise of Fô, for the highest wisdom of the Chinese consists in that, and they end where the Europeans begin, and with their so many thousand letters they do not go further than our students of Rhetoric. At every step they speak of Dragons which are sacred in upper China only. They imagine titles and dignities in Indian Kings as is the case in China, giving them their own terms. They make the obsequies of Fô take place according to the Chinese fashion, except the cremation, and they suppose white to be the colour of mourning, which is a thing peculiar to China and Japan alone. They say he was placed in a coffin, which is not the practice among the heathen there [India], but in China to be without it is to be deprived of the sacred burial, as amongst us. They erected large monasteries for Bonzes though the Yogis and Bragmanes and the like in India do not live in Monasteries (those of Ceylon have monasteries, I think) though they have very large temples. They consider shaving essential to their Order, though in India the Yogis grow their hair matted, and are thereby distinguished from the others. (The Ganezes of Ceylon also cut their hair.) They forbid eating any living thing, but the Lamas of Tartary do not imitate them in this, for they eat meat like tigers without giving more time for cooking than what is spent in their prayers, and once that is over, they eat it without any addition of bread or vegetables; and for these and other reasons I am persuaded that many things in these scriptures have been changed, as has been the case with many other sects of China.

These Bonzes do not wage any campaign against us, for there they are not esteemed as they are in Japan, nor are they men of letters, but low and despicable people, for no grave person becomes a Bonze, and they adopt this mode of life merely for a living, for entrance into it is cheap, and one finds these do-nothings at every turn; and being such, they receive no kind of reverence. The greatest use of their monasteries is that they serve as inns for wayfarers, to whom they hire them readily for payment, which makes them the more despised, and there are some well-known charges made against them at every turn and even in their books, and they are called by the name [of that crime], and in their histories many wicked and deceitful deeds are ascribed to them, and if they are true, it is strange that there should be any one who becomes a Bonze or gives them to eat. As they are ignorant, even when they dispute with us, which is rare, they grant whatever we want. In Japan however they have great authority.

Such is the summary of Father Thomas Pereyra, from which it appears that in their practices they do not differ greatly from what we have said of the Chingalas, and that their Ganezes in point of estimation and nobility resemble rather the Bonzes of Japan. And as it has been observed that the Ganezes of Ceylon, the Talpoys of Arracan, Pegu, Siam and other neighbouring Realms, as well as the Lamazes of Tartary agree with the Bonzes of China and Japan in the essentials of their sect and profession, it is easy to understand that the Buddum of Ceylon, the Fô of China, the Xaka of Japan is the same as the Xekia of India, for the word Buddum is only an adapted name, and in Ceylon it means Saint by antonomasia. And if those who had read the documents of Ceylon had been more curious and had not been weary of giving us more detailed information, we could have shown more clearly from what they relate of his life the additions made by Chinese malice.

If intelligent Europeans wonder, considering what it is that such intelligent people embrace as true, let them remember what heathen Europe so pertinaciously believed and worshipped. The fact is the Devil has forestalled everything. When we preach to the heathens of hither India, they reply that they also have a Trinity, and that their Vixnu incarnated himself times out of number; if we preach to those of farther India and of Ceylon (for this Sect has disappeared from many parts of India wherein it began), they reply that their Buddum or their Fô or their Xaka also took the shape of a man, though he was an eternal being. And as the

Religious of this Sect have a great reputation outside China, it is a very difficult matter to convert any of his sectaries, which has been the experience especially in the Kingdoms of Arracan, Pegû, Siam, Laos and others of lesser name. In the sixth part of our *Missionario* we treat more fully on this subject and of the Sects of the one and the other India, refuting them in the best way that God was pleased to enlighten us, wherein the zealous and the curious can read it, for here we are only concerned with the information which we were able to obtain about the Island of Ceylon.[16]

♦ GUY TACHARD (1651–1712)

One of the six Jesuits in Louis XIV's second delegation to Siam was Guy Tachard. After meeting with the Thai king, the other five Jesuits continued to China, while the Chevalier de Chaumont, the Abbé de Choisy, and Father Tachard sailed back to Paris, taking with them a Siamese delegation to Louis' court. Upon his return to Paris, he published A relation of the voyage to Siam. *In it, he wrote, "I shall not so much enlarge upon the Customs and Government of the Siamese as upon their Religion, which I have taken great care to be informed of, and have learnt many particulars relating thereunto, which, as I think, will be very acceptable to the curious. I owe almost all of them to a Siamese Church-man who came to France with the Ambassadors of the King of Siam."*

Tachard's description of the Buddha is one of the most detailed of the period; three excerpts follow. The first describes the state of Buddhahood in general terms; here, God = Buddha. In this passage, Tachard's tone is generally one of detached reportage. In the second passage, he turns to the biography of the Buddha (whom he calls Sommonokhodom), which he finds to be "a monstrous mixture of Christianity and the most ridiculous Fables." He is particularly interested in the Buddha's antagonist, his cousin (Tachard calls him his brother), Devadatta (Tachard calls him Thevathat). The French delegation's interest focused particularly on Devadatta's attempts to kill the Buddha; several pages about Devadatta between the second and third excerpts have not been included here. In the third excerpt, Tachard explains that the success of the Jesuit mission was thwarted by a terrible mistake: the Siamese believed that Jesus is Devadatta.

———

The Religion of the *Siamese* is very odd, and cannot be perfectly understood but by the Books that are written in the *Balis* Language, which is the Learned Language, and hardly understood by any, except some of their Doctors. Nor do these Books neither always agree amongst themselves. This following account of their Religion is the most exact that possibly I could attain to.

The *Siamese* believe a God, but they have not the same notion of him that we have. By that word they understand a being perfect after their manner, consisting of Spirit and Body, whose property it is to assist men. That assistance consists in giving them a Law, prescribing them the ways of living well, teaching them the true Religion, and the Sciences that are necessary unto them. The perfections which they attribute unto him are all the moral virtues, possessed by him in an eminent degree acquired by many acts, and confirmed by a continual exercise in all the Bodies he hath past through.

He is free from passions, and feels no motion that can alter his tranquillity; but they affirm that before he arrived at that State, he made so prodigious a change in his Body by struggling to overcome his Passions, that his blood is become white. He hath the Power to appear when he pleases, and also to render himself invisible to the eyes of men; and he hath such wonderful agility, that in a moment he can be in any place of the world he pleases.

He knoweth all without having ever learnt any thing from men, whose Doctor and Master he himself is, and that universal knowledg [*sic*] is inherent in his state, having possessed it from the instant that he was born God; it consists not as ours does, in a train of consequences, but in a clear, simple and intuitive vision, which all at once represents to him the Precepts of the Law, Vices, Virtues, and the most hidden secrets of Nature, things past, present and come, Heaven, Earth, Paradice, Hell, this Universe which we see, and even what is done in the other Worlds which we know not. He distinctly remembers all that hath ever befallen him from the first transmigration of his Soul, even to the last.

His body is infinitely more radiant than the Sun, it lights that which is most hidden, and by the help of the light that it diffuses, a man here below upon Earth, might, that I may make use of their expression, see a grain of Mustard seed placed in the Highest Heavens.

The happiness of that God is not compleat, but when he dies never to be born again: for then he appears no more upon the Earth, nor is he any more subject to Misery. They compare that death to a torch extinct, or to a sleep that renders us insensible of the Evils of Life, with this difference that when God dies, he is exempted from them for ever, whereas a man asleep is but free from them for a certain time.

This reign of every Deity lasts not eternally, it is confined to a certain number of years, that's to say, until the number of the elect who are to be sanctified by his

Merits be accomplished; after which he appears no more in the World but slides into an Eternal repose, which was thought to have been a real annihilation, because they were not rightly understood. Then another God succeeds to him, and governs the Universe in his place, which is nothing else but to teach men the true Religion.

Men may become Gods, but not till after a very considerable time; for they must needs have required a consummated Virtue; Nor is it enough to have done a great many good Works in their Bodies where their Souls have lodged, they must also at every good Action they do, have an intention of meriting Divinity, they must have intimated that intention, by invoking and taking to witness the Angels who preside in the four Parts of the World, at the beginning of their good work; and they must have poured out Water, imploring the Succours of the She-tutelary Angel of the Earth, called *Naang pprathoram*; for they believe, as we shall shew hereafter, that there is a diversity of Sex amongst Angels as well as amongst Men. They who desire to be Gods carefully observe that Practice.

Besides that state of Divinity to which the most perfect aspire, there is another not so high, which they call the state of Sanctity. It is enough for being a Saint, that having past through several Bodies, one has acquired many Virtues, and that in the Acts which men do they have proposed the acquisition of Sanctity. The Properties of Sanctity are the same with those of Divinity. The Saints possess them, as well as God does, but in a far more imperfect degree; besides that, God has them of himself, without receiving them from another, whereas the Saints derive them from him by the Instructions he gives them. It is he who teaches them all those Secrets whereof he hath a perfect Knowledg. And therefore it is that if they be not born whilst he is in the world, since they cannot receive his Documents, they are not sanctified. So that it is their custom in doing good Works, to desire the Grace to be born again at the same time their God is. What we have said of the Deity, that it is not consummated till God dying upon Earth, ascends up into Heaven, that he may no more appear here below, ought in like manner to be understood of Sanctity; for it is not perfect till the Saints die, not to be born again, and till their Souls be carried into Paradice, there to enjoy eternal Felicity.[17]

I thought fit to premise all these things before I came to speak of *Sommonokhodom* (so the *Siamese* call the God whom at present they adore) because they are necessary to the understanding of his History. That History, after all, is a monstrous mixture of Christianity and the most ridiculous Fables. It is at first supposed that *Sommonokhodom* was born God by his own virtue; and that immediately after his

Birth, without the help of any Master, to instruct him, he acquired by a meer [sic] glance of his Mind, a perfect knowledg of all things relating to Heaven, the Earth, Paradice, Hell, and the most impenetrable Secrets of Nature; that at the same time he remembred all that ever he had done in the different Lives he had led; and that after he had taught the People those great Matters, he left them written in Books, that Posterity might be the better for them.

In these Books he reports of himself, that being become God, one day he desired to manifest his Divinity to Men by some extraordinary Prodigy, He then sate under a Tree called *Ton ppô*, which for that reason the *Siamese* reverence as some sacred thing, and look upon it as a happy Presage for the places where it grows, being perswaded that it would be a great sin to do the least hurt to that Tree. He adds, that presently he found himself carried up into the Air in a Throne all shining with Gold and precious Stones, which came out of the Earth in the place where he was; and that at the same instant Angels coming down from Heaven, rendered him the Honours and Adorations that were due unto him. His Brother *Thevathat* and his Followers could not without extream Jealousie behold the Glory and Majesty that environed him. They conspired his Ruin, and having stirred up the Beasts against him, engaged with him in a War. Though he was all alone, he was not terrified by that multitude of Enemies, he resisted all their Attempts without being shaken, and by virtue of his good works which defended him, the shafts they darted at him, were changed into so many Flowers, which far from hurting him, served only to encrease his Honour. In the mean time he confesses that in the brunt of the Battle, when he was most in danger, it was but in vain that he had his recourse to the good works he had done in keeping the Nine first Commandments of the Law, which he found were not sufficient to defend him in this pressing Necessity. But being armed with the tenth Command, which he had inviolably observed, and which enjoyns the practice of Charity towards Men and Beasts, he easily triumphed over his Enemies; and in this manner he obtained that victory. The Female Guardian-Angel of the Earth (for we have already distinguished two Sexes amongst the Angels); coming to him, at first adored him, then turning towards *Thevathat* and his Adherents, she made known to them that *Sommonokhodom* was really become God. She told them, that she had been a Witness of his good Works; and to convince them of that shewed them her own Hair still dripping with the Waters that he poured out in the beginning of his good Actions. Hence came the superstitious Custom of the *Siamese* of shedding Water in the beginning of their good works, whereof we have spoken several times already, and which the *Siamese* religiously observe since that time. In fine, she exhorted them to render him the Adorations that he deserved; but finding them to be hardned and obstinately resolved not to hearken to her Remonstrances, she squeezed her wet hair, and pressed out of them an Ocean of Water, wherein they were all drowned.

It is also found written in the books of *Sommonokhodom*, that from the time he aspired to be God, he had returned into the World five hundred and fifty times under various shapes; that in every Regeneration, he had been always the Chief, and, as it were, Prince of the Animals under whose shape he was born; that many times he had given his Life for his Subjects, and that being a Monkey, he had delivered a Town from a horrible Monster that wasted it; that he had been a most potent King, and that seven days before he obtained the Sovereign Dominion of the Universe, he had retired in imitation of some Anchorites, with his Wife and two Children into remote Solitudes; that there he was dead to the World and his Passions in such a degree that without being moved he suffered a *Baramen* who had a mind to try his Patience and carry away his Son and Daughter, and torment them before his face. Nay his mortification went a great deal farther, for he even gave his Wife to a poor Man that begged an Alms, and having put out his own eyes he sacrificed himself by distributing his flesh amongst the Beasts, to stay the hunger that pressed them. From thence they take occasion again to find fault with the Christian Religion, which enjoyns not Men to comfort and assist Beasts in their necessities. These are the rare actions which the *Talapoins* in their Sermons propose to the people for imitation, and the examples they make use of to encline them to virtue.[18]

After all the outrages that *Thevathat* had done to his Brother without any respect to Nature or even to Divinity. It was but just he should be punished. And so the *Siamese* Scriptures make mention of his punishment, and *Sommonokhodom* himself relates that after he became God, he saw that wicked Brother of his in the deepest place of Hell. He was in the eight Habitation, that is to say, in the place where the greatest Offenders are tormented, and there by a terrible punishment, he expiated, all the sins that he had committed, and especially the injuries he had done to me. Explaining afterwards the pains which *Thevathat* was made to suffer, he says that he was fastened to a Cross with great nails, which piercing his hands and feet, put him to extreme pain, that on his head he had a Crown of Thorns, that his Body was full of wounds, and to compleat his Misery, the Infernal place burnt him without consuming of him. So sad a spectacle moved him to compassion; he forgot all the wrongs his Brother had done him, and could not see him in that condition without taking a resolution to help him. He proposed to him then these three words to be adored, *Ppu thang, Thamang, Sangkhang* [that is, the three jewels: the Buddha, the dharma, and the saṃgha], sacred and mysterious words for which the *Siamese* have a profound veneration, and whereof the first signifies God, the second the word of God, and the third the imitator of God; promising him, that if he would accept so easie and reasonable a condition, to deliver him from all the pains to which he was condemned. *Thevathat* consented to adore the first two words, but he never would adore the third, because it signified Priest or Imitator of God, protesting that Priests were sinful Men that deserved no respect. To punish him for that Pride, he still suffers and will suffer for a great many years to come.

Tho there be many things that keep the *Siamese* at a distance from the Christian Law, yet one may say, nothing makes them more averse from it than this thought. The similitude that is to be found in some points betwixt their Religion and ours, making them believe that Jesus Christ, is the very same with that *Thevathat* mentioned in their Scriptures, they are perswaded that seeing we are the Disciples of the one, we are also the followers of the other, and the fear they have of falling into Hell with *Thevathat*, if they follow his Doctrine, suffers them not to hearken to the propositions that are made to them of embracing Christianity. That which most confirms them in their prejudice, is that we adore the Image of our Crucified Saviour, which plainly represents the punishment of *Thevathat*. So when we would explain to them the Articles of our Faith; they take us always up short, saying that they do not need our Instructions, and that they know already better than we do, what we have a mind to tell them.

But it is time to return to *Sommonokhodom* whose Story we have interrupted; he had run over the World, declaring to Mankind good and evil, and teaching them the true Religion, which he himself wrought that he might leave it to Posterity. He had even gained several Disciples, who in the condition of Priests were to make a particular Profession of imitating him, in wearing a habit like to his, and in observing the Rules that he gave them, when, at length, he attained to the fourscore and second year of his age, which was also the Age of that Monster, which heretofore he killed as we have already said. One day as he sate in the middle of his Disciples teaching them, he saw the same Monster in shape of a Pig, running with incredible Fury, and he made no doubt but that it had a design to be revenged. Knowing then that the time of his departure out of the World drew nigh, he foretold it to his Disciples, and shortly after having eaten a piece of the Pig which he had seen, he was taken with a violent Cholic which killed him.

His Soul ascended to the eight Heaven, which is properly Paradise called *Nyr-*

uppaam, it is no more subject to miseries and pain, but there enjoys perfect bliss. For that reason it will never be born again, and that is the thing they call being annihilated. For by that term they understand not the total destruction of a thing reduced to nothing; but their meaning is, that one appears no more upon Earth, tho he live in Heaven. His body was burnt; and his bones, as they say, have been preserved to this present. One part of them are in the Kingdom of *Pegu*, and the other in *Siam*. They attribute a wonderful Virtue to these bones, and they affirm that they shine with a Divine splendor. Before he died, he ordered his Picture to be drawn after his Death, for fear Men might by little and little suffer his Person to wear out of their remembrance, and at long run forget him for good and all. He would have the same honours rendred to him in that Image which were due to his Divinity. He left also the print of one of his feet in three different places, in the Kingdom of *Siam*, the Kingdom of *Pegu* and the Isle of *Ceilan*. People go thither in Pilgrimage from all parts, and yearly honour these prints with singular Devotion.

The *Siamese* pretend also that they have part of *Sommonokhodom*'s hair, which he had cut off after he became God: The other part was by Angels carried up into Heaven. It is their custom to upbraid us that we have not respect enough for holy Images, for Sacred Books, and for the Priests. The Truth is, no People can have greater Veneration for those things than they have. By a precept of their Law they are commanded to honour them: but it is not enough for them to respect the Priests and the Divine Scriptures; the Vestments of the one, and the Characters of the other wherein their Law is written, is to them also an object of Religious Worship. Nay they think it is a most laudable action, and excellent virtue to do good to the *Talapoins*, and that their Cloaths and the Beads which they receive from them have the power to cure Diseases. They imagine also that in their Books there is a divine virtue, and that if one understood it and knew how to use the words of them, he might work great wonders. And therefore of the three ways of working Miracles; the first is to understand aright how to make use of the word of God; the second, to be instructed in the Doctrine of the Anchorites; and the third is the assistance of Devils. This last, however, they condemn, but they mightily approve of the two former, boasting that they alone know these admirable secrets.[19]

✦   NICOLAS GERVAISE (CA. 1662–1729)

Nicolas Gervaise was a French missionary to Siam, living there from 1681 to 1685. After returning to France, at the urging of friends he gathered his notes from his time overseas and in 1688 published Histoire naturelle et politique du royaume de Siam

(The Natural and Political History of the Kingdom of Siam). He seems to have conceived of the book as a source of previously unknown information about Siam that would be useful to his compatriots traveling there on either political or religious missions.

Two excerpts are provided, the first concerning the state of Buddhahood and the second the life of the Buddha (Sommonokodom). Father Gervaise reports that according to the Chinese, the Buddha was a Chinese ambassador sent as an envoy to Siam, where he married the king's daughter and became the ruler of the kingdom, before he renounced the world. The Siamese, however, say he was the son of the king of Siam.

––––––

FIRST CHAPTER, THE CREED OF THE SIAMESE

I do not intend to relate here all the stories within which the Siamese hide the mysteries of their religion: for, although they may be well woven with wit and told in a pleasant manner, nevertheless, they are so obscure that it would be difficult to find the meaning of them, and they are so long that it would be hard to contain them all in one volume. I shall dwell only on the chief points of their creed. I shall explain as clearly as I can their opinion on the Transmigration of Souls, and I shall relate briefly what I have learnt about the God they worship, of the cult they practice towards Him, of the ministers who serve Him, of their traditions, ceremonies, temples and all that concerns the practice of their religion.

The Siamese recognize a Sovereign Being whom they call *Pra* or *Pra pen chaou*, that is to say, God, Who is the Lord. Their idea of Him is altogether different from ours, for they do not believe Him to be the first Principle and Author of all things. According to them, the world has neither Creator nor Master, but is the work of chance, and all the parts composing it came together of themselves. The earth has always existed, or, rather, no time is known when it did not exist. A number of spirits are scattered throughout this vast universe, and keep order and peace, maintaining the regularity of its movements. Some of them are purely spiritual: others are confined within bodies capable of doing good and evil, and of acquiring by the merit of their good deeds, supreme power over all others. Thus divinity is but the price and reward of virtue. Souls do not arrive at this consummation of glory and happiness except after much time and trouble: two thousand years is not long enough to render them worthy of divinity. Before this comes to pass it is necessary for them to pass through various states of being, and fulfil these conditions exactly to the letter. In proportion as they progress and strengthen themselves in the practice of doing good, they purify and ennoble themselves, so to speak; so that after having appeared first in the form of some ordinary man, they are reborn as a mandarin, and in succeeding generations they become successively prince, king, priest, saint, angel, and lastly, god, if they have always persevered without interruption or rest in the exercise of good works.

When by favour of moral virtues a soul is elevated from degree to degree to the highest point of perfection, and is purer than gold that has passed through the crucible, it no longer feels any cravings of the passions or weaknesses of human nature. It must be reborn for the last time and come in human guise to rectify the abuses prevalent in this world, to teach men a new law, and to receive the honour due to it. This new God soon announces His existence by the radiance spread by His person, twenty times more brilliant than the sun and stars, and by a great number of miracles. He raises the dead, He makes the blind to see, moves mountains, penetrates the most hidden secrets of nature and science: all creatures and the elements are subject unto Him; animals hearken to His voice and obey Him; diseases, unhappiness, and even death yield to Him; and demons tremble in His presence and, convinced of their impotency and weakness, they recognize that everything must yield to His absolute power. After having passed several years in teaching men and bestowing upon them innumerable graces, He suddenly disappears and goes to take his place in *Nyreupane* (Nirvana) that is, a place of rest and pleasure, the dwelling place of the gods, where, they spend their time for all eternity in providing for their own happiness and think only of enjoying the fruits of their labours in complete tranquillity. When they enter this dwelling place, they no longer have anything to do with other creatures, and heaven and earth, henceforth unworthy of their care, no longer receive from them either protection or assistance.

Siamese Doctors of Religion express the state of the gods in *Nyreupane* in these terms: *Pra chaou caou Nyreupane dapsoun pai leou*, which means, *God the Lord has entered into Nirvana and now is nonexistent*. They give a mystic sense to these words, and they say that by the word *dapsoun* they do not mean a physical and total annihilation of being, but merely exemption from all the imperfections to which They were subject before They were deified, or, that They are nonexistent as far as men and animals are concerned, since to these They are as if They no longer existed: to these They exist eternally, sunk in contemplation and love of Themselves, tasting all the innumerable pleasures that can be imagined by those who feel them. They place this *Nyreupane* above the heavens and indicate neither the extent nor form of it. Four gods have already entered it in the manner I have just described. They are called *Concoussone, Conadom, Cahdsop* and *Sommonokodom.* The Siamese worship the last-named at the present time. They await a fifth Who is to come within a few centuries and Who will reinstate the law in its pristine purity, and when He has entered *Nyreupane,* they will worship Him as long as the law lasts and until another God comes to re-establish it. Then Sommonokodom will remain buried in eternal oblivion and He will be honoured no more.

They believe in a paradise and a hell which are temporal and transient. In paradise there are various dwelling places where souls are happy in proportion to the good they have done. Those found sinless at the time of death are immediately taken up by the sole merit of their good deeds. While they are there they console themselves that they have left their past wretchedness, and try to attain bliss, until the severe law of destiny and order that is of Nature compels them to return anew into the conventional human shape for their last work, for there in Nyreupane, they have none but gods whose state is fixed and permanent.

In hell, which is situated directly in the centre of the earth under a huge sea forty nine thousand leagues in depth, there are as many punishments as there are kinds of crimes committed—a punishment to fit every crime. Those who are guilty of some sin when they die are carried away by the weight of their iniquities and without any judgment than that of their own conscience. They dwell there as long as it is necessary for the expiation of their sins, and then they enter the body of some animal, more or less noble according to the seriousnesss [*sic*] of their crimes, and passing thus from kind to kind, they continue to be reborn as animals until they are sufficiently purified to become men again. Few people escape hell, for they go there for the least sin.

They recognize two kinds of angels: the first are purely spirits without the least admixture of matter; the second are corporeal and have a diversity of sex. They are subject to the same order of nature as men are, although their changes are not as frequent, and some of them are over sixty thousand years in one state of being. Their functions are to govern the celestial bodies and other parts of the world, to administer justice, protect the good people, punish the wicked, to act as guardians to men and to save empires from ruin. Each has his special territory: his nation, his town, his village, in proportion to his merit and ability. The Peguans and Cochin-Chinese place the angels above all others. Amongst them, that which concerns the business of everyday life and the needs of nature, all utensils, all corners of the house, have their tutelary angel in the same way as the ancient heathens assigned a special god to the vilest of functions and to actions which decency forbids us to mention.

These, then, are the principal articles of the creed of the Siamese, and the very foundations of their religion. The priests who are the trustees of this doctrine envelop it in a thousand fictitious tales to render it more venerable by reason of its obscurity and vagueness. The low-class people who usually revere only those things which they do not know or understand, are ignorant of the mysteries of metempsychosis (transmigration of souls), and content themselves with worshipping the statue of Sommonokodom which is made of lime and brick, to which they attribute all the good and evil that happens to them.

The King and several lords of the Court are more enlightened than the rest, have a theology of their own. The introspection of their own minds has brought them to discover that Sommonokodom, having been mortal, cannot have become a god. Furthermore, they do not consider Him to be more than a person of extraordinary virtue who has left good maxims and good examples to be followed. Moreover, they recognize a Supreme and Perfect Being Who has created the heavens and the earth and keeps them alive. But they imagine that He keeps them for His own diversion, for the entertainment He finds in the diversity of languages, customs, dresses, and even religions which exist among men. They believe that this medley produces the same effect as the variety of flowers in a flower-bed, as the different dishes of a meal, or as the diversity of offices in the palace of a prince. It is their idea that thus God has been pleased to cause men to honour and serve Him in different ways; that we should believe them all to be good since all have the same object and lead man on towards his end, as the various roads lead at last to the same city.[20]

FOURTH CHAPTER.

THE ORIGIN OF THEIR RELIGION

The era of this religion is very vague, and one cannot tell very exactly when it began nor in what manner it was established. Common opinion says it is about two thousand years old, and the Siamese would like to believe that it originated in their country. Those who have voyaged along the Coromandel coast think that this religion came from the Brahmins by reason of the great similarity that exists between them and the Siamese in religion. The Chinese maintain that the glory is due to their country. It is seen in their books, which are exceedingly old, that Sommonokodom was Chinese. An emperor of China, they say, had sent his ambassador to Siam, and he acquitted himself so well that the King of Siam gave him his daughter in marriage and made him his successor. After having reigned several years to the people's liking, this ambassador voluntarily abdicated his sovereign power and retired to the woods, where the austerity of his life did not, however, prevent his being followed by a great number of people who placed themselves under his guidance. He taught them, not only by his own example, but also by means of precepts full of admirable wisdom. After his death his disciples spread his teaching, and, in order to immortalize their gratitude and his memory, they built temples in his honour and erected statues to him. As century followed century these statues served to cast the Siamese into the practice of idolatry, and led them to look upon Sommonokodom as a God, and, finally, in order to justify their worship of him and to legalize their errors, they invented those stories which their unfortunate posterity have received as fixed truths and articles of faith.

The Siamese accept a part of these stories and add many others which the Chinese writers do not mention. If their stories are to be believed, then Sommonokodom was the son of a King of Siam, whose period and name I have not been able to discover. His father having died, he ascended the throne and ruled so gently and justly that he soon became the joy of his subjects. But this prince had already passed through all the degrees of metempsychosis, and, aspiring to a higher state, he resolved to put aside his crown, to withdraw from the world that he might more promptly fulfil the measure of good works which it was yet necessary for him to perform in order to arrive at Divinity. In the depths of the forests where he had hidden himself, he began to exercise upon himself unheard of severities: he afflicted his body, he mortified his senses, he reduced himself to eating only one handful of rice per day, and afterwards nothing but a single grain. He deprived himself of everything for the poor who had recourse to him, and his charity went to the extent that he even gave one of his eyes as alms. In this manner, which is unknown to the rest of men, he succeeded in subduing his passions and triumphing over the rage of demons and the malice of the enemies which his brother, Tevatat had stirred against him. After this, an Angel from Heaven, having come down to congratulate him on the fortunate success of his works, ordained him to be priest, and at the same time shaved his head and his eyebrows, and told him that the time had come for him to proclaim the new law and to show men the way of salvation. Sommonokodom, impatient to see the accomplishment of his desires, then received under his guidance all whom he had formerly refused through his humility and modesty. He made them priests by means of the same ceremonies that the angel had observed with regard to himself. He then expounded to them the profound mysteries of transmigration, and declared to them that, as Nature had subjected them to so many different cycles, they could not free themselves from their present servitude except by doing good works, that virtue alone led to rest and glory, and than [*sic*] all other possessions were frail and perishable, but that such virtue would never perish. He did not mislead them into thinking that the way was anything but difficult. He showed them that they must tread the path of sorrow, persecutions and injuries, that it was not enough to conquer self alone if one were not ready to sacrifice self still further in the service of others. But he moved them by pictures of the greatness and certainty of reward. He comforted them with the examples of the life he had led in the wilderness and convinced them that the practice of virtue was not impossible to any but those who did not love virtue or lacked courage. The reputation of his sanctity relighted the fires of jealousy in the heart of his brother, Tevatat. This superb spirit, to whom the new order of things gave umbrage, conspired to supplant his brother or to get rid of him. The more easily to surprise him, he joined his brother's band of disciples. This ruse did not succeed, and so he used open force, also with quite as little success. Sommonokodom, who from the beginning had known of his evil intention, upset all the intrigues without the least difficulty, and being content to oppose this violence and deceit with much patience and gentleness, he confounded this wretch and forced him to withdraw. Tevatat did not long survive his shame. He was attacked by a dangerous disease for which his friends could find no remedy other than that of taking him to Sommonokodom and imploring the latter's mercy. But he died on the way, and was thrown over the abyss. There, bound to a cross, he expiates, in torment, the horrible crime that he had attempted to commit. After the death of Tevatat, Sommonokodom, being as far above humanity as he was above envy and malice, appeared robed in all the attributes of Divinity: His face became so radiant that no-one could withstand the brilliance. His power and His goodness manifested themselves in an infinite number of miracles. The Siamese still say that He was one day on a hill near Louvo (Lopburi), when He leapt upon another hill situated in the kingdom of *Lancas*, (Lanka, or Ceylon) three years' journey from Siam by the roads, and that, in leaping he implanted the shape of his foot upon the rock. They call it by the Bali name of Pra-Bata, that is to say, Sacred Foot Print. This imprint, which may still be seen to this day, resembles the footprint of a man, but it is a cubit long. It is respectfully covered with a sheet of gold which is enclosed in another sheet of the same metal. It is uncovered only on certain Feast days, or when the King commands it to be uncovered. Near to the place where is found this so-called imprint of the foot of Sommonokodom, they have built a temple and a monastery, which demonstrate the extent to which the devotion of the Siamese kings displays their magnificence. It is their custom to go thither in March every year on a pilgrimage. Lastly, they add that Sommonokodom, after having established His law and accomplished His ministry, divested Himself before the eyes of men, and entered Nyreupane (Nirvana) where, with the other gods, He shares happiness that shall know no end.

In this we see the least part of the marvels which the Siamese proclaim concerning their Lawgiver, but they are the chief and most universally received amongst them. I have taken them from the books which are usually accepted by the people and the monks, and I have omitted to gather several instances and facts that are recounted only by writers who, themselves, add scarcely anything in the matter of faith, and I leave there also, those writers who say that Sommonokodom was born of a virgin the last time He came into the world, that He had formerly been a bull, as His name appears to signify, that he died once through having eaten too much pork, and a thousand and one other similar tales. I have thought that it is sufficient to show the nature of the spirit with which the Siamese endow this extraordinary Personage and what has been the source of the errors amongst which these people have been groping for so many centuries.[21]

◆ SIMON DE LA LOUBÈRE (1642–1729)

In 1687, Louis XIV sent a third mission to Siam, led by Simon de la Loubère. Born into a distinguished provincial family, de la Loubère was something of a prodigy, having composed a Latin tragedy and a French comedy by the age of sixteen. He served as a diplomat in Switzerland before being chosen by the king to lead the embassy to Siam. He arrived in Bangkok in October that year and departed on January 3, 1688. His stay was therefore brief, but upon his return to France he produced a remarkable report for the king, published in Paris and Amsterdam in 1691 as De royaume de Siam *(The Kingdom of Siam); it was translated into English two years later. It deals with a wide range of Thai life and culture, including religion.*

Like his compatriots before him, de la Loubère was very interested in Devadatta (here, Thevetat) and had the Thais compose a book about him in Pāli. The translation of that text forms a substantial second of part 2 of his report. What follows, however, is a section on the Buddha himself, who, according to de la Loubère, killed his wife and children and fed them to monks. De la Loubère concludes with a wildly mistaken discussion of the etymology of the name Somono-Codom, and goes on to draw a number of false conclusions from it.

———

'Tis no fault of mine that they gave me not the life of *Sommona-Codom* translated from their Books, but not being able to obtain it, I will here relate what was told me thereof. How marvellous soever they pretend his Birth has been, they cease not to give him a Father and a Mother. His Mother, whose Name is found in some of their *Balie* Books, was called, as they say, *Maha Maria*, which seems to signifie the *great Mary*, for *Maha* signifies *great*. But it is found written *Mania*, as often as *Maria*: which proves almost that these are two words *Man-ya*, because that the *Siameses* do confound the *n* with the *r* only at the end of the words, or at the end of the Syllables, which are followed with a Consonant. However it be, this ceases not to give attention to the Missionaries, and has perhaps given occasion to the *Siameses* to believe, that *Jesus* being the Son of *Mary*, was Brother to *Sommona-Codom*, and that having been crucified, he was that wicked Brother whom they give to *Sommona-Codom*, under the Name of *Thevetat*, and whom they report to be punished in hell, with a Punishment which participates something of the Cross. The Father of *Sommona-Codom* was, according to this same *Balie* Book, a King of *Teve Lanca*, that is to say, a King of the famous *Ceylon*. But the *Balie* Books being without Date, and without the Author's Name, have no more Authority than all the Traditions, whose Origin is unknown. This now is what they relate of *Sommona-Codom*.

'Tis said, that he bestowed all his Estate in Alms, and that his Charity not being yet satisfied, he pluck'd out his Eyes, and slew his Wife and Children, to give them to the *Talapoins* of his Age to eat. A strange contrariety of Idea's in this People, who prohibit nothing so much as to kill, and who relate the most execrable Parricides, as the most meritorious works of *Sommona-Codom*. Perhaps they think that under the Title of Property a Man has as much Power over the Lives of his Wife and Children, as to them it seems he has over his own: For it matters not if otherwise the Royal Authority prohibits particular *Siameses* from making use of this pretended Right of Life and Death over their Wives, Children and Slaves; whereas it alone exerts equally over all its Subjects, it may upon this Maxim of the despotic Government, that the Life of the Subjects properly belong to the King.

The *Siameses* expect another *Sommona-Codom*, I mean another miraculous man like him, whom they already name *Pra Narotte*, and whom they suppose to have been foretold by *Sommona-Codom*. And they before-hand report of him, that he shall kill two Children which he shall have, that he will give them to the *Talapoins* to eat, and that it will be by this pious Charity that he will consummate his Vertue. This expectation of a new God, to make use of this Term, renders them careful and credulous, as often as any one is proposed to them, as an extraordinary Person; especially if he that is proposed to them, is entirely stupid, because that the entire Stupidity resembles what they represent by the Inactivity and Impassibility of the *Nireupan*. As for example, there appeared some year since at *Siam*, a young Boy born dumb, and so stupid, that he seemed to have nothing humane but the Shape: yet the report spread itself through the whole Kingdom, that he was of the first men, which inhabited this Country, and that he would one day become a God, that is to say arrive at the *Nireupan*. The People flocked to him from all parts, to adore him and make him Presents, till that the King fearing the consequences of this Folly, caused it to cease by the Chastisement of some of those, that suffered themselves to be seduced. I have read some such think in *Tofi's India Orientale*, Tom. I. page 203. He reports that the *Bonzees* of *Cochinchina*, having taken away from them a stupid Infant, show'd him to the People as a God, and that after having inrich'd themselves with the Presents which the People made him, they published that this pretended God would burn himself; and he adds that they indeed burnt him publickly, after having stupefied his Senses by some Drink, and calling the insensible state, wherein they had put him, Extasie. This last History is given as a crafty trick of the *Bonzees*, but it demonstrates, as well as the first, the Belief which these People have, that there may daily spring up some new God, and the Inclination which they have to take extream Stupidity, for a beginning of the *Nireupan*.

Sommona-Codom being disingaged, by the Alms-deeds which I have mentioned, from all the Bands of Life, devoted himself to Fasting, to Prayer, and to the other Exercises of the perfect Life: But as these Practices are possible only to the *Talapoins*, he embraced the profession of a *Talapoin*; and when he had heaped up his good works, he immediately acquired all the Priviledges thereof.

He found himself endowed with so great a Strength, that in a Duel he vanquished another man of a consummated Vertue, whom they call *Pra Souane*, and who doubting of the Perfection whereunto *Sommona-Codom* was arrived, challenged him to try his Strength, and was vanquisht. This *Pra Souane* is not the sole God, or rather the sole perfect Man, which they pretend to have been contemporary with *Sommona-Codom*. They name several others, as *Pra Ariaseria*, of whom they report that he was forty Fadoms high, that his Eyes were three and a half broad, and two and a half round, that is to say, less in Circumference than Diameter, if there is no fault in the Writing from whence I have taken this Remark. The *Siameses* have a time of Wonders, as had the *Ægyptians* and the *Greeks*, and as the *Chineses* have. For Instance, their principal Book, which they believe to be the work of *Sommona-Codom*, relates, that a certain Elephant had Three and thirty Heads, that each of its Heads had seven Teeth, every Tooth seven Pools, every Pool seven Flowers, every Flower seven Leafs, every Leaf seven Towers, and every Tower seven other things, which had each seven others, and these likewise others, and always by seven; for the numbers have always been a great Subject of Superstition. Thus in the Alcoran, if my Memory deceives me not, there is an Angel with a very great number of Heads, each of which hath as many Mouths, and every Mouth as many Tongues, which do praise God as many times every day.

Besides corporal strength, *Sommona-Codom* had the power of doing all sorts of miracles. For example, he could make himself as big and as great as he pleas'd: and on the contrary, he could render himself so little, that he could steal out of sight, and stand on the head of another man, without being felt either by his weight, or perceived by the Eyes of another. Then he could annihilate himself, and place some other man in his stead: that is to say, that then he could enjoy the repose of the *Nireupan*. He suddenly and perfectly understood all the things of the World: He equally penetrated things past and to come, and having given to his body an entire Agility, he easily transported himself from one place to another, to preach Vertue to all Nations.

He had two principal Disciples, the one on the right Hand, and the other on the left: they were both plac'd behind him, and by each other's side on the Altars, but their Statues are less than his. He that is plac'd on his right Hand is called *Pra Mogla*, and he that is on his left Hand is called *Pra Scaribout*. Behind these three Statues, and on the same Altar, they only represent the Officers within the Palace of *Sommona-Codom*. I know not whether they have Names. Along the Galleries or Cloysters, which are sometimes round the Temples, are the Statues of the other Officers without the Palace of *Sommona-Codom*. Of *Pra Mogla* they report, that at the request of the damned he overturned the Earth, and took the whole Fire of Hell into the hollow of his Hand: but that designing to extinguish it, he could not effect it, because that this Fire dried up the Rivers, instead of extinguishing, and that it consumed all that whereon *Pra Mogla* placed it: *Pra Mogla* therefore went to beseech *Pra Pouti Tchaou*, or *Sommona-Codom*, to extinguish Hell Fire: but though *Pra Pouti Tchaou* could do it, he thought it not convenient, because, he said, that men would grow too wicked, if he should destroy the Fear of this Punishment.

But after that *Pra Pouti Tchaou* was arrived at this high Vertue, he ceased not to kill a *Mar*, or a *Man*, (for they write *Mar* and *Man*, though they pronounce always Man) and as a Punishment for this great fault, his Life exceeded not Eighty years, after which he died, by disappearing on a sudden, like a Spark which is loft in the Air.

The *Man* were a People Enemies to *Sommona-Codom*, whom they called *Paya Man*; and because they suppose that this People was an Enemy to so holy a Man, they do represent them as a monstrous People, with a very large Visage, with Teeth horrible for their Size, and with Serpents on their Head instead of Hair.

One day then as *Pra Pouti Tchaou* eat Pig's flesh, he had a Chollick fit which killed him: An admirable end for a man so abstemious: but it was necessary that he died by a Pig, because they suppose that the Soul of the *Man* whom he slew, was not then in the Body of a *Man*, but in the Body of a Pig: as if a Soul could be esteemed, even according to their Opinion, the soul of a *Man*, when it is in the Body of a Pig. But all these inventers of Stories are not so attentive to the Principles of their Doctrine.

Sommona-Codom before his Death, ordered that some Statues and Temples should be Consecrated to Him, and since his Death he is in that state of repose, which they express by the word *Nireupan*. This is not a place but a kind of Being: for to speak truly, they say *Sommona-Codom* is no where, and he enjoys not any Felicity: he is without power, and out of a condition to do either good or Evil unto Men: expressions which the *Portugueses* have rendered by the word Annihilation. Nevertheless on the other hand the *Siameses* do esteem *Sommona-Codom* happy, they offer up Prayers unto him, and demand of him whatever they want: whether that their Doctrine agrees not with itself; or that they extend their worship beyond their Doctrine: but in what Sense soever they attribute Power to *Sommona-Codom*, they agree that he has it only over the *Siamese*, and that he concerns not himself with other People, who adore other Men besides him.

As therefore they report nothing but Fables of their *Sommona-Codom*, that they respect him not as the Author of their Laws and their Doctrine, but at most as him who has re-established them amongst Men, and that in fine they have no reasonable Memory of him, it may be doubted, in my Opinion, that there ever was such a man. He seems to have been invented to be the Idea of a Man, whom Vertue, as they apprehend it, has rendered happy, in the times of their fables, that is to say beyond what their Histories contain certain. And because that they have thought necessary to give at the same time an opposite Idea of a Man, whom his wickedness has subjected to great Torments, they have certainly invented that *Thevetat*, whom they suppose to have been Brother to *Sommona-Codom*, and his Enemy. They make them both to be *Talapoins*, and when they alledge that *Sommona-Codom* has been King, they report it, as they declare he has been an Ape and a Pig. They suppose that in the several Transmigrations of his Soul he has been all things, and always excellent in every kind, that is to say he has been the most commendable of all Pigs, as the most commendable of all Kings. I know not from whence Mr. *Gervaise* judges that the *Chineses* pretend that *Sommona-Codom* was of their Country: I have seen nothing thereof in the Relations of *China*, but only what I have spoken concerning *Chekia* or *Chaka*.

The Life of *Thevetat* was given me translated from the *Baly*, but not to interrupt my discourse, I will put it at the end of this Relation. 'Tis also a Texture of Fables, and a curious specimen of the thoughts of these men, touching the Vertues and Vices, the Punishment and Rewards, the Nature and the Transmigrations of Souls.

I must not omit what I borrow from Mr. *Harbelot*. I have thought it necessary to consult him about what I know of the *Siameses*; to the end that he might observe what the words which I know thereof, have in common with the *Arabian*, *Turkish* and *Persian*: and he informed that *Suman*, which must be pronounced *Souman*, signifies *Heaven* in *Persian*, and that *Codum*, or *Codom*, signifies *Ancient* in the same tongue; so that *Sommona-Codom* seems to signifie the *eternal*, or *uncreated Heaven*, because that in *Persian* and in *Hebrew*, the word which signifies Ancient implys likewise *uncreated* or *eternal*. And as touching the *Baly* Tongue, he informed me, that the ancient *Persian* is called *Pahalevi*, or *Pahali*, and that between *Pahali* and *Bahali* the *Persians* make no Difference. Add that the word *Pout*, which in *Persian* signifies an *Idol*, or *false God*, and which doubtless signified *Mercury*, when the *Persians* were Idolaters, signifies *Mercury* amongst the *Siameses*, as I have already remark'd. *Mercury*, who was the God of the Sciences, seems to have been adored through the whole Earth; by reason doubtless that Knowledge is one of the most essential Attributes of the true God. Remarks which may hereafter excite the curiosity of the learned men, that shall be designed to travel into the East.

But I know not whether to this hour it is not lawful to believe that this is a proof of what I have said, that the Ancestors of the *Siameses* must have adored the Heaven, like the ancient *Chineses*, and as perhaps the ancient *Persians* did, and that having afterwards embraced the Doctrine of the *Metempsychosis*, and forgot the true meaning of the name of *Sommona-Codom*, they have made a man of the Spirit of Heaven, and have attributed unto him all the fables that I have related. 'Tis a great Art to change the belief of the People, to leave unto them their ancient words, by cloathing them with new Idea's. Thus, it may be, that the Ancestors of the *Siameses* have thought that the Spirit of Heaven ruled the whole Nature, though the modern *Siameses* do not believe it of *Sommona-Codom*: they believe on the contrary, as I have said, that such a care is opposite to the supream felicity. They believe also that *Sommona-Codom* has sinned, and that he has been punished, at the time that he was worthy of the *Nireupan*, because they believe the extream virtue impossible. They believe that the worship of *Sommona-Codom* is only for them, and that amongst the other Nations there are other men, who have render'd themselves worthy of Altars, and which those other Nations must adore.[22]

✦ LOUIS LE COMTE (1655–1728)

Louis le Comte was a French Jesuit missionary, and among the six Jesuit scientists assigned to the first delegation sent by Louis XIV to the court of Siam in 1685. At the conclusion of the negotiations, he was one of the five Jesuits who proceeded to China, arriving in 1688. He returned to France three years later, and published his Nouveau mémoire sur l'état présent de la Chine *(New Memoir on the Present State of China) in 1696. The passage below is from the English translation, published in the following year.*

After Matteo Ricci's decision to "draw close to Confucianism and repudiate Buddhism," Jesuit descriptions of the Buddha in China were consistently negative, as we see here. For Father le Comte, Buddhism is "the second Sect," after what we today call Confucianism.

———

The second Sect which is prevalent in China, and is more dangerous and more universally spread than the former, adore an Idol which they call *Fo* or *Foë* as the only god of the World. This Idol was brought from the *Indies* two and thirty years after the Death of JESUS CHRIST. This Poyson began at Court, but spread its infection thro' all the Provinces, and corrupted every Town: so that this great body of Men already spoiled by Magick and Impiety, was immediately infected with Idolatry, and became a monstrous receptacle for all sorts of Errors. Fables, Superstitions, Transmigration of Souls, Idolatry and Atheism divided them, and got so strong a Mastery over them, that, even at this present, there is no so great impediment to the progress of Christianity as is this ridiculous and impious Doctrine.

No body can well tell where this Idol *Fo*, of whom I speak, was born; (I call him an Idol and not a Man, because some think it was an Apparition from hell) those who with more likelihood say he was a Man, make him born about a thousand years before JESUS CHRIST, in a Kingdom of the *Indies* near the Line, perhaps a little above *Bengala*. They say he was a Kings Son.

He was at first called *Che-Kia*; but at thirty year of age he took the name of *Fo*. His Mother who brought him into the World thro' her right side, died in Childbirth: she had a fancy in her Dream that she swallowed an Elephant, and for this reason it is that the *Indian* Kings pay such honour to white Elephants: for the loss of which, or gaining some others they often make bitter Wars.

When this Monster was first born he had strength enough to stand alone, and he made seven steps, and pointed with one Hand to Heaven, and the other to the Earth. He did also speak, but in such a manner as shewed what Spirit he was posses'd withal. *In Heaven or on the Earth*, says he, *I am the only person who deserve to be honoured.* At seventeen he married, and had a Son, which he forsook as he did all the rest of the World, to retire into a Solitude with three or four *Indian* Philosophers, whom he took along with him to teach. But at thirty he was on a suddain possessed, and as it were fulfilled with the Divinity, who gave him an universal knowledge of all things. From that time he became a God, and began by a vast number of seeming Miracles, to gain the Peoples admiration. The number of his Disciples is very great, and it is by their means that all the *Indies* have been poysoned with his pernicious Doctrine. Those of *Siam* call them *Talapoins*, the *Tartars* call them *Lamas* or *Lama-sem*, the *Japoners Bonzes*, and the *Chinese Hocham*.

But this Chimerical God found at last that he was a Man as well as others. He died at 79 years of Age; and to give the finishing stroke to his Impiety, he endeavoured to persuade his Followers to Atheism at his Death, as he had persuaded them to Idolatry in his Life time. Then he declared to his Followers that all which he had hither told them was enigmatical; and that they would be mistaken if they thought there was any other first Principle of things beside nothing; *It was*, said he, *from this nothing that all things sprang, and it is into this nothing that all things must return. This is the Abyss where all our hopes must end.*

Since this Impostor confessed that he had abused the World in his life, it is but reasonable that he should not be believed at his death. Yet as Impiety has always more Champions than Virtue, there were among the *Bonzes* a particular Sect of Atheists, formed from the last words of their Master. The rest who found it troublesome to part with their former prejudices, kept close to their first Errors. A third sort endeavoured to reconcile these Parties together, by compiling a body of Doctrine, in which there is a twofold Law, an interior and an exterior. One ought to prepare the mind for the reception of the other. It is, say they, the mould which supports the material 'till the Arch be made, and is then taken away as useless.

Thus the Devil making use of Mens Folly and Malice for their destruction, endeavours to erase out of the minds of some those excellent ideas of God which are so deeply ingraved there, and to imprint in the minds of others the Worship of false Gods under the shapes of a multitude of different Creatures, for they did not stop at the Worship of this Idol. The Ape, the Elephant, the Dragon have been worshipped in several places, under pretence perhaps that the God *Fo* had successively been transmigrated into these Creatures. *China* the most superstitious of all Nations, increased the Number of her Idols, and one may now see all sorts of them in the Temples, which serve to abuse the folly of this People.[23]

Engelbert Kaempfer was born in Westphalia, the son of a Lutheran pastor. Trained as a physician, he served as secretary in a Swedish delegation to Persia, departing in 1683 and arriving in the capital of Isfahan in January 1684. When it was time to return to Sweden, Kaempfer decided to leave the delegation and journey east alone. He traveled extensively in the employ of the Dutch, stopping in Arabia, the Malabar Coast in southwest India, Sri Lanka, Bengal, and Sumatra before reaching Batavia (Jakarta) in Indonesia, the headquarters of the Dutch East India Company, in September 1689. Eight months later, he again put to sea, having been appointed physician to the Dutch embassy to Japan. Before proceeding north, the ship first sailed to Siam, eventually reaching Japan in September 1690. Kaempfer would spend the next two years there. At that time, the Dutch were restricted to Dejima, an artificial island in Nagasaki Bay.

There Kaempfer received invaluable service from a young Japanese, Imamura Gen'emon Eisei, appointed as his servant. Kaempfer taught him to read and write Dutch, instructed him in anatomy and medicine, and paid him a handsome salary. In turn, Eisei provided Kaempfer with a great deal of information and also procured books for him, explaining their contents. In the course of his two-year stay, Kaempfer was twice allowed to make the long journey from Nagasaki to Edo (Tokyo), where he met the Tokugawa shogun, seeing a great deal of Japan along the way. He left in November 1692.

Engelbert Kaempfer died in his home city of Lemgo on November 2, 1716, with his extensive writings left unpublished. His history of Japan, written in High Dutch, was translated into English and published in London in 1727 as The History of Japan, giving an Account of the ancient and present State and Government of that Empire. *The book contains much information about Buddhism that would be repeated in other works over the course of the eighteenth century. Indeed, Kaempfer's work was a major source for Bernard Picart's* Cérémonies et coutumes religieuses de tous les peuples du monde *(Religious Ceremonies and Customs of All the Peoples of the World) as well as Diderot and d'Alembert's* Encyclopédie *(both discussed in the next chapter). For the European encounter with the Buddha, Kaempfer is a figure of particular importance; he put forth two of the most influential views about the Buddha, views that we might call "the two-buddha theory" and "the African hypothesis."*

Two passages from Kaempfer are provided here, one about the Buddha in Siam and the other about the Buddha in Japan.

In viewing these Temples I took notice, as of something particular, that I met with no images of beasts, and Idols of a monstrous figure, as the Brahmines and Chinese have in theirs, for all their idols within the Temples are represented in human shape, either sitting, or standing, tho' without them, as for instance on the gates, entries, pyramids, particularly in these two squares, we are now speaking of, appear as by way of ornament many monstrous images, with hideous frightful faces. . . .

The Pyramids standing in those Squares are built in honour of certain gods, to whom they are dedicated and named after them. They are commonly provided with shelves on which the Devotees place their offerings for the benefit of the priests.

In the other Square (*See Tab.* V *Fig.* 1) within its walls were rang'd Flower-pots and Boxes for plants. There stood also within it several *Topoo* Trees, in the East Indies call'd *Rawusith*, and *Bipel*. This is a sort of a Milk or Fig Tree, of the size of a beach, with extended branches, a smooth grey bark, and round but long pointed leaves, bearing a round fruit, which is insipid, and nourishment only for Bats. All the Pagans of these parts hold it to be holy, and pleasing to the Gods, for as much as their great Saint *Sammana Khodum* always chose to sit under it, and for this reason they love to plant it near their temples, if the Soil and Climate will allow it. The like holiness is ascrib'd to another Milk or Fig Tree, whose branches bending towards the ground take root in it, after they touch it, and form as many new Stems, by which means it extends it self far round about: It hath leaves not unlike those of the Lauro-Cerasus, but larger and bears a fruit like the other, which bats love to eat. The Ceylonese call it also *Budhum Gas*, that is *Budhum's* Tree. But it is difficult to plant and not proper to stand near the temples by reason of its spreading so far. The second square contain'd two remarkable Temples, the first of which represented on each door in the porch two Savages with heads of Devils (*See Tab.* V *Fig.* 2) and at the back door were painted two Portugueze as big as the Life. A great festival is yearly celebrated in this Temple. There stood besides in this second square some other Chapels with Idols in them, and also divers fine pyramids, some of which are gilt over, and others full of monstrous figures. It would be too tedious to describe each of them in particular, and I think it sufficient to have given the figures of the most remarkable ones in *Tab* VI. *Fig.* 1. 2. 3. 4. 5. 6. 7. . . .

The Religion of these People is the Pagan Doctrine of the *Brahmans*, which ever since many Centuries hath been profess'd amongst all the Nations from the River Indus to the extremity of the East, except that at the Court of the Grand Mogul, and in his great Cities, as also in *Summatra*, *Java*, *Celebes*, and other neighbouring Islands the Mahometism has gain'd so much ground, that it seems to prevail above it. This general Paganism, (which is to bedistinguish'd from the Religion of the old Persians worshipping the Sun, now almost extinct) tho' branch'd out into several Sects and Opinions, according to the various Customs, Languages, and Interpretations, yet is of one and the same Origine. The Siamites represent the first Teacher of their Paganism in their Temples, in the figure of a Negro sitting, of a prodigious size, his hair curl'd, the skin black, but as it were out of respect gilt over, accompanied on each side by one of his chief Companions, as also before and around him by the rest of his Apostles and Disciples, all of the same colour and most in the same posture. They believe according to the Brahmans, that the Deity dwelt in him, which he prov'd by his Doctrine, Way of Life, and Revelation. For *Wistnu*, by which they mean the Deity, having already many hundred thousands of years before assum'd different forms, and visited the World eight different times appear'd the ninth in the person of this Negro, whom for this reason they stile *Prahpuditsau*, that is to say, the Saint of high descent; *Sammana Khutama*, the Man without Passions: *Prah bin Tsjau*, the Saint who is the Lord; or plainly *Prah*, the Saint, or *Budha'* (or *Phutha'* in one syllable, according to their guttural pronunciation, like that of the Hottentots). The Ceylanese call him *Budhum*, the Chinese and Japanese *Sacka*, or *Siaka*, or plainly *Fotoge*, that is, the Idol, and with an honourable Epithet *Si Tsun*, the great Saint.

About his origine and native Country, I find the account of those Heathens do not agree. The Siamites call the Country of his nativity *Lanca*, which is the Island of *Ceylon*, from whence they say, their Religion was first brought over to them, and afterwards further propagated through the neighbouring Countries as far as *China* and *Japan*. Accordingly there are still to be seen some foot steps of their Religion, as well of that which they exercis'd before, as of the other sprung up in the room of it, on the top of a high mountain in the Island of *Ceylon*, by the Europeans call'd *Pico d'Adam*, which they look upon as holy, and in their Maps place it in the Centre of the World. The Ceylonese themselves call the Country of his nativity *Macca desia*, meaning by it the Kingdom of *Siam*, for they make use of the Pali, or Bible of the Siamites, which the Peguans call Maccatapasa, in their *Khom*, or Language of the *Khomuts*, owning that they had it from the Siamites. The Chinese and Japanese pretend that this Saint, and the Doctrine he reveal'd, had their origine in the Country of *Magatta*, or as the Japanese call it, *Tensik Magatta Kokf*, that is the Heavenlandish *Magatta*, which according to their description and opinion is the Continent of *India*, including *Pegu* and *Siam*, adding withal, that *Siaka* was the Son of the King of those Countries, the Inhabitants of which ascribe to each other the origin of their Teacher, a Prophet, as it seems, being always thought the greater for being of a foreign Country. The *Benians* and learned *Brahmans* believe that *Budha* had neither Father nor Mother, and consequently own, they know nothing of his birth and native Country. They represent him in the figure of a man with four arms, and as for the rest have no other Legends concerning his miracles and actions, besides a tradition of his adorable piety having now for 26430 years been sitting on a *Tarate* flower, and praising the Supreme God ever since 21639 years (reckoning from the 1690 year of Christ), when he first appear'd and reveal'd himself to the world. But the Siamites, and other Nations lying further East, have whole Books full of the birth, life and miracles of this God *Prah*, or *Siaka*. I am at a loss how to reconcile these various and opposite accounts, which I have gather'd in the abovesaid Countries, unless by supposing, what I really think to be the true opinion, *viz.* that the Siamites and other Nations lying more Easterly have confounded a younger Teacher with *Budha'* and mistaken the former for the latter, which confusion of the Gods and their names is very frequent in the Histories of the Greeks and Egyptians; so that *Prah* or *Siaka*, is not the same with *Budha*, much less with *Ram*, or *Rama*, as he is call'd by Father Kircher in his *Sina Illustrata* [1667 Latin edition, p. 152a] the latter having appear'd many hundred thousand years before, but that he was some new Impostor who set up but about five hundred years before Christ's nativity. Besides this, many circumstances make it probable, that the *Prah*, or *Siaka*, was no Asiatick, or Indian, but some Egyptian Priest of note, probably of *Memphis*, and a Moor, who with his Brethren being expell'd their native Country, brought the Egyptian Religion into the Indies, and propagated it there, and this for the following Reasons.

1. There appears in several material Points a conformity between this Eastern, and the Ancient Egyptian Paganism; for the Egyptians represented their Gods, as these Heathens now do, in the form of different sorts of Animals and human Monsters; whereas their Neighbours in *Asia*, as for example, the Persians, Chaldeans, and other Nations professing the same Religion, worship'd rather the Luminaries of the Heavens, particularly the Sun, and the Fire, as being its Image; and it is probable, that before the introduction of the present Paganism among the Indians, they had the same sort of worship with the neighbouring Chaldeans and Persians. For as it cannot be suppos'd, that these sensible Nations liv'd without any Religion at all, like the brutal Hottentots, it is highly probable, that they rever'd the divine Omnipotence by worshiping, according to the Custom of the Chaldeans, the Sun, and other Luminaries of the Firmament, as such parts of the Creation, which

most strike the outward senses, and fill the understanding with the admiration of their unconceivable proprieties. And there are still to this day among those Heathens some remains of the Chaldean Religion, consisting in a worship paid to the Sun and the Stars, which however is not taught by their Priests, but only tolerated like some supererogatory worship, just as there remain even in Christian Governments, certain ancient pagan customs and superstitions, especially the Bachanals. Two Articles in the Egyptian Religion, which were most religiously maintain'd, were, the Transmigration of Souls, and a Veneration for Cows, particularly for the holy Cow at *Memphis*, call'd *Apis*, or *Serapis*, which had divine honours paid her, and was serv'd by Priests. Both these Articles are still observ'd among the Asiatick Heathens, particularly those that inhabit the West-side of the Ganges; for no body there dares to kill the least and most noxious Insects, as being animated by some transmigrated human Soul; and the Cows, whose Souls they think are by frequent transmigrations, as it were, deified, are serv'd and attended with great veneration, their Dung being burnt to ashes is turn'd into holy Salve, their Urine serves for holy Water, the Image of a Cow possesses a peculiar Chapel before their Temples, is every day honour'd with fresh flowers, and hath sweet-scented oyl poured upon her. It is also remarkable, that the nearer those Heathens are to *Egypt*, the greater Zeal appears among them with relation to these two Articles, and the more remote they are from it, the more they abate in it, so that in *Siam* and the more Eastern Kingdoms, even the Priests themselves make no scruple of eating Cows Flesh, provided they have not given occasion, nor consented to their killing; nor doth the opinion of the transmigration of the Souls prevail there so much, as it does among the *Benjans* in *Hindostan*, for the Inhabitants of the East-side of the *Ganges* grant no quarters to Fleas or Flies, that attack their Skin. I shall barely mention, that among these Asiatick Heathens we meet not only with the greater Deities of the Egyptians, but also with the lesser, tho' they are disguised by other names, and fabulous circumstances, which however might be easily clear'd up and reconcil'd.

2. It is observable, that twenty three Centuries ago, or according to the most exact computation in the five hundred and thirty sixth year before Christ's nativity, *Cambyses*, the Persian Tyrant, subverted the Religion of the Egyptians, kill'd their *Apis*, or *holy Cow*, the Palladium of their Worship, and murder'd, or exil'd their Priests. Now if one considers that the Siamites, reckoning, their *Soncarad*, or Ecclesiastical *Epocha* from the death of their great Saint, their 2233–4th year falls in with our present 1690th year after Christ's nativity, it will appear, that the said *Epocha* agreed with that time, and that it may be concluded from thence, that then a notable Priest of *Memphis*, to whom they gave the name of *Budha*, *Siaka*, or the

great Saint, fled with his Brethren into India, where he publish'd his Doctrine, which was so well receiv'd, that it spread to the extremity of the Orient.

3. This Saint being represented with curled Hairs, like a Negro, there is room to conclude, that he was no native of India, but was born under the hot Climate of Africa, considering that the Air in India produces on its black Inhabitants none of that curl'd Wool, but long and black Hair, quite lank, and very little curl'd: And tho' the Siamites crop theirs, so as to leave it only of the length of a Finger; yet as it stands on end like bristles, it is easily distinguish'd from the woolly Curls of a Negro, and consequently it is more probable, that *Budha* was of African, than of Siamite extraction.[24]

OF THE BUDSDO, OR FOREIGN PAGAN WORSHIP, AND ITS FOUNDER

Foreign Idols, for distinction's sake from the *Kami*, or *Sin*, which were worshipp'd in the country in the most ancient times, are call'd *Budsd* and *Fotoke*. The Characters also, whereby these two words are express'd, differ from those of *Sin* and *Cami*. *Budso*, in the litteral sense signifies the *way of Foreign Idols*, that is, the *way of worshipping Foreign Idols*. The origine of this religion, which quickly spread thro' most *Asiatick* Countries to the very extremities of the East, (not unlike the *Indian* Fig-tree, which propogates itself, and spreads far round, by sending down new roots from the extremities of its branches,) must be look'd for among the *Brahmines*. I have strong reasons to believe, both from the affinity of the name, and the very nature of this religion, that its author and founder is the same person, whom the *Brahmines* call *Budha*, and believe to be an essential part of *Wisthnu* [*sic*] or their Deity, who made its ninth appearance in the world under this name, and in the shape of this Man. The Chinese and Japanese call him *Buds* and *Siaka*. These two names indeed become in success of time a common Epithet of all Gods and Idols in general, the worship of whom was brought over from other Countries: sometimes also they were given to the Saints and great men, who preach'd these new doctrines. The common people in *Siam*, call him *Prah Pudi Dsau*, that is, the *Holy Lord*, and the learned among them, in their *Pali* or holy language, *Sammona Khodum*. The Peguans call him *Sammana Khutama*. (*See* Book I. Ch. II.)

His native country, according to the Japanese (with regard to whom he is chiefly consider'd in this place) is *Magattakokf*, or the Province *Magatta* in the Country *Tensik*. *Tensik*, in the litteral sense, signifies a *Heavenly country*, a *Country of Heavens*. The Japanese comprehend under this name the Island of *Ceylon*, the Coasts of *Malabar* and *Cormandel*, and in general all the Countries of South *Asia*, the continent as well as the neighbouring Islands, which are inhabited by Blacks, such as the *Peninsula* of *Malacca*, the Islands of *Sumatra, Java*, the Kingdoms of *Siam, Pegu*, &c.

He was born in in [*sic*] the twenty-sixth year of the reign of the Chinese Emperor *Soowo*, who was fourth Successor of the famous *Suno Buo*, on the eighth day of the fourth month. This was according to some the year before our Saviour's Nativity 1029, and according to others 1027, (when I was in *Siam*, in 1690), the *Siamites* then told 2232 years from their *Budha*, who, if he be the same with the *Siaka* of the Japanese, his birth comes up no higher than 542 years before Christ. His father was King of *Magattakokf*, a powerful Kingdom in the Country *Tensikf*. I conjecture this to be the Island of *Ceylon*. The Kingdom of *Siam* indeed is so call'd to this day by the common People in *Japan*.

Siaka, when he came to be nineteen years of age, quitted his Palace, leaving his wife and an only son behind him, and voluntarily, of his own choice, became a disciple of *Arara Sennin*, then a Hermit of great repute, who liv'd at the top of a mountain call'd *Dandokf*. Under the inspection of this holy man he betook himself to a very austere life, wholly taken up with an almost uninterrupted contemplation of heavenly and divine things, in a posture very singular in itself, but reckon'd very proper for this sublime way of thinking, to wit, sitting cross-legg'd, with his hands in the bosom placed so, that the extremities of both thumbs touch'd one another: A posture, which is thought to engage one's mind into so profound a meditation, and to wrap it up so entirely within itself, that the body lies for a while as it were senseless, unattentive, and unmoved by any external objects whatsoever. This profound Enthusiasm is by them call'd *Sasen* and the divine truths revealed to such persons *Satori*. As to *Siaka* himself, the force of his Enthusiasm was so great, that by its means he penetrated into the most secret and important points of religion, discovering the existence and state of Heaven and Hell, as places of reward and punishment, the state of our Souls in a life to come, the transmigration thereof, the way to eternal happiness, the divine Power of the Gods in the government of this world, and many more things beyond the reach of humane understanding, which he afterwards freely communicated to the numerous crowds of his disciples, who for the sake of his doctrine and instructions follow'd him in flocks, embracing the same austere way of life, which he led himself.

He liv'd seventy-nine years, and died on the fifteenth day of the second month, in the year before Christ 950.

The most essential points of his doctrine are as follows.

The souls of men and animals are immortal: Both are of the same substance, and differ only according to the different objects they are placed in, whether human or animal.

The souls of men after their departure from their bodies, are rewarded in a place of happiness, or misery, according to their behaviour in this life.

The place of happiness is call'd *Gokurakf*, that is, *a place of eternal pleasures*. As the Gods differ in their nature, and the souls of men in the merit of their past actions, so do likewise the degrees of pleasure and happiness in their Elysian Fields, that every one may be rewarded as he deserves. However the whole place is so throughly fill'd with bliss and pleasure, that each happy inhabitant thinks his portion the best, and far from envying the happier state of others, wishes only for ever to enjoy his own.

Amida is the sovereign Commander of these heavenly Stations, (for all his doctrine hath not been introduc'd by the *Brahmines*, till after our Saviour's glorious resurrection). He is look'd upon as the general Patron and Protector of human Souls, but more particularly as the God and Father of those, who happily transmigrate into these places of bliss. Through his, and his sole mediation, Men are to obtain absolution from their sins, and a portion of happiness in the future Life.

Leading a virtuous Life, and doing nothing that is contrary to the Commandments of the Law of *Siaka*, is the only way to become agreeable unto *Amida*, and worthy of eternal happiness.

The five Commandments of the Doctrine of *Siaka*, which are the standing rule of the life and behaviour of all his faithful adherents, are call'd *Gokai*, which implies as much, as the *five Cautions*, or *Warnings*. They are,

Se Soo, the Law not to kill any thing that hath Life in it.

Tsu To, the Law not to steal.

Sijain, the Law not to whore.

Mago, the Law not to lie.

Onsiu, the Law not to drink strong Liquors; a Law which *Siaka* most earnestly recommended to his Disciples, to be by them strictly observe'd.[25]

◆ IPPOLITO DESIDERI (1684–1733)

Ippolito Desideri was born in Tuscany and entered the Jesuit order in 1700, studying at the Collegio Romano. Following two years as an instructor in theology, he requested permission to become a missionary. After audiences with Pope Clement XI and Cosimo III dei Medici, he made his way to Genoa, where he sailed for India on November 23, 1712, arriving in Goa five months later. Assigned to the Tibet mission, Father Desideri and another priest, the Portuguese Manoel Freyre, eventually set off on the trip north, making their way to Leh, the capital of Ladakh, the westernmost Tibetan domain. They remained in Leh for fifty-two days. Desideri wished to found the mission there, but his fellow priest, and superior, insisted that they continue eastward to Lhasa. They were able to survive the difficult seven-month journey thanks to the protection of a Mongol princess, who allowed the two priests to join her caravan. They reached Lhasa on March 18, 1716.

After just a month in Lhasa, Desideri's companion decided to return to India, leaving Desideri alone—and the only European, and sole Christian—in Tibet. Tibet was ruled at that time by a Mongol chieftain, Lhazang Khan, and Desideri was granted an audience. Apparently impressed by the Tuscan's resolve to teach Tibetans the route to heaven, and his declaration that he wished to remain in Tibet for the rest of his life, the khan granted Desideri permission to stay, offer-

ing lodging and support. He arranged for Desideri to live at Ramoche, also known as Shidé, in Lhasa, and then at Sera, a monastery of some 5,500 monks on the outskirts of the city, one of "three seats" of the Geluk sect. Desideri's notes from his studies, preserved in the Jesuit archives in Rome, trace his course through a young monk's textbooks on elementary logic through to the masterworks of the tradition.

In 1719, the Capuchins, who had arrived in the fall of 1716, presented him with an official letter from the Propaganda Fide ordering the Jesuits to leave Tibet. After failed appeals to the Pope and his Jesuit superiors, Desideri reluctantly did so, arriving in Kathmandu in Nepal on January 20, 1722.

Desideri returned to Rome on January 23, 1728. The last years of his life were consumed with composing long defenses of his work, as well as the remarkable account of his time in Tibet, the Relazione de' viaggi all' Indie e al Thibet *(Report on Travels to India and Tibet). His works would remain unread and unknown for more than a century.*

In his Relazione, *Desideri describes the religion of Tibet, in Italian, to his fellow Roman Catholics. In this long work, he mentions the Buddha, whom he refers to as Sciacciá-Thubbá (Shakya thub pa, the Tibetan version of Śākyamuni), relatively rarely, identifying him as the "Lawgiver of the Thibettans." Although noting his Indian origins, Desideri seems to regard Sciacciá-Thubbá only as the founder of the religion of the Tibetans; he does not identify him with the Xaca of the Japanese, the Fo of the Chinese, or the Sommonocodom of the Siamese.*

In the passage below, Desideri describes with great accuracy the Buddha's decision to descend from the Tuṣita heaven and begin his last rebirth. However, Desideri sees something suspicious in the language used.

———

Having accepted this fable, they state that their lawgiver, having attained the state of a *Cian-giub-sem-ba* [*byang chub sems dpa'*, or bodhisattva] was totally freed from the necessity of being reborn, but nevertheless subjected himself voluntarily to the suffering of further births in order to lead other living beings to the good, which in their opinion is the ministry proper to a Cian-giub-sem-ba. He was especially moved by the desire to bring about the salvation of the Lhà among whom he was reborn and remained a long while, until he found himself among the Lhà who dwell on that part of Mount Ri rab ccenbo [Mount Meru] called Kaa-ndèn [Dga' ldan or Tuṣita]. Then, remembering our lowly world, he regarded each region most attentively and pondered how it had been reduced to a most deplorable condition of spiritual ruin by the blindness, the passions, and wickedness of human beings, beyond any help or redress. He then generated the highest compassion for them and decided to come to earth himself and be reborn as a human being to deliver humankind from evil and to lead them to eternal salvation. In one of the numberous and very large volumes of the Kâa-n-ghiùr [Bka' 'gyur, the Tibetan canon] called Ngṅombarè-n-giunvee-do, that is, the history of his last advent in the world, the Tibetans' lawgiver describes how he glanced down upon the world and resolved to leave Kaa-n-dèn and the supremely happy state of a Lhà and descend to earth and be reborn in the human condition. He employs a manner of speaking and tone in making his decision and expresses such thoughts as he had on that occasion and subject that make it seem as if it were the Devil himself speaking in the guise of a man, or through the mouth of a man, and that he had undertaken to behave, as we say, like a monkey, by fully imitating everything our ascetics and contemplatives are wont and capable of expressing in order to make us comprehend the decree of the Most Holy Trinity for the salvation of mankind which the Divine Word accepted in coming to earth and becoming a man, in order to be our Savior, at the cost of his degradation, his passion, and his holy death.

After a long series of very tender and moving speeches, the Tibetans' lawgiver adds that once he had made his resolution, he glanced over the world another five times to determine the five special qualities of his advent: his caste or tribe, his country, his time, his family, and the woman from whom he would be born and take a human body. The special gifts and perfections he sought in the woman whom he had to choose as his mother are also like another copy made by the said infernal monkey of what our ascetics and contemplatives are wont to say about the Divine Word's election of the Most Holy Virgin to be elevated to the great dignity of the Mother of God Incarnate. Another copy is his moving speech of how, before coming to be born into the world as a man and embarking on the great task of leading the world to the good and to salvation, he offered to endure insults, pains, hardships, and whatever might serve the goal that he had undertaken.

After specifying the above-mentioned five special qualities and having chosen the tribe of the Brahmans, that is, the priests, the country of Benares in the great empire of Hindustan, the royal family of the Sciaccià, and the particular woman who would become his mother, he describes the fantastic marvels and prodigies attending his conception. He then goes on to describe how during his conception and throughout all the time he was in his mother's womb, and at the time of his birth, he had perfect awareness and intelligence and full freedom and quickness of will, all of which were employed during that whole time in his principal actions and his understanding. To this he adds that while he was in his mother's womb, he was totally free of every stain and uncleanness, which he strives hard to describe using various locutions and diverse similes. Indeed, he adds that his body, despite being shut up in his mother's womb, was not only very clean and bright in itself, but what's more, it radiated its effulgence outward, transmitting its radiance to his mother's womb first of all. Afterward, speaking of his approaching birth, he says of himself that as he had nothing in common with other human beings insofar as he was not conceived like them, it did not suit him to be born as others are, but in an absolutely extraordinary and astonishing way, which he then proceeds to describe in the following manner.

He says that when the time came for him to be born, his mother felt a great desire to go out and amuse herself in the delightful and magnificent garden of her royal palace. As she slowly strolled through the garden in the company of a large entourage of noble maids of honor and court ladies, enjoying the amenities of that place, there suddenly appeared an especial rarity, a tree bursting into bloom with the most extraordinarily beautiful and deliciously fragrant flowers. As soon as his mother saw this wonder, she was carried away by the most acute desire to gather some of these flowers with her own hands. She hurriedly ran to it, and as soon as came beneath the tree, she raised her arm toward the branches and in the act of plucking a flower with her hand, to the great wonder and astonishment of all who were present, and without her feeling the slightest discomfort, an opening appeared between her upraised arm and her hip, and she gave birth in an unprecedented manner to her son Sciaccià-Thubbà, who entered the world surrounded by light and with a lovely and joyful expression. Then the opening immediately closed up, without leaving even the slightest scar. He adds that no sooner was he born than a great multitude of gods descended from the sky, celebrating his birth with great rejoicing, poetry, music, and singing his praises, which he himself relates with figures and allegories entirely appropriate for a world-savior.

He recounts similar marvels and excellences about his boyhood and youth: how when he came to study writing, oratory, arithmetic, astronomy, and astrology, he was found at his first lessons in all of these subjects to be so perfect that he had already surpassed his own teachers. Afterward, speaking about the knightly arts and feats of strength he tells things that ought to astonish his credulous followers and make them raise their eyebrows. He goes on to relate how having reached a certain age, his parents, the king and queen, married him to a most accomplished, great, and beautiful princess. But after living some time among luxuries and amusements, he said that finally, on a certain occasion, like one who wakes from a peaceful sleep and returns to his senses, an overwhelming sentiment of the vanity of all things was kindled in his heart. Having seriously considered that he had not come to the earth to pass his time amid luxuries and amusements but to toil for the conversion of humankind and the salvation of the world, he resolved to abandon his father, mother, wife, kingdom, and everything, and with all his might fulfill all that had been preordained on his coming to earth. Once he imparted the resolution to his wife, her crying and shouts made the matter known. His father and mother could not by any means dissuade him from that upon which he had so firmly resolved. Every other effort having failed, they finally settled upon the expedient of imprisoning him in a fortress with high ramparts, several circuits of walls, moats, and bastions, and well guarded by loyal guards and numerous sentries. However, all their scrupulous care was in vain, every obstacle worthless, and every precaution useless, as he overcame every impediment and left the fortress without anyone's awareness or resistance, not knowing when or from where he had left, and in what direction he was traveling. His father sent out numerous troops through every region to bring him back, but in vain, as it proved impossible to trace him.

After hurrying away in that manner he freed himself from all encumbrances and distractions of his parental home, of the kingdom to which he had been the designated heir, and of the entire world and its diversions. He hid himself away in a remote and desolate solitude, where he devoted himself to the continual practice of contemplation, complete and utter poverty, and an unparalleled abstinence to the point where he did not eat anything for long periods of time. After spending a long time in this austere and withdrawn life, he began preaching, which was so effective that he was able to convert every kind and condition of person and lead them to the good. Great troops of men and women continually flocked to him, leaving their homes and the world, becoming his disciples and dedicating themselves to the religious life. Finally, after converting countless living beings through his preaching, the effectiveness of his example, and the splendor of the miracles that he performed, and having established his law for their benefit and salvation, he left this world and passed into eternal rest in the blessed company of the other Sanghieê kon-cciòa [*sangs rgyas dkon mchog*, or buddhas].

This is what the credulous and deceived Tibetans state and lovingly believe about their lawgiver Sciaccià-Thubbà, whose statues and images represent him as a man sitting cross-legged, in a plain habit appropriate to a monk, with a rosary in his hand, and his ears pierced with very large holes, according to the custom of both ancient and modern penitents among the pagans of Hindustan. Lastly, he is represented with a shaven head, following the usage of the monks and lamas of this country.[1]

François Valentijn was a Dutch clergyman who served in the Dutch East India Company as a pastor and missionary in what is today Indonesia. He was based on the island of Ambon (or Amboina), where he worked from 1685 (when he was nineteen years of age) to 1694 and served again from 1705 to 1713. Upon his return to his native city of Dordrecht, Reverend Valentijn wrote a lengthy history of the Dutch East India Company and the lands visited by its officers. Oud en Nieuw Oost-Indiën (Old and New East Indies), *published between 1724 and 1726 in five volumes and eight folios, contains a total of 4,631 pages and 1,050 illustrations. The fifth volume includes a long section on Ceylon, which was under Dutch control at the time. The following passage is drawn from that section, in an 1827 translation that appeared under the title "The Great Buddhoo" in* Asiatic Journal and Monthly Register for British India and its Dependencies.

Valentijn never visited Ceylon. Like many writers about Asia of the day, he drew heavily from the work of others, including the papers of the Dutch East India Company as well as material he acquired from his compatriots who had served in Ceylon: former Dutch governors Rijckloff van Goens, who served from 1675 to 1679; Cornelis Joan Simons, who served from 1703 to 1706; and Adam van der Duyn, who served between 1699 and 1708, later becoming Commander of Jaffna. Also like writers of that period, Valentijn borrowed information from published sources, often without attribution, including Diogo de Couto and João Ribeiro among the Portuguese and Robert Knox among the English.

In what follows, he gives a particularly violent account of the Buddha's enlightenment and its aftermath, noting at the end that the Buddha destroyed those who refused to believe in his teachings.

THE Singhalese speak much of the Prophet Buddhoo, who appeared in the Island of Ceylon 622 years before Christ, and who introduced the Buddhist religion among them.

The sangetaris, or priests, say that this holy man came from the east, and that his footstep is as yet to be seen on the top of Adam's Hill, or Devinagerie Gallé, where he gave them their laws engraved on tables of stone. It is said that he was twelve feet high, but if we consider the calculation of their time, no dependence can be placed on their story, and they often contradict each other.

Thus, they say that, prior to the coming of Buddhoo into the world, he lived in the fourth heaven, called Toésietlénom Devilokenaye, where he reigned over a million of angels: seeing that the people then on earth were living without laws or religion, and that they would all be lost, he pitied them, resolved to save them, and therefore entered into the maternal womb of the Empress Mahamaye Devi; which event took place on the day of the full moon in July, 622 years before the birth of Christ. He was born in a most miraculous manner at mid-day, on a Tuesday (being the day of the full moon which happened in the month of May following), in the palace of the Emperor Soedoedenoe Rajoero, at Kiemboulat Poerre, the capital of the kingdom of Madde Mandalum. The Emperor was delighted at the birth of this child, and ordered that he should be called Sidditure Coemarea, which means "the prince who can do every thing he wishes." He performed many wonderful things before the age of sixteen: at that age he was married to the Princess Jasoedera, who was born at the same time and hour as Buddhoo was. She was the daughter of the King Andesah Rajoero, and the Queen Amoetanam Bisso, who were equal in rank with the parents of Buddhoo; he lived with his wife Jasoedera for thirteen years, and had a son who was called Rahoele Coemarea. After the birth of this son he left his wife, and retired into the woods, where he lived in great misery for six years. While he was in the woods, a throne of diamonds and other precious stones descended from heaven, in which he entered and returned from the woods, when he immediately became a Buddhoo. In this throne he was protected by the three following gods: Theacre Areme, Wishnu, and Mahaswere, with swords in their hands. The devils, on hearing of the birth and wonders of Buddhoo, feared that he would drive them away from the world and destroy them; and they consulted with their king, Wasse-Mantimande, how to dispute the laws and religion of Buddhoo, which the people were fast following. Thereupon they all appeared with arms, and fell upon Buddhoo in order to destroy him. But his strength and power were far superior; at his command all the grass of the earth, the branches and leaves of the trees turned into swords and other warlike instruments; and with great violence destroyed (or overcame) all the devils. After this victory over them, he entitled himself, for a week, "*Guntuma Buddhoo*," which means, "the conqueror of his enemies." The next week after the conquest there had been much rain, when the devils conspired again to disturb Buddhoo; and as they were approaching him, whilst seated under a large tree, a snake came forward and sheltered him with his head; the devils, on seeing this, were much terrified, and returned back quietly.

The third week after the first conquest, the devils appeared again, in the character of dancing girls, to endeavour by this means to captivate him; but he immediately destroyed them all.

The fourth week he caused great honours to be paid to the tree under which he was seated when the snake appeared and sheltered him.

The fifth week a throne of rubies descended from heaven, in which he entered to receive a message that was brought to him from heaven.

The sixth week he came out of this throne and proceeded towards the tree kir-ryupaloe; whilst seated under it, he perceived a great number of angels: thereupon he immediately began to worship and praise God.

The seventh week he retired to the city called Sewet Noere, where the emperor Coesele Maha Rajoero had prepared a palace for him; the palace was called Jat-tewarrene, to erect and prepare which the emperor spent all his fortune: this palace was built that Buddhoo might live in it, and receive the visits of the emperors, kings, and princes that came to see him, and also to teach them his doctrine. He had five apostles; two of them were always standing at his right side, two on the left, while the fifth served him; besides these five apostles he had 500 writers, through whom he proclaimed his doctrines throughout that part of the world; those that did not receive and believe it he destroyed. He also distributed many good books for the guidance of the people. He was thus employed during forty-five years, till he arrived in the country of Coeserane Noevere, where he lodged in the King's garden; a bed was prepared for him there, and on this bed he expired, in the month, the day, and the hour of his birth. Whilst his writers were lamenting his loss, his spirit appeared and addressed them in the following words: "Be by no means sorry, for the hour is come that I must leave this world; but burn my remains, and deposit my bones in a grave, and preserve by all means my doctrine." And he especially directed that they should preserve it, particularly at Ceylon, Siam, and Arracan, as the generation of the Emperor Soedoedeno Rajoero would reign in those places.[2]

✦ JEAN FRÉDÉRIC BERNARD (1683–1744) AND BERNARD PICART (1673–1733)

As seen in the previous chapter in works like Purchas His Pilgrimage, *the seventeenth century saw the beginnings of compilations of travelers' accounts from around the world. In the eighteenth century, this trend continued and became more specialized, with works devoted to specific topics. In Amsterdam between 1723 and 1743, a nine-volume work was published with the title* Cérémonies et coutumes religieuses de tous les peuples du monde. *It was published in English between 1733 and 1739 as* The Ceremonies and Religious Customs of the Various Nations of the Known

World. *It was the work of the French bookseller Jean Frédéric Bernard and Bernard Picart, the greatest engraver of the day. Although remembered especially for Picart's remarkable engravings, the work was highly influential in its day and remains an invaluable compendium of information about the religions of the world as they were understood during the French Enlightenment.*

Because it described the religious practices of a wide range of nations and regions, it provided an opportunity to compare what would come to be called Buddhism across a wide geographical range. Thus, a number of selections from "Picart," as the work is commonly called, are provided here, describing the Buddha in Laos, Tonkin (modern Vietnam), Sri Lanka, China, and Japan. In these selections, we begin to see the repetition and revision of elements we have encountered from the previous century.

The first section, on Laos, begins with a description of Xaca and the previous buddhas, and goes on to explain that the buddha of the future (unnamed here) will burn the scriptures and destroy the temples of Xaca; according to Buddhist doctrine, Maitreya will appear when all the teachings of Śākyamuni have disappeared. The passage also includes an interesting claim about the relationship of Xaca and Jesus.

ON THE RELIGION OF THE PEOPLE OF LAIES, LANGIENS, OR LAOS

BEFORE this Restoration of the Earth to its primitive State, four Deities condescended to govern and preside over it. Three of them, weary at last of the important Charge, resigned their Guardianship, and went higher towards the North, to taste the uninterrupted Joys of Solitude and Retirement. Now the sole acting God that remained, and who, as they insist, was *Xaca*, was still to live and reign for some thousands of Years. This *Xaca*, being fully determined to attain to the highest Pitch of Perfection imaginable, sunk at last into that happy State of Annihilation: But he took particular Care beforehand to direct, that Mankind should build Temples and Idols in Commemoration of his godhead; promising at the same Time, that he would fill those sacred Edifices, set apart for Divine Worship, with an Emanation of his Virtue, which should amply make amends for the Want of his personal Appearance, and would effectually breathe into the Idols some Degree of his divine Influence. Thus these Statues participated of the divine Nature of *Xaca*, pursuant to his gracious and express Promise, when he sunk down into *Nireupan*, or the ever-blessed State of Annihilation. From hence the Worship of Images, and such other Objects, in which the divine Spirit, as they imagined, delighted to reside, was first instituted and annointed. This Idea is not so extravagant, but that something very much resembling it has imperceptibly crept into divers other Religions.

When the Term of *Xaca's* Reign shall be expired, another god, say the Natives of *Laos*, will arise, who shall demolish these Temples, break down these Idols, burn the sacred Writings which contain the Commandments of *Xaca*, and after he has thus persecuted *Xaca's* Disciples, and prohibited all divine Worship in general, he shall dictate new Laws, and elect new Ministers. They assert, likewise, that there was a perfect Harmony and Agreement established between *Xaca* and the God of the Christians; that the former has made Choice of the East for his particular Residence, and resigned the West to the Direction of the latter, who made a despicable Figure there, and had at first but a very pitiful retinue: In Process of time, however, he performed Wonders, had Attendants without Number, and gained inexhaustible Treasures. In short, they add a thousand Stories more wild and extravagant than all the Riffraff we have already related.

On some particular Days in the Year, the Statue of *Xaca* is with great Solemnity exposed to publick View on some spacious and elevated Place, in order for the Devotees to assemble there, and pay their divine Adoration to it. No one presumes to approach it without some Free-Will Offering in his Hand, which the *Talapoins* always convert to their own private Emolument. The Natives of *Langiens*, says our Author, who seems to be one of our honest Missionaries, that will never be suspected a Haretick, behave very devoutly and are religious beyond Imagination. So far are they from entertaining the least sacrilegious Thought of pillaging this Statue of all its costly Decorations, that they impoverish themselves to testify their Zeal and Veneration for it. What a pity 'tis, that a people so pious, and so well disposed, should be blind, and so confirmed in Ignorance and Error!

Thus have I given you a true Account of what I found most remarkable, with respect to the People of *Laos*, which is in a great measure conformable to the Tenets of the *Siamese*. One may perceive, even from the dark and confused narration of Father *Marini*, that the People of *Laos* have some Idea of the fallen Angels, and of theirs, and the evil *Genii's* familiar Conversation with the Female Sex. The Blacks are the legitimate Offspring of those Demons. *Xaca*, of whom we shall treat more at large hereafter, is in all Probability no other than *Sommona-Codom*.[3]

Picart's section on northern Vietnam (Tunquin) provides what is by now a fairly familiar account. It makes reference to Xaca's two doctrines: a secret doctrine of atheism (although the term is not used here) and a public doctrine of rewards and pun-

ishments in accordance with one's deeds. Also detailed here is the number of years one must pass in the cycle of transmigration before reaching "the happy State of Perfection."

The common People, indeed, for the Generality, are Admirers and Followers of *Xaca*, whom father *Tassanier* calls *Chaca*, and *Tavernier*, *Chacabout*. Our Jesuitical Missionary is of Opinion, that this *Xaca* was a *Jew*, because he seems to be acquainted with the *Jewish* Writings. 'Twould be as difficult, however, to maintain this Assertion, as to demonstrate that *Xaca* was *Pythagoras* himself. He at first attempted to captivate the Affections of the People, by being seemingly very contemplative, and by affecting a modest and humble Deportment. He conceal'd himself for six Years successively in a Wilderness, and in this State of Solitude and Retirement compos'd those most remarkable Doctrines, which afterwards he preach'd to his Disciples. He attempted to persuade them, that there was no such Thing as a Divine Providence; that the Soul was mortal, and that there were no Punishments or Rewards in a Future State. In order to imprint on the Minds of the People a more aweful Regard and Veneration for him, he boldly assured them, that two *Demons* inspired him with all those dangerous Doctrines which he was oblig'd to preach up for the Instruction of Mankind. This dangerous Tenet, however, was reserved only for a select Number of his favourite Disciples. As for the Generality of his Followers, he recommended the Transmigration of souls as an Article of their Belief, and gave them ten Commandments, the same in Effect with those of *Laos* and *Siam*. *Xaca* likewise maintain'd, That it was requisite for all such as aim'd at the highest Pitch of Perfection, to renounce the Pomps and Vanities of the World, to have Pity and Compassion on their Fellow Creatures, and to succour and relieve them under all their Distresse; to employ their precious Hours in Meditation, and endeavour, as much as in the lay, to subdue their inordinate and unruly Passions. And, moreover, that all such as after this Life ended, should have disobey'd his Doctrines, or contemned his Laws, should suffer Punishment in ten distinct Places; after which they should revive, in order only to die and suffer again; that their State and Condition should be one eternal Round of Deaths, Resurrections, Pains, and Torments. On the contrary, that such as had religiously practiced his Maxims, and kept his Commandments, should be rewarded in Proportion to their Perfection, and their Faith. Those that had made the slowest Advances towards Perfection, should be exposed for the Space of 5000 Years to a restless Transmigration; such as had made a greater Progress, for 4000, and those that had happily arrived within one Degree of the Achme, or Pitch of Perfection, for 300 Years; and the last, who should have fulfilled his Commandments with the utmost Strictness, should enjoy everlasting Happiness, and never be liable more to any future Transmigrations. *Xaca* assured his Disciples, that even he was obliged to die, and revive ten Times successively, before he could obtain to that happy State of Perfection. He taught his Disciples two and forty Years, and by his last Will and Testament, engaged one of his greatest Favourites to maintain and confirm the Truth of his Precepts by this short Form, *Thus it is in the Book*; Words of the same Import and Signification with those the *Pythagoreans* made use of to vindicate the Truth of their Doctrine, *Our Master says so*. After the Death of *Xaca*, his Doctrine spread over a great part of *Asia*, particularly the Eastern Part of it.[4]

Picart's brief section on Sri Lanka notes that Buddu may have in fact been St. Thomas, the apostle said to have brought the Gospel to India. It also recounts very briefly the story of the Portuguese seizure and destruction of a tooth relic of the Buddha in 1561. As the story notes, although destroyed by the Portuguese in Goa, the relic miraculously reappeared in Sri Lanka.

THE Inhabitants of *Ceylan*, like the other *Indians*, are all Pagans. The *Chingulese* indeed worship one God, the Creator of the Universe; but they believe there are Deities who are subordinate to him, who act as his Deputies, and are establish'd in such Posts as he thinks most convenient for them. Thus Agriculture is the peculiar Province of one, Navigation of another, *&c*. All these Idols, are represented by fantastic and monstrous Figures. One of them is form'd like a Giant, and by them called *Buddu*, who formerly liv'd a very holy and penitent Life. The *Chingulese* reckon their Years from the Time that he lived amongst them, and by Computation we find, according to *Ribeyro*, that he lived about the fortieth Year of the Christian Æra, and was supposed to be St. *Thomas*. They further add, that this *Buddu*, who was not born in their Country, died on the Continent; which, we are told, agrees with the Opinion that the Christians of St. *Thomas* have of that Apostle's Death. The Tooth of an Ape, which a *Portuguese* Viceroy caused be burnt in the Year 156[1] was formerly ador'd as one of *Buddu's*. In vain did the *Portuguese* attempt by this Means to put a Stop to their idolatrous Worship of that sacred Relick. Superstition, which is never at a loss for new Devices, gave out, that the tooth made its Escape out of the Hands of the Profane, and took Refuge upon a Rose. It is *Buddu's* peculiar Province to watch over, and save Men's Souls. We shall have Occasion in another Place to make Mention of *Buddu*, where we shall endeavour to shew, that 'tis much more reasonable to suppose he was *Fo* and *Xequia*, than St. *Thomas*.[5]

Picart's account of the Buddha in China begins with a by now familiar lament about his role in turning China to idolatry, and then proceeds with an account of his birth. The major part of the description, however, deals with his deathbed confession that everything is nothing. As a result, Buddhism comprises two sects: the idolaters who follow his earlier teachings, and the atheists who follow his final recantation.

A DISSERTATION *ON THE* RELIGION

OF THE CHINESE

BUT the *Jesuits* who have oblig'd us with the History of *China*, assure us, that the most fatal Blow Religion ever felt, was given her by *Fo* and his Disciples. This *Fo* began to flourish and meet with universal Approbation amongst the *Chinese*, about two and thirty Years after the Death of *Jesus Christ*. His Idol, they say, was brought thither from *India*. The Minds of the People were perfectly dispos'd to give it a favourable Reception, and at that Juncture Superstition and Idolatry gain'd Ground apace. Some have asserted, that this *Fo* was a *Ghost* who broke loose from the infernal Regions; but not to dwell on such a chimerical Suggestion, what follows is the best and most rational Account, in our Opinion, that can be given of him. Others, therefore, inform us, that he was born in *India*, about one thousand Years before Christ, and that he was of Royal Extraction; that at first his Name was *Che-kia*, or *Xe-quia*; but when he had attain'd the Age of thirty Years, he chang'd it into *Fo*. As *Laokun* sprang from his Mother's Left Side, so *He* miraculously issued from his Mother's Right, who died in her Labour. Some Time before his Birth, she dreamt that she had swallowed (others say that she was brought to the Bed of) an Elephant, and this awful Dream is the original Cause of that Reverence and Respect which the Kings of *India* pay to their white Elephants. This *Fo* was blest with uncommon Strength, and could stand alone as soon as ever he was born. He took seven Steps, pointing with one Hand to the Heavens, and with the other to the Earth. His Tongue likewise was immediately loosen'd; he spoke at his very Birth, and gave all about him a surprising Characteristick of his Mission. *I am*, said he, *the only Being to whom Honour is due, upon Earth, or in the Heavens.* When he was seventeen Years of Age, he married, and had a Son, whom he soon after abandon'd, as he did all the rest of Mankind. He withdrew into a solitary Desart, with three or four favourite Philosophers, whom he made choice of for the Direction of his future Conduct. At thirty two he began to be inspir'd; he was then posses'd with, and full of the Deity, and at once became omniscient. From that Moment he was constituted a god, and establish'd the Veneration and Respect which the People had for him by innumerable *Miracles*, or rather, (not to profane that sacred Term, the true and genuine Signification whereof a great Part of those who profess themselves Christians are perfect Strangers too,) by Impostures and Delusions. In a very short Time he had a prodigious Train of Admirers and Disciples, who, in Imitation of their new God, chang'd their Names according to the various Countries where they propagated their Doctrine. But this Deity himself at last was convinced, that he was but a Man, like those who ador'd him; for he died in the seventy ninth Year of his Age; and when he found himself at the Point of Expiration, that the Measure of his Iniquities might be full, he endeavour'd to inspire and poison his Followers with his atheistical Principles. He told them ingenuously, *That till that Time he had talk'd to them in obscure and unintelligible Terms; but don't deceive yourselves,* said he, *and vainly imagine to find out of* Nothing *the first Principle of all Things; for from* Nothing *all Things deriv'd their Beings, and to* Nothing *will they all return. This is the dark Abyss of all our Hopes.* This Doctrine, perhaps, notwithstanding the Horror and Detestation which it naturally creates at first View, might appear less shocking and insupportable, if we would reconcile it with the Principles of the *Siamese,* by substituting the Idea of their *Nireupan* in Lieu of that abominable *Nothing.* But be that as it will, by this Recantation, he divided his Disciples into two Sects, one of which follow'd literally the Doctrines which *Fo* taught in his Life-Time; that is to say, Idolatry; the other embrac'd the dying Words of their great Master, as fundamental Articles of their Faith, and openly declare themselves profest Atheists. This Sect, if we may credit Father *Gobien,* is strenuously oppos'd by that of the *Philosophers,* whose Doctrine favours another kind of Libertinism. Some have attempted to reconcile these direct Contradictions of *Fo,* by the Supposition that he laid down a double Law; that is, in their Terms, an *external* and an *internal* Law. The former is preparatory to, and directs us to the latter, and is afterwards of no Manner of Importance; no more than the Props which support an Arch-Roof, when the Work is completed. But after all, it must be acknowledg'd, that amidst these various Opinions, and those which we shall treat of in the Sequel of this Discourse, some are very dark and obscure, and others seem very loose and licentious, either on Account of their having been injudiciously related, or from the dangerous Consequences that may actually be drawn from them. Father *Kircher* has given us a farther Account of this *Fo,* which shall be inserted hereafter in its proper Place.[6]

Picart's description of the Buddha in Japan, after some familiar remarks on his origins, pays particular attention to the meditation posture in which the Buddha con-

templated "the most hidden Mysteries of Religion." Picart notes, "The Reader might reasonably expect to have seen him in a more painful Attitude."

THE Sect or Religion of *Budsito* came from *India* to Japan. We have already mentioned the Progress which this new Religion made, and the Schism thereby created amongst the *Sinto's*, of whom one Party rigidly adher'd to *Sintoism*; the other, by some commodious Concessions, found out a Method to reconcile the Opinions of the *Budsdoists* and those of the *Sintoists* together. We are informed, that the literal Sense and Signification of the Term *Budso*, is, the *Way of foreign Idols*, that is to say, the Manner in which they are to be worshipped. The Founder of this Sect, in all Probability, is the same with *Budhu, Siaka,* or *Xaquia, Sommona-Codom,* &c. The *Japanese* assert, That he was a Native of that Country, where he is worshipped under the Denomination of *Budhu* and *Sommona-Codom*, and are of Opinion, he was born in the Reign of one of the Emperors of *China*, who lived about a thousand Years before the Nativity of *Jesus Christ*. Without perplexing ourselves here about the true and genuine Name of this Founder of *Budsdoism*, and without making any Enquiry whether he be the same with those just before-mentioned, or any other, we shall always, for the future, in Conformity to *Kaempfer*, call him *Siaka*. The Reader, we are sensible, may justly charge us with some Tautologies, but they are absolutely necessary, to give him an adequate Idea of this Sect of *Japan*.

SIAKA was the Son of one of the King's of *Ceylan*. When he was but nineteen Years of Age, he not only abandoned all the Pomps and Vanities of the World, but his Wife too and only Son, to become the Disciple of a celebrated Anchoret. Under this great Master he made a very considerable Progress in the State of Contemplation; and the more effectually to wean his Thoughts from all external Objects, he habituated himself to sit in such a Posture, as, according to the Disciples of *Siaka*, engages the Mind so intensively, that a Man thereby descends, as it were, into himself, and is wholly wrapped up in his own Ideas. We are obliged to make use of these formal Terms, to give you the Energy and full Force of their enthusiastic Expressions. *Siaka's* Posture abovementioned, was this. He sat with his Legs a-cross directly under him, and his Hands laid one over another, in such a Manner as that the Tip of his Thumbs met close together. The Reader might reasonably expect to have seen him in a more painful Attitude; 'twas in this Situation, however, that the Divine Truths were revealed to this Enthusiast; that he penetrated into the most hidden Mysteries of Religion, and discovered the Existence both of Heaven and of Hell; that he entertained an adequate Idea of the State of Souls after their

Separation from the Bodies which they animated, and all their various Transmi-
grations; that he was fully appris'd of their Rewards and Punishments in another
Life; together with the Omnipotence of the gods, and their Divine Providence, &c.
On this Revelation he grounded his System, and in Process of Time confirmed his
Disciples in the stedfast Belief of it.[7]

◆ JEAN BAPTISTE DU HALDE (1674–1743)

*When Ignatius Loyola formed the Society of Jesus, he required that his missionar-
ies send back detailed reports and letters describing their activities and the peoples
and places they encountered. These reports (called* relation *in French and* relazione
in Italian; hence Desideri's Relazione *above) became crucial sources of information
about the world beyond Europe. In France, these reports and letters were gathered together and published in thirty-four volumes between 1702 and 1776 as* Lettres édifi-
antes et curieuses *(Edifying and Curious Letters). They were widely read and highly
influential during the Enlightenment. The editor of the series between 1709 and 1743
(producing volumes 9 through 26) was the Jesuit priest Jean Baptiste du Halde. From
these (and previous studies of China), he composed the four-volume* Description
géographique, historique, chronologique, politique et physique de l'empire de la
Chine et de la Tartarie chinoise *(Geographical, Historical, Chronological, Political
and Physical Description of the Empire of China and Chinese Tartary) in 1743. Although Father du Halde never traveled to China, and is said to have never left Paris,
his book was highly influential, being read and praised by Voltaire and other luminaries of the age.*

*In the following unflattering portrait of the Buddha, we see a variety of elements
encountered in earlier sources.*

———

OF THE SECT OF FO, OR FOË

For the space of 270 Years the Emperors of the Dynasty of *Han* possessed the Im-
perial Throne, and about sixty-five years from the Birth of Christ the Emperor
Ming ti introduced a new Sect into *China* still more dangerous than the former
[Daoism], and has made a much more rapid Progress.

This Prince happened to dream one Night, and among other things there
occurred to his Mind a Sentence which *Confucius* often repeated, *viz., That the
Most Holy was to be found in the West*; upon this he sent Ambassadors into the
Indies to discover who this Saint was, and to seek for the true Law which he there

taught; the Ambassadors supposed they had found him among the Worshippers of the Idol *Fo* or *Foë*, and they transported this Idol into China, and with it the Fables wherewith the *Indian* Books were filled.

This Contagion, which began in the Court, soon got ground in the Provinces, and has spread thro' all the Empire, wherein Magick and Impiety had already made too great havock.

It is hard to say in what part of the *Indies* this Idol was, and if the extraordinary things that its Disciples relate of it are not so many Fables purposely invented, one would be apt to believe, with St. *Francis Xavier*, that he was rather a Demon than an ordinary Man.

They relate that he was born in that part of *Indies* which the Chinese call *Chung tien cho*, that his Father was the King of this Country, and that his Mother was called *Mo ye*, and died soon after he has born; when she conceived she almost constantly dreamed that she had swallowed an Elephant, and hence arise the Honours that the Kings of the *Indies* pay to white Elephants, and often make War to gain possession of this Animal.

Hardly, *say they*, was this Monster separated from his Mother, but he stood upright and walked seven Paces, pointing with one Hand to the Heaven, and the other to the Earth; nay he likewise spoke and pronounced distinctly these following Words, *There is none but myself in the Heaven or on the Earth that ought to be adored.*

At the Age of Seventeen he married three Wives, and had a Son called by the *Chinese Mo heou lo*; at the Age of Nineteen he forsook his Wives, and all earthly Cares, to retire into a solitary Place, and put himself under the guidance of four Philosophers called by the *Indians, Joghi*; at Thirty he was wholly inspired by the Divinity, and became *Fo* or Pagod, as the *Indians* call him, looking upon himself as a God; he then applied himself wholly to propagate his Doctrines, the Devil always helping him out at a dead Lift, for by his Assistance he did the most wonderful things, and by the novelty of his Miracles filled the People with Dread, and procured himself great Veneration; the *Chinese* have described these Prodigies in several large Volumes, and represented them in several Cuts.

It is scarcely credible how many Disciples this chimerical God gained, for they reckon eighty thousand who were busy in infecting all the East with his impious Tenets; the Chinese call them *Ho chang*; the *Tartars, Lamas*; the *Siamese, Talapoins*; the *Japanese*, or rather the *Europeans, Bonzes*: Among this great number of Disciples there were ten of greater Distinction as to Rank and Dignity, who published five thousand Volumes in honour of their Master.

However, this new God found himself mortal as well as the rest of Mankind, for at the Age of seventy-nine the Weakness of his Body gave him notice of his approaching End, and then to crown all his Impieties he broached the Venom of Atheism.

He declared to his Disciples that till that Moment he had made use of nothing but Parables, that his Discourses were so many Enigmas, and that for more than forty Years he had concealed the Truth under figurative and metaphorical Expressions, but being about to leave them he would communicate his true Sentiments, and reveal the Mystery of his Doctrine: *Learn then*, said he to them, *that the Principle of all things is Emptiness and Nothing; from Nothing all things proceeded, and into Nothing all will return, and this is the end of all our Hopes*; but his Disciples adhered only to his first Words, and their Doctrine is directly opposite to Atheism.

However the last Words of this Impostor laid the Foundation of that celebrated Distinction, which is made in his Doctrine into Exterior and Interior, of which I shall speak hereafter: His Disciples did not fail to disperse a great Number of Fables about his Death, and easily persuaded a simple and credulous People that their Master had been born eight thousand times, that his Soul had successively passed thro' different Animals, and that he had appeared in the Figure of an Ape, a Dragon, and Elephant, &c.

This was plainly done with a design to establish the Worship of this pretended God under the shape of various Animals, and in reality these different Creatures, through which the Soul of *Fo* was said to have passed, were worshipped in several Places; the *Chinese* themselves built several Temples to all sorts of Idols, and they multiplied exceedingly throughout the Empire.

Among the great Number of Disciples that this chimerical Deity made, there was one more dear to him than all the rest, to whom he trusted his greatest Secrets, and charged him particularly to propagate his Doctrine; he was called *Moo kia ye* [Mahākāśyapa]; he commanded him not to amuse himself with bringing Proofs and tedious Arguments to support his Doctrine, but to put, in a plain manner, at the Head of his Works which he should publish these Words, *It is thus that I have learned*.[8]

♦ ADRIANO DI ST. THECLA (1667–1765)

The Italian missionary to Vietnam, a monk of the Discalced (or Barefoot) Augustinian Order, Adriano di St. Thecla arrived in what is today northern Vietnam on April 29, 1738. He quickly gained the ability to read Hán, that is, classical Chinese, with Vietnamese pronunciation as well as to speak vernacular Vietnamese. In his Latin work Opusculum de Sectis apud Sinenses et Tunkinenses (A Small Treatise on the Sects among the Chinese and Tonkinese), he provided a more elaborate account of how Buddhism entered China: the story of the dream of the emperor Ming, retold by Matteo Ricci. At the conclusion of the passage below, referring to Ricci's claim that the Golden Man was really Jesus, Father Adriano notes that "this fact became known from the Christian books," then goes on to provide the traditional Chinese account, concluding, "From this it has been discovered that the aforementioned emperor sent [ambassadors] to India with the intention to bring to China the book and the image of Thích Ca [Śākya] called Phật [Buddha], but [the emperor] did not send them to the remotest West or Europe or even to Palestine to bring from there the image as well as the doctrine of the saintly people who lived there."

––––––

During the rule of the Han dynasty, the Phật sect was brought to China from India by order of the Emperor Minh Đê (Mingdi) in the eighth year of his reign, approximately in the seventieth year after Christ was born. These events are narrated in the Christian books, and first of all in the book *Văn Lâm Quảng (Wen Lin Guang)*, in the following way: they say that Han Minh Đê (Han Mingdi) saw in a dream a man with a golden body sixteen cubits tall. Being asked by the emperor who he was, he responded that he was a man from the western region. When this dream was presented to the royal dream interpreters to get them to provide its interpretation, they said that holy men had always been in the West, and they congratulated the emperor for catching sight of a holy man; they also interpreted that dream [to predict] that the emperor would be prospering for a long time. Because of this the emperor himself wanted to go to the West to inquire there and bring back the image and the law of that holy man. Since the dream interpreters were against the trip of the emperor because in his absence the state might be thrown into turmoil, he sent two ambassadors, named Thái Am (Cai An) and Tân Cảnh (Qin Jing), to look [for the image and the book] and bring them to him. When they came to India, or Thiên Trúc, they still had not covered half of the way to the remote West, but, terrified by the incommodities and difficulties of [going] the rest of the way, they took an image of an idol and the books that were kept there [in India] and brought them to the emperor, pretending that they brought the image and the books of the holy man of the West. Deceived by their words, the emperor trustingly accepted the cult of Phật and ordered his subjects to construct everywhere temples for this idol, and forbade under penalty of death that anyone should kill an animal in the future, according to the doctrine of this sect. This fact became known from the Christian books.[9]

✦ ANTONIO AGOSTINO GIORGI (1711–1797)

The two-buddha theory, encountered in chapter 3 in the passage from Engelbert Kaempfer, next appears in 1762, and in Latin, in a work entitled Alphabetum Tibetanum (Alphabet of Tibet). *A summary of the records of the Capuchin mission to Lhasa (1708–45) by the Augustinian friar Antonio Agostino Giorgi, it is a huge and vexing text, filled with some accurate information and much fantastical theorizing, with words in Greek, Hebrew, Arabic, Devanagari, and Tibetan script appearing on many of the work's more than nine hundred pages. Father Giorgi's tome remained an influential source on Tibet into the nineteenth century; it was cited favorably by Kant himself.*

For Giorgi, as for Kaempfer, there were two buddhas, separated by long periods of time; the first was of Egyptian origin and associated with the Egyptian god Osiris. But whereas for Kaempfer the second buddha came to India some five centuries before the birth of Christ, for Giorgi he arrived there after Christ's resurrection. Indeed, this figure, whom Giorgi calls Butta, impersonated Christ. The friar goes on to explain, quite mistakenly, that the Tibetans were so taken with this Butta that they named their country for him; the Tibetan word for "Tibet" is Bod.

———

We have exposed him as twins, namely as *Butta* and *Xaca*: a first one, whose arrival was nearly a thousand years before Christ and a second one, who has become known to the Tibetans only after [Christ's] ascension. We have seen both as similar, with the same name homonymous and fabulous. However, the first one was fabricated by heathen myths, the second one was invented by Gnostic, Basilidian, Manichean, and sacrilegious legends of the Pseudo-Christians. This new *Butta*, who was excogitated by the Gnostics at the end of the first century of the Christian calendar, became known to the Scyths, Indians, Chinese, and Tibetans. We have said that he [claimed to be] God's son Jesus Christ himself, born of a virgin mother, conceived by the Holy Spirit, filled with the Holy Spirit. . . . However, the ancients and the pagans have with utmost irreverence dressed him in filthy and horrible rags of the virgin born *Butta*. We have also demonstrated, how *Mani's* tricks were so advanced that he strived to be regarded by the Tibetans as the *Butta* himself and as heavenly spirit.[10]

*Perhaps the most celebrated work of scholarship of the French Enlightenment was
Denis Diderot and Jean le Rond d'Alembert's* Encyclopédie, ou Dictionnaire raisonné des sciences, des arts et des métiers *(Encyclopedia, or Systematic Dictionary of the Sciences, Arts, and Crafts), published in seventeen volumes of text and
eleven volumes of plates between 1751 and 1772. We read in volume 15 of the* Encyclopédie *(published in 1765) this entry on Siaka (that is, Śākyamuni, the "sage of the
Shakya clan," one of the epithets of the Buddha).*

———

SIAKA, religion of, (Hist. mod. Superstition) this religion, which is established
in Japan, has as its founder *Siaka* or *Xaca*, who is also called *Budso*, & his religion *Budsodoism*. It is believed that the *buds* or the *siaka* of the Japanese is the
same as the *foë* of the Chinese, & the *visnou*, the *buda* or *putza* of the Indians, the
sommonacodum of the Siamese; for it seems certain that this religion came originally from the Indies to Japan, where previously only the religion of the *sintos* was
professed. The Budsodoists say that *Siaka* was born around twelve hundred years
before the Christian era; that his father was a king; that his son left his father's palace, abandoned his wife and son, in order to embrace a penitent and solitary life,
and in order to devote himself to the contemplation of celestial things. The fruit
of these meditations was to penetrate the depths of the most sublime mysteries,
those of the nature of heaven and hell; the state of souls after death; their transmigration; the path to eternal felicity, and many other things well beyond ordinary
men. *Siaka* had a great number of disciples; feeling that he was near the end, he
declared to them that throughout his life, he had wrapped the truth in a veil of
metaphors and that it was finally time to reveal an important mystery to them.
There is, he said, *nothing real in the world, but nothingness and the void: this is the
first principle of all things; do not seek anything beyond, and do not place your confidence in anything else.* After this impious plea, Siaka died at the age of seventy-
nine years; his disciples accordingly divided his law into two parts; one exterior,
which is taught to the people; the other interior, which is only communicated to a
small number of proselytes. This latter consisted in establishing the void and nothingness, as the principle and end of all things. They claim that the elements, men,
and generally all creatures are formed of this void, and reenter it after a certain
time through a dissolution of parts; such that there is only a single substance in

the universe, which diversifies itself into particular beings, and for a time receives different modifications, although at bottom it is always the same: almost like water is always essentially water, though it takes the form of snow, rain, hail, or ice.

As for the exterior religion of *budsdoism*, the principal points of its doctrine are, (1) that the souls of men and of animals are immortal; that they are originally of the same substance, and that they differ only according to the different bodies they animate. (2) That the souls of men that have separated from the body are rewarded or punished in another life. (3) That the abode of the blessed is called *gokurakf* [*gokuraku*; the heaven of Sukhāvatī]; men enjoy a happiness there proportionate to their merit. Amida is the chief of the celestial domains; it is only through his meditation that one can obtain remission of one's sins, and a place in heaven, this is what makes Amida the object of worship by the followers of *Siaka*. (4) This religion accepts that there is a place called *dsigokf* [*jigoku*; hell]; where the wicked are tormented according to the number and quality of their crimes. Jemma [Enma; Yama, the king of hell] is the sovereign judge of these places; he has a great mirror before him, in which he sees all the crimes of the damned. Their torments only last a certain time, at the end of which the unfortunate souls are returned to the world to animate the bodies of impure animals, whose vices accord with that which soils their souls; from these bodies, they pass successively into those of more noble animals, until they are able to reenter a human body, where they can gain or lose anew. (5) The law of *Siaka* forbids killing any living creature, stealing, committing adultery, lying, and using strong drink. This law prescribes, in addition to that, very bothersome duties, and the continual mortification of the body and spirit. The bonzes or monks of this religion punish the least faults of those under their direction with the utmost severity and in the cruelest manner; these monks are of two kinds, ones called *genguis* and others called *goguis*. They lead an extraordinarily penitent life, and their countenance is something hideous. The people believe them to be saints, and dare not resist their orders, however barbarous they might be, even though their performance must lead to death. These monks make the pilgrims who visit the temple of *Siaka* pass through the cruelest trials, in order to force them to confess their crimes before allowing them to pay homage to this god.

This religion has its martyrs, who give their lives voluntarily in the hope of rendering themselves pleasing to their gods. One sees, along the coasts of the sea, boats filled with fanatics, who after attaching a stone around their neck, throw themselves into the depths of the sea. Others enclose themselves in caves that are walled up, and remain there to die of hunger. Others jump into the abyss of volcanoes. Some crush themselves under the wheels of chariots on which Amida and other gods of their religion are carried in procession; these scenes recur every day, and the so-called martyrs themselves become objects of veneration and worship by the people.

There are several solemn festivals that the followers of the religion of *Siaka* celebrate. The main one is that which is called the *festival of the man*. The statue of the god *Siaka* is carried in procession on a litter. That of his mistress then appears. This latter meets as if by chance the statue of his legitimate wife: then those who carry it begin to run to one side and other, and seek to express by their actions the chagrin that the encounter with a preferred rival caused this unfortunate spouse; this chagrin is communicated to the people, who usually begin to burst into tears. The litters are approached confusedly as if to take sides with the god, his wife, and his mistress, and after some time, each retires peaceably to his own home, after having taken the deities to their temples. These idolaters have another singular festival, which seems made to decide, arms in hand, the precedence that the deities deserve. Horsemen armed from head to foot, inflamed by drunkenness, carry on their back the gods of whom they are the champion; they engage in combat that is nothing less than a game, and the field of battle ends in being covered with the dead; this festival serves as a pretext for those who have personal injuries to avenge, and often the cause of the gods provides the place for the animosity of men.

The religion of *Siaka* has a sovereign pontiff, called *siako*, bishops who are called *tundes* [*tôdô*] and monks or bonzes called *xenxus* [*zenshū*; Zen sect] and *xodoxins* [*jodoshin*; Jōdoshinshū]. See *these different articles*.[11]

✦ VOLTAIRE (1694–1778)

Voltaire (the pen name of Françoise-Marie Arouet) was a towering figure of the French Enlightenment, a renowned man of letters and a prolific author of influential works in a wide range of genres, including poetry, drama, and novels, as well as works of history, philosophy, and science. His satiric wit and scathing criticism of many of the French institutions of the day, including the Roman Catholic Church, resulted in various periods of imprisonment and exile; some of his works were banned, others were burned. Yet he became a legendary figure during his lifetime, counting some of the leading thinkers in Europe as his friends and supporters.

Inspired by the success of the Encyclopédie *of Diderot and d'Alembert, in 1764 he published his own* Dictionnaire philosophique. *It was hailed by some (including*

Frederick the Great of Germany and Catherine the Great of Russia) and condemned by others. Both the acclaim and the condemnation derived, at least in part, from his criticism of the Roman Catholic Church. His dictionary also contained negative portrayals of Judaism and Islam.

Voltaire also criticized Buddhism (although he did not use the term), but he praised the Buddha, or, as he called him, *Sammonocodom*, adopting the Thai term. Voltaire read widely, and knew the accounts of the delegations that Louis XIV had sent to Siam, including those of Guy Tachard and the Abbé de Choisy (both are discussed in chapter 3). Drawing from these, he wrote his own entry on Sammonocodom for his dictionary. He uses it as an occasion not so much to discuss the Buddha and his teachings but to decry a tendency that he observes in all religions, past and present: the compulsion of later generations to deify the founder, who was in fact not a god but simply a teacher of morality and ethical precepts. We will see echoes of Voltaire, expressed with rather less wit and irony, in Burnouf (see chapter 5).

——

SAMMONOCODOM OR SOMMONA-CODOM

I recall that *Sammonocodom*, the god of the Siamese, was born from a young virgin and was raised on a flower. In the same way, *Gengis* [Khan]'s grandmother was impregnated by a ray of sunlight. In the same way, the Emperor of China, *Kienlong* [Qianlong], at present reigning so gloriously, asserts outright in his beautiful poem on *Moukden* that his great-grandmother was a very beautiful virgin, who became mother to a race of heroes by eating cherries. In the same way, *Danaë* was the mother of *Perseus* and *Rhea-Silvia* was mother of *Romulus*. In the same way, the Harlequin, looking upon all that happens in the world, said with good reason, *Tutto il mondo è fatto come la nostra famiglia* [The whole world is like our family].

The religion of the Siamese proves to us that never did a lawmaker teach bad morals. See, O reader, how the teaching of *Brama*, of *Zoroaster*, of *Numa*, of *Thaut* [Thoth], of *Pythagoras*, of *Mahomet*, and even of the fish *Oannès*, is absolutely the same. I have often said that one would throw stones at a man who would teach lax morals, and this is why the Jesuits themselves were such austere preachers.

The rules that *Sammonocodom* gave to his disciples the Talapoins [monks] are as severe as those of *St. Basil* and *St. Benedict*.

Avoid songs, dances, assemblies, everything that might soften the soul.
Do not have gold or silver.

Speak only of justice and work only for justice.

Sleep little, eat little, keep only one robe.

Never mock.

Meditate in private, and reflect often on the fragility of human affairs.

By what fate, by what fury, did it happen that in all countries, the excellence of such a holy and necessary morality has always been disgraced by extravagant tales, by prodigies more laughable than all of the fables of Metamorphoses? Why is there not a single religion whose precepts do not come from a sage and whose dogmas are not of a madman? (You understand that I make an exception of our religion, which is infinitely wise in every sense).

Is it not that the lawmakers were content to give reasonable and useful precepts, while the disciples of the first disciples and the commentators wanted to go one better? They said, "We will not be sufficiently respected if our founder was not in some way supernatural and divine. It is absolutely necessary that our *Numa* had a rendezvous with the nymph *Egérie*, that one of *Pythagoras*' thighs was made of pure gold, that *Sammonocodom*'s mother was a virgin when she gave birth to him, that he was born on a rose and that he became god."

The first Chaldeans passed down to us nothing but very honest moral precepts, but that does not suffice: it is even more wonderful that these precepts were proclaimed by a pike that emerged twice a day from the bottom of the Euphrates to deliver a sermon.

Have these unhappy disciples, these odious commentators not seen that they will alarm the human race? All reasonable people say, "Here, these are very good precepts." I myself would have said the same, but those are impertinent doctrines, absurd and repugnant—quite able to discredit the best precepts. What comes from this? These reasonable people have passions just like the Talapoins, and the stronger these passions become, the bolder they come to say out loud: "My Talapoins have deceived me about the doctrine, they may as well have deceived me about the maxims that contradict my passions." So they shake the yoke, since it had been put on badly; they no longer believe in GOD, because they see well that *Sammonocodom* is not god. I have already warned my dear readers about this several places, when I was in Siam, and I beseeched them to believe in GOD despite the Talapoins. The Reverend Father *Tachard*, who so amused himself on the ship with the young midshipman *Destouches* who later composed the opera *Issé*, knew well that what I say is very true.

About a younger brother of the god Sammonocodom

See whether I have been mistaken in urging you frequently to define your terms in order to avoid ambiguity. A foreign term that you translate very badly with the word God plunges you a thousand times into extremely clumsy errors. The supreme essence, the supreme intelligence, the soul of nature, the great being, the eternal surveyor who has put everything in order, weight, and measure: this is GOD. But when one gives the same name to *Mercury*, to Roman emperors, to *Priapus*, to the divinity of the breasts, to the divinity of the buttocks, to the god fart, to the god of the commode, one no longer understands, one no longer knows where one is. A Jewish judge, a sort of bailiff, is called god in our holy Scriptures. An angel is called god. One gives the name gods to the idols of the small nations neighboring the Jewish horde.

Sammonocodom was not god properly speaking, and a proof that he is not god is that he became god, and that he had a brother named *Thevatat* who was hanged and who was damned.

After all, it is not unusual that in a family there is a clever man who makes a fortune, and another unwise one who is a hardened criminal. *Sammonocodom* became a saint, he was canonized in the Siamese manner, and his brother, who was a badly behaved rascal and was placed on the cross, went to hell where he remains today.

Our travellers have reported that when we wanted to preach about a crucified God to the Siamese, they mocked us. They told us that the cross could well be the instrument of torture of God's brother, but not of a God himself. This reason seems plausible enough, but it is not convincing as good logic. Because, since the true God gave *Pilate* the power to crucify him, he could, with even stronger reason, have given him the power to crucify his brother. In fact, JESUS-CHRIST had a brother, *St. Jacques* [St. James], who was stoned. He was no less God. The bad deeds imputed to *Thevatat*, brother of the god *Sammonocodom*, are again a weak argument against the Abbé de *Choisi* and Father *Tachard*, for it could have just as easily happened that *Thevatat* might have been unjustly hanged, and that he might have deserved heaven rather than damnation. All of this is extremely delicate.

As for the rest, one wonders how Father *Tachard* could have learned Siamese so well in such a short time that he could debate with the Talapoins?

One replies that *Tachard* knew the Siamese language in the same way that *François-Xavier* knew the language of India.[12]

✦ PETER SIMON PALLAS (1741–1811)

Peter Simon Pallas was a German naturalist who in 1767 was invited by Catherine the Great to join the faculty of the Academy of Sciences in St. Petersburg. He would become a favorite of the tsarina, later serving as tutor to her grandsons Alexander (who would become Tsar Alexander I) and Constantine. Between 1768 and 1774, Pallas led a scientific expedition through many Russian provinces, collecting specimens of flora, fauna, and minerals. Like other naturalists of the day, his detailed reports, from which an excerpt appears below, also included descriptions of the cultures he encountered. In the region between the Black Sea and the Caspian Sea he came upon the Kalmyks, ethnic Mongols who had settled in the Lower Volga region in the early seventeenth century. They were adherents of Tibetan Buddhism. Unlike many other Europeans who saw images of buddhas and bodhisattvas, Pallas identifies the male figures as female.

————

During the past golden-age, several of the thousand Burchans or idols of that happy period, appeared on earth, in order to reform mankind. For example, at that time, when the life of man had decreased to 40,000 years, appeared in the empire of Enednai (which, perhaps is that of the Mogul), *Ebdefchi-Burchan*, (the destroyer), and preached religion. At the decline of the human life to 30,000, he was followed by *Altan-Dschidakti-Burchan*, (the golden unalloyed). When life fell to 20,000 years, came *Gerel-Sakiktschi-Burchan*, (the preserver of the world),* and after him, *Mafsuschiri-Burchan*, upon this world; and finally, when the limits of man's age dropped to one hundred years, the great Burchan, and founder of the doctrine of Lama, *Dschakshimuni* came down and preached to the sixty-one nations of the earth. But it is to be lamented, say they, that each listened to the doctrine with different ears, it having produced as many religions and languages as there are nations. . . .

I have mentioned the time when the Burchans or gods of the Kalmucks were raised from mortality. They are so numerous, and they relate so much of each, as to fill whole folios; but their tales are so confused and the Kalmuck Clergy so ignorant, that it is difficult to make out the context, without translating and comparing many of their writings. So far it is certain, that these Burchans have originated

---

* *One might suppose, that under this and the preceding name, lies some obscure and deformed tradition of the Saviour.*

FROM 1701 TO 1800

from holy men, or men pretending to holiness, who have asserted that they passed through many bodies before they were regenerated, or from fabulous persons or deformed idols of some other more ancient religion. I could not absolutely find out whether, besides these Burchans, they admit of some higher supreme being, or, whether they account for the first operative principles in the manner of *Epicurus*; but from what has been related, I should rather suppose the latter to be the case. Good and bad events are governed by the Burchans, and good or malignant aerial spirits. There seems to be degrees of rank among their Burchans, at least they differ much from one another in power and occupation. I think they look upon Burchan *Abida*, as the most exalted of the whole, though the supposed founder of the superstitions of Lama, *Dshakshimuni* is more popularly worshiped and known. It's [*sic*] image is almost always seen among the Kalmuck idols.

It is remarkable that almost all their idols, except the *Dalai-Lama* and some other priestly-looking images, are represented as women, with the flaps of their ears long and pierced, having Indian ornaments, and their feet turned underneath themselves, or else in a sitting posture; yet I saw some standing images with many arms and faces.[13]

◆ GUILLAUME LE GENTIL (1725–1792)

Evidence of the absence of Buddhism in India is found in the account of the remarkable French astronomer Guillaume le Gentil, who in 1761 participated in an international scientific project to measure the distance from the earth to the sun. For this endeavor, over one hundred observers were dispatched to follow the path of Venus across the sun from various points on the globe. Le Gentil was assigned to the French colony of Pondicherry on the east coast of India. But by the time he arrived, the British had captured the colony. Moreover, on June 6, 1761, the date that the observations had to be made, he was at sea, and the rolling of the ship made accurate observations impossible. Undeterred, le Gentil decided to remain in Asia until Venus could again be viewed, eight years hence. By this time, Pondicherry was back in French hands. Le Gentil built an observatory and waited for the appointed day, June 3, 1769. The day was cloudy. Almost driven to madness, he eventually returned to Paris, where he found himself declared dead and his wife remarried.

In 1780, le Gentil published an account of his travels in two volumes, entitled Voyage dans les mers de l'Inde, fait par ordre du roi, à l'occasion du passage de Vénus sur le disque du soleil le 6 Juin 1761, et le 3 du même mois 1769 *(Voyage in the Seas of India, Made by Order of the King, on the Occasion of the Passage of Venus*

Across the Disk of the Sun on June 6 1761 and on the 3rd of the Same Month 1769). *In the passage below, he describes something he saw near Pondicherry.*

———

There was then in those parts of India, and principally on the Coromandel Coast and in Ceylon, a form of worship about whose dogmas we are absolutely ignorant. The god Baouth, of whom nothing more than the name is known today in India, was the object of this worship; but it has been completely abolished; although some families of Indians might still be found, separated from and scorned by the other castes, who remain faithful to Baouth, and who do not recognize the religion of the Brames [Brahmins].

I have not heard that there are these families in the vicinity of Pondichéry; yet there is something most noteworthy, which none of the travelers who discuss the Coromandel Coast and Pondichéry have noticed, found a short league south of the town, on the plane of Virapatnam, and rather near the river, a granite statue very hard and very beautiful: this statue, around three feet to three and a half feet in height, is sunk in the sand up to the waist, and doubtless weighs many thousand; it is as if it was abandoned in the middle of this vast plain. I cannot give a better idea of it than to say that it exactly conforms to and resembles the Siamese *Sommonacodum*; its head is the same shape, it has the same facial features, its arms are in the same attitude, and the ears are absolutely similar. The form of this divinity, which has certainly been made in this country, and which does not resemble in any way the present-day divinities of the Gentiles [Hindus], struck me when I passed this plain. I found various information about this singular figure; the Tamoults [Tamils] all assured me that it was Baouth, who was no longer looked to and whose worship and festivals ceased after the Brames made themselves masters of the peoples' belief.[14]

✦ WILLIAM HURD

At the end of the eighteenth century, William Hurd, a British clergyman about whom little is known, published A New Universal History of the Religious Rites, Ceremonies, and Customs of the Whole World. *Unlike Picart, discussed earlier in this chapter, it was published in a single large volume (790 pages), and like Picart it would be reprinted many times in the subsequent decades. In his preface, Hurd explains that "there is no other Book in our Language, nor indeed in any other, on an enlarged plan; for blending Instruction with Entertainment, this work will lead mankind to set a proper value on the great truths of the Protestant Religion; and it is hoped that the*

Author's sincere endeavours to diffuse useful knowledge amongst all ranks of people, will meet with general approbation and applause." Yet despite his claims of original-ity, he draws heavily from Picart—all the copper engravings, with the exception of the frontispiece, are copied from that work. Much is drawn from Picart in the text as well, but Hurd often adds his own embellishments, as we see in these selections on Siam and Ceylon.

————

[DESCRIBING "*THE* RELIGION
IN THE KINGDOM OF SIAM"]

The grand object of worship in Siam is *Sommona Codom*, of whom they give us the following account: They say he was born of a virgin, through the influence of the sun; and that when the virgin found herself with child, she was so much affected, that she went and hid herself in a desart, in order to conceal her shame from the world. There, on the banks of a lake, she was delivered of a most beautiful child, but having no milk, wherewith to suckle him, and unwilling that he should die, she jumped into the lake, and set him upon a flower which blowed of itself, for his more commodious reception, and afterwards inclosed him in a cradle.

From the moment he was born, without the assistance of a tutor, he instructed himself, and acquired a perfect knowledge of all things relating to heaven, earth, paradise, and hell, with all the mysteries of nature. He taught the people to believe that angels visited him, as he sat under a tree, and that they worshipped him. But, although he was born in such a miraculous manner, yet they tell us, he had a brother named *Thevatat*, who being jealous of him, conspired his downfall; but *Sommona Codom* prevailed, and *Thevatat* was sent to be tormented in hell. They tell us further, that the guardian angel of the earth, whom they make a female, endeavoured to pre-vail with the enemies of *Sommona Codom*, to adore him as a god; but they refusing, she squeezed her watery locks, and poured forth a deluge, which destroyed them.

Before *Sommona Codom* began to aspire at the godhead, he had appeared five hundred and fifty times in the world, under various forms, and always assumed that which was the most beautiful at each period. He frequently laid down his life for the good of his people, and accustomed himself so much to mortification and penance, that he suffered a bramin to take his son and daughter from him, and put them to the most exquisite tortures before his face. He was so charitable, that he once gave his wife to a poor man who implored charity. Whatever an European may think of this benevolent action, we are assured, that the people of Siam con-sider it as one of the most illustrious virtues in his life.

After he had renounced the pomp and vanities of the world, he applied himself to all the austerities of a devotee. He fasted, prayed, and performed all the religious duties common in the country, and rose to such strength of body, and perfection of mind, that he overcame, in single combat, a saint of consummate virtue. He had the power to work miracles, and he could make himself invisible, in order to know what secret things were transacting in the world. He flew as swift as the wind, from place to place, in order to preach virtue and morality; but one day forgetting himself, he killed a man, for which he was put to death. The person whom *Sommona Codom* murdered, was, what the people of Siam call, a heretic; for these idolators have heretics among them, as well as we Christians. It was not long before *Sommona Codom* made his appearance again in the world, and the first thing he desired was, to eat the flesh of the hog into which the soul of him whom he murdered had entered, in order to be revenged on his murderer.

Accordingly, as he was teaching his disciples one day, a piece of the flesh of this hog was brought him, and he ate a part, but being taken ill with it, he told his disciples to build temples and altars to his memory, and then died. Ever since his death, he has enjoyed *Nireupan*, or perfect tranquillity, being subject to no sort of pain, trouble, or sorrow.

He left the print of his feet in three different parts of the world, viz. in the kingdoms of Siam and Pegu, and in the island of Ceylon. To those places, whole crowds of pilgrims resort annually, where they offer up their prayers to him. These pilgrims are permitted to see the bones of *Sommona Codom*, but they shine with such resplendant lustre, that they cannot behold them a minute at a time.[15]

[DESCRIBING "*THE* RELIGION OF CEYLON"]

The inhabitants of Ceylon are all Pagans, for although some of them acknowledge there is one Supreme God, yet they allow of many subordinate ones to act under him; and this was the idolatry of the ancient Greeks and Romans. Thus they have gods for agriculture, some for navigation, for sickness, and for almost every thing. All their idols are represented by the most fantastic and monstrous images. One of these is formed like a giant, and by them called *Buddu*, who lived a very holy and penitent life. The inhabitants reckon their years from the time this *Buddu* lived, and as it agrees with the fortieth year of the Christian Æra, most of the Jesuits are of opinion, that he was St. Thomas the Apostle.

They add further, that this *Buddu*, who was not born in their country, died on the continent, and the time of his death agrees with that of the Apostle St. Thomas, although it is much more probable that he was a native of China, and perhaps the same person whom they call *Fo*, for we cannot depend on the truth of their chronologies. The tooth of an ape, which a Portuguese governor caused to be burnt, was formerly adored as one of *Buddu's*. In vain did the Portuguese attempt, by this means, to put an end to their superstition, and idolatrous worship; for they gave it out that the tooth made its escape from the hands of its enemies, and took refuge on a rose. It is the province of *Buddu* to watch over and protect the souls of men, to be with them in this life, and to support them when dying.

The devil is also worshipped here, under the name of *Jaca*, and their religious motives arise from fear. They often sacrifice all they have to this infernal spirit; and although the Jesuits said all they could to persuade them to desist from such abominable idolatry, yet it was all in vain; for ignorant as these people are, they made answer, that they sacrificed to the devil to procure his friendship and favour. They are extremely fond of miracles, otherwise they could not have believed that the tooth of *Buddu* made its escape from the fire, but they have others no less wonderful.

One of their pagods or temples, had been shut up many years, and totally deserted by the devotees, who formerly came to it to worship; for the king of the country had given out, that the image placed in it, was not capable of working miracles, and therefore he ordered his subjects to treat it with every mark of ignominy, to the no small loss of the priests.

The priests, however, who generally know how to be revenged on those who meddle with what they consider as their temporal interest, resolved to take part with their insulted god. One day, as the king went into the long deserted temple to mock at the image, the priests had so contrived matters, that the sovereign was like to have paid dear for his impiety. Fire issued out of the mouth of the image, his eyes sparkled resentment, and in his hand he held a scymiter, ready to plunge into the heart of the royal unbeliever. His majesty, conscious of his guilt, acknowledged it, begged pardon in the most supplicant manner, and adored the deity that threatened to punish him. The devotees thronged in crowds to the pagod; worship was re-established there, and the god was adored with as much fervency as ever. From that time, the natives of Ceylon have there worshipped *Buddu* as the guardian of their island, and of the whole universe; and they are of opinion, that the world can never be destroyed while this image stands in his temple. In sickness, in adversity, and under all sorts of afflictions, they make their addresses to this image, and in every house there is a basket of flowers devoted to his service, and kept to make a part of their freewill-offerings.[16]

◆   JEAN-BAPTISTE GROSIER (1743–1823)

In 1065, the emperor of China instructed the scholar Sima Guang and a team of assistants to write a comprehensive history of China covering from 403 BCE to 959 CE. They completed the task nineteen years later, publishing the 294-volume Comprehensive Mirror to Aid the Government *(Zizhi Tongjian), known in English as "The Great Chinese Annals." In the twelfth century, the famous Neo-Confucian scholar Zhu Xi produced a condensed version. During the Qing dynasty, this version was translated into Manchu, which in turn was translated into French by the Jesuit missionary Joseph-Anna-Marie de Moyriac de Mailla; he completed the work in twelve volumes in 1730. He sent it back to France for publication, but because of the suppression of the Jesuits, it lay unpublished for almost fifty years, until the abbé and Jesuit Jean-Baptiste Grosier published it in twelve volumes between 1777 and 1783. The Abbé gave it the title* Histoire générale de la Chine, ou Annales de cet Empire; traduit du Tong-kien-kang-mou par de Mailla *(General History of China, or Annals of this Empire; translated from the Tongjian Gangmu by de Mailla). However, he felt that the translation would not be comprehensible to European readers without an introduction, and so in 1786 he published* De la Chine, ou description générale de cet empire, rédigée d'après les Mémoires de la mission de Pékin. *It was translated into English two years later as* A General Description of China: Containing the Topography of the Fifteen Provinces which Compose This Vast Empire.

Although he had the translation of the Chinese text before him, Grosier relied not so much on the Chinese text but on previous Jesuit reports, as we see in the chapter below. We find here, yet again, the story of the Buddha's deathbed recantation, which does not appear in Buddhist accounts. Grosier concludes his discussion of Buddhism with, "Can any one believe that a philosophy so extravagant and absurd would have found partisans in China! The emperor Kao-tsong, however, became so much infatuated with it, that he abdicated the throne, in order that he might be more at liberty to indulge himself in the practice of this extravagant doctrine, which entirely destroys morality, subverts society, and tends to annihilate that reciprocal relation which unites men together."

————

CHAP. IV

Sect of the God Foe, or Fo

This sect, still more pernicious, and much wider diffused throughout China than the preceding, came originally from India. The doctors of *Tao-ssé* had promised to a prince of the *Tchou*, and brother of the emperor *Ming-ti*, to make him enter into communion with the spirits. This credulous and superstitious prince, having heard of a celebrated spirit in India, named *Fo*, by continued importunities prevailed on his brother to send an embassy to this foreign deity. The officer who was charged with this commission set out, accompanied by a train of seventeen persons, and directed his course towards India. As soon as he arrived at the place of his destination, he found there only two *Cha-men*, or votaries of *Fo*, whom he carried with him to China. He collected, at the same time, several images of the god *Fo*, or *Boudha*, painted on fine chintz, with forty-two chapters of the canonical books of the Indians, which he placed, together with the images, upon a white horse. This embassy returned to the imperial city in the eighth year of the reign of *Ming-ti*, and the sixty-fifth of the Christian æra. All historians agree, that the doctrines and worship of *Foe* were at that epoch first introduced into China, where, in a short time, they made a rapid progress.

We have no certain knowledge of the birthplace of this pretended god. His followers relate that he was born in one of the kingdoms of India, situated near the line, and that his father was a king. They assure us that his mother, who was named *Mo-yé*, brought him into the world by the left side, and that she expired soon after her delivery; that at the time of her conception, she dreamed that she swallowed an elephant, and that this strange dream gave birth to the particular veneration, which the kings of India have always shewn for a white elephant. "As soon as this extraordinary child was born," add they, "he has strength enough to stand erect without assistance; he walked seven steps, and pointing with one hand to the heavens, and with the other to the earth, cried out—*In the heavens and on earth there is no one but me who deserves to be honoured.*"

At the age of seventeen he espoused three wives, by one of whom he had a son called by the Chinese *Mo-heou-lo*. At nineteen he abandoned his home, his wives, his children, and all the cares of life, and retired to a vast desert followed by four philosophers, to whose care he committed himself. At the age of thirty, he felt himself all on a sudden filled with the divinity, and he was metamorphosed into *Fo* or *Pagod*, according to the expression of the Indians. He had no sooner become a god, than he thought of establishing his doctrine, and of proving his celestial mission by performing miracles. The number of his disciples was immense, and they soon spread his ridiculous errors through every part of India, and the higher extremities of Asia.

The priests attached to the worship of *Fo* are called *Talapoins* by the Siamese, *Lamas* by the Tartars, *Ho-chang* in China, and *Bonzes* in Japan; they are generally known by Europeans under the latter appellation.

One of the principal errors propagated by *Fo* is the doctrine of metempsychosis of which he appears to have been the inventor. As he lived five hundred years before Pythagoras, and as we know that the Grecian philosopher travelled through Egypt, and several parts of India, there can scarcely be a doubt of his having borrowed this notion from some of the disciples of *Fo*. This doctrine of the transmigration of souls has given rise to that multitude of idols, which are reverenced in every place where the worship of *Fo* is established. Quadrapeds, birds, reptiles, and the vilest animals had temples, and became objects of public veneration, because the soul of the god in his transmigrations and metamorphoses might have inhabited their bodies.

We shall conclude the chapter with the account given by the bonzes of this pretended deity. He had attained to age of seventy-nine, when he perceived by his feebleness and infirmities, that his borrowed divinity could not prevent him from paying the debt of nature like other men. He was unwilling to leave his disciples without revealing to them the whole secret and hidden mysteries of his doctrine. Having therefore called them together, he declared, that till that moment he had always thought proper to speak to them in parables, and that for the space of forty years, he had disguised the truth under figurative and metaphorical expressions; but being on the point of bidding them a long farewell, he would disclose his real sentiments, and unveil the whole mystery of his wisdom. *Learn then*, said he, *that there is no other principle of all things, but a vacuum and nothing; from nothing all things have sprung, to nothing they must again return, and there all our hopes end.*

An infinitude of fables were spread by his disciples after his death. They affirmed that their master was still in life, that he had been already born eight thousand times, and that he had appeared successively under the figures of an ape, lion, dragon, elephant, &c. Among his disciples, there was one who had been dearer to him than all the rest, to whom he committed his most secret thoughts, and whom he entrusted with the care of propogating his doctrine; he is called by the Chinese *Moo-kia-yé*. He desired him never to attempt to support his tenets by proofs and long reasoning, and commanded him to put only at the beginning of the books which he published: *Thus have I learned.* In one of his works the same *Fo* had made mention of another master still more ancient than himself, whom the Chinese name *O-mi-to*, and the Japanese *Amida*. The bonzes assure us that the latter became so eminently holy, that it is at present sufficient only to invoke him in order to obtain immediate pardon from the greatest crimes: The Chinese therefore on almost every occasion have continually in their mouth these two names, *O-mi-to, Fo!* [in fact, it is one name: Amituo fo in Chinese; Amitābha Buddha in Sanskrit].[17]

✦ SIR WILLIAM JONES (1746–1794)

Sir William Jones was the most famous British orientalist of the nineteenth century. From an early age, he excelled at the study of languages, especially Persian, and after his studies at Oxford supported himself as a translator and language teacher. He later turned to the law and in 1783 was appointed a junior judge at the Supreme Court of Bengal. Upon his arrival in Calcutta (today spelled Kolkata), he developed a strong interest in classical Indian culture, learning Sanskrit and eventually translating Hindu poems and law codes. The year after his arrival in India, Jones founded (with others) the Asiatick Society, and served as its first president (in 1825, the antique k was dropped from the organization's name, which became the Asiatic Society of Bengal in 1832). In "On the Hindus," his Third Anniversary Discourse delivered on February 2, 1786, Jones famously speculated that Sanskrit, Greek, and Latin come from the same source. But later in that same lecture, a portion of which follows, he also commented on the Buddha's hair.

Four years later, Jones wrote about the Buddha at greater length. In the second passage below, he comments on a contradiction. His Brahmin informants speak of the Buddha in negative terms, and yet the Buddha is considered the ninth avatar of the Hindu god Vishnu. Jones seeks to resolve this contradiction by proposing his own version of the two-buddha theory, which had been propounded by Engelbert Kaempfer a century before.

The letters on many of those monuments appear, as I have before intimated, partly of Indian, and partly of Abyssinian or Ethiopick, origin; and all these indubitable facts may induce no ill-grounded opinion, that Ethiopia and Hindustan were peopled or colonized by the same extraordinary race; in confirmation of which, it may be added, that the mountaineers of Bengal and Bahar can hardly be distinguished in some of their features, particularly their lips and noses, from the modern Abyssinians, whom the Arabs call the children of Cush: and the ancient Hindus, according to Strabo, differed in nothing from the Africans, but in the straitness and smoothness of their hair, while that of the others was crisp or wooly; a difference proceeding chiefly, if not entirely, from the respective humidity or dryness of their atmospheres; hence the people who received the first light of the rising sun, according to the limited knowledge of the ancients, are said by Apuleius to be the *Aru* and Ethiopians, by which he clearly meant certain nations of India; where we frequently see figures of Buddha with curled hair apparently designed for a representation of it in its natural state.[18]

I have long been convinced, that, on these subjects, we can only reason satisfactorily from written evidence, and that our forensick rule must be invariably applied, to take the declarations of the Brahmans most strongly against themselves, that is, against their pretensions to antiquity; so that, on the whole, we may safely place Buddha just at the beginning of the present age: but what is the beginning of it? When this question was proposed to Radhacant, he answered: "Of a period comprising more than four hundred thousand years, the first two or three thousand may reasonably be called the beginning." On my demanding written evidence, he produced a book of some authority, composed by a learned *Goswami*, and entitled *Bhagawatamrita*, or, the *Nectar* of the *Bhagawat*, on which it is a metrical comment; and the couplet, which he read from it deserves to be cited: after the just mentioned account of Buddha in the text, the commentator says, "He became visible, the-thousand-and-second-year-of-the-Cali-age being past; his body of-a-colour-between-white-and-ruddy, with-two-arms, without-hair on his head."

Cicata, named in the text as the birth place of Buddha, the *Goswami* supposes to have been Dhermaranya, a wood near Gaya, where a colossal image of that ancient deity still remains: it seemed to me of black stone; but, as I saw it by torchlight, I cannot be positive as to its colour, which may, indeed, have been changed by time.

The Brahmans universally speak of the Bauddhas with all the malignity of an intolerant spirit; yet the most orthodox among them consider Buddha himself as an incarnation of Vishnu: this is a contradiction hard to be reconciled; unless we cut the knot, instead of untying it, by supposing with Giorgi, that there were two Buddhas, the younger of whom established the new religion, which gave so great offence in India, and was introduced into China in the first century of our era. The Cashmirian before mentioned asserted this fact, without being led to it by any question that implied it; and we may have reason to suppose, that Buddha is in truth only a general word for a philosopher: the author of a celebrated Sanscrit dictionary, entitled from his name *Amaracosha*, who was himself a Bauddha, and flourished in the first century before Christ, begins his vocabulary with nine words, that signify heaven, and proceeds to those, which mean a deity in general; after which come different classes of gods, demigods, and demons, all by generick names; and they are followed by two very remarkable heads; first, (not the general names of Buddha, but) the names of a Buddha-in-general, of which he gives us eighteen, such as *Muni, Sastri, Munindra, Vinayaca, Samantabhadra, Dhermaraja, Sugata*, and the like; most of them significative of excellence, wisdom, virtue, and sanctity; secondly, the names of a particular-Buddha-*Muni*-who-descended-in-the-family-of-Sacya (those are the very words of the original), and his titles are, *Sacyamuni, Sacyasinha, Servarthasiddha, Saudhodani, Gautama, Arcabandhu,* or kinsman of the sun, and *Mayadevisuta,* or child of Maya: thence the author passes to the different epithets of particular Hindu deities. When I pointed out this curious passage to Radhacant, he contended, that the first eighteen names were general epithets, and the following seven, proper names, or patronymicks, of one and the same person; but Ramalochan, my own teacher, who, though not a Brahman, is an excellent scholar and a very sensible unprejudiced man, assured me, that Buddha was a generick word, like *Deva*, and that the learned author, having exhibited the names of a *Devata* in general, proceeded to those of a Buddha in general, before he came to particulars: he added, that Buddha might mean a sage or a philosopher, though Budha was the word commonly used for a mere wise man without supernatural powers. It seems highly probable, on the whole, that the Buddha, whom Jayadeva celebrates in his Hymn, was the *Sacyasinha*, or Lion of Sacya, who, though he forbad the sacrifices of cattle, which the *Vedas* enjoin, was believed to be Vishnu himself in a human form, and that another Buddha, one perhaps of his followers in a later age, assuming his name and character, attempted to overset the whole system of the Brahmans, and was the cause of that persecution, from which the Bauddhas are known to have fled into very distant regions. May we not reconcile the singular difference of opinion among the Hindus as to the time of Buddha's appearance, by supposing that they have confounded the two Buddhas, the first of whom was born a few years before the close of the last age, and the second, when above a thousand years of the present age had elapsed? We know, from better authorities, and with as much certainty as can justly be expected on so doubtful a subject, the real time, compared with our own era, when the ancient Buddha began to distinguish himself; and it is for this reason principally, that I have dwelled with minute anxiety on the subject of the last *Avatar*.[19]

♦ THOMAS MAURICE (1754–1824)

Thomas Maurice was an English clergyman who, although he never traveled to India, wrote extensively about it, drawing from the burgeoning publications of the day. In 1783, he set to work on what would eventually become the three-volume History of Hindostan. *However, in 1789, he suspended work on the project in order to write a more polemical work, one which sought to refute the claims originating in Paris that the accounts in Hindu and Christian scriptures were astronomical and natural allegories, and that elements of the Bible, including the Pentateuch, derived ultimately from Hindu sources. Maurice thus responded to Voltaire and his followers, or "the French infidel school," as he called them, in his six-volume* Indian Antiquities, *published between 1792 and 1796.*

Here, he is content to give an astronomical interpretation to the Buddha, making him the planet Mercury and the day of the week Wednesday.

———

While in these remote northern regions it would be improper to pass unnoticed by the ancient race and religious rites of Scandinavia, I have elsewhere endeavoured, by a chain of strong evidence, to demonstrate that their first celebrated god Oden, or Woden, was no other than the Taut of Phœnicia, the Hermes of Egypt, the elder Buddha or Boodh of India, the Fo of China, and the Mercury of Greece and Rome. In short, that the religion of almost every nation of the earth, previous to the happy diffusion of the Christian doctrine, exhibited little else besides the shattered fragments of one grand system of primitive, I do not say the earliest, theology, once prevalent in the Greater Asia. Not the least forcible of the arguments adduced to support this hypothesis, an hypothesis that gives to Britain, in the earliest periods of the world, a colony of Brahmins, or at least of Brahmin-taught sages of the sect of Boodh, are those derived from the striking similitude of the superstitious ceremonies instituted and observed in those respective regions, and the very singular circumstance of the Indian god and planet Boodh, under the name of Woden and Mercury, conferring his name, over all the northern and western empires of Europe, upon one particular day of the week. This remarkable fact is evidenced in the instance of the BOODH WAR, or dies Mercurii, of India being the very same fourth day of the week which the Scandinavians consecrated to Oden, which our Anglo-Saxon ancestors denominated Woden's dag, and which we call Wednesday.[20]

♦   LOUIS-MATHIEU LANGLÈS (1763–1824)

Louis-Mathieu Langlès served as conservator of Oriental manuscripts at what is today the Bibliothèque Nationale in Paris (called at the time the Bibliothèque du Roi). In 1795, inspired by Voltaire and with the support of the Count de Volney (1757– 1820), he was named director of the École Spéciale des Langues Orientales Vivantes (today the Institut National des langues et civilisations orientales), an institution where the study of Asia and its languages took place free from the assumptions of biblical theology. Indeed, Langlès would argue that the Pentateuch in the Bible was an abridgment of Egyptian books, and that those Egyptian books derived originally from the five Vedas of India. Thus, whereas scholars of the previous century, such as Athanasius Kircher, saw a movement (in his case, of idolatry) from Egpyt to India to China, Langlès saw India as a cradle of civilization whose influence spread to Egypt in the West and China in the East.

Langlès was also a prolific translator and editor, rendering the early volumes of Asiatick Researches *into French. He also translated the accounts of a number of travelers to Asia, including the Swedish botanist C. P. Thunberg (1743–1828), who served in the Dutch East India Company in Japan in 1775 and 1776. At Thunberg's mention of the Buddha, Langlès provides a long footnote, from which the following passage is drawn. Here, like other scholars of his day, Langlès finds the Buddha everywhere, but unlike others, he traces his origins to Tibet.*

———

Without wishing to engage ourselves in chronological discussions, as uncertain as they are superfluous, we allow ourselves to believe, following to original fragments preserved in several ancient languages, that we have identified the same legislator in the *Boutta* of the ancient Gymnosophists, the *Sammana-Kantama* of the Peguans, the *Sammana-Coudom* of the Siamese, the *Foé* of the Chinese, the ancient *Boudso* or *Chaca* of the Japanese, the *Vichnou* of the Hindus in one of his incarnations, the *Lama* of the Tibetans, the *Baouth* of the Singhalese, the *Thic-Ca* of the Tonquinese, the *Thoth* of the Egyptians, the *Boa* of the Tungus, the *Torus* of the Laplanders, the *Ouden* or *Woden* of the gothic nations, to whom Wednesday is further dedicated in the name *Woden-tag*, Wednesday in English (*Boud-Var* in Sanskrit), *Mercurii dies*; Mercury, Hermes, Toth and Boudh are but the same person.

The comparison of the books or the original fragments that remain for us from the different Legislators in addition comes to support the identity I wish to establish, and it is in Tibet that original prototype must be sought. The Lama is the Sovereign Pontiff, the spiritual Father of the Chinese, the Tartars, and of northern Asia. It is to the temple of Lhassa that the Priests of these countries go to study theology and Tibetan, which is the sacred language of these different nations or Tartar hordes.[21]

◆   PAULINUS A S. BARTHOLOMAEO (1748–1806)

The Carmelite missionary to Malabar in southern India, Paulinus a S. Bartholomaeo, published in 1790 the first European grammar of Sanskrit, entitled Dissertatio Historico-Critica in Linguam Samscrdamicam *(Historical-Critical Disserta-*

tion on the Sanskrit Language). *Father Paulinus considered the several epithets of the Buddha contained in the fifth-century Sanskrit thesaurus, the* Amarakoṣa, *and came to the conclusion that the Buddha was not a man but a planet. He described the Buddha in his 1796* Viaggio alle Indie orientali, *published in English in 1800 as* A Voyage to the East Indies, *from which the following is taken.*

————

The next in order among the celestial gods is *Budha*, that is, the intelligent, the vigilant, the crafty, the acute. He is supposed to be a bosom friend of *Shiva*, and supplies the place of his private secretary. This office has been conferred on him by the Indian mythologists; because, according to their ideas, each planet is governed by a particular genius; and because *Budha* represents Mercury, which is nearest the sun. This god is said to have been the author of a great many books, and to have invented arithmetic, the art of writing, geometry, astronomy, and, in short, all those sciences which have been cultivated and improved by the industry of man. The opinion of those who consider him as having been really a writer, a king, a legislator, is ridiculous.[22]

✦ FRANCIS WILFORD (1761–1822)

Francis Wilford was born in Hanover and joined the army of the British East India Company in 1781 as a member of the Hanoverian reinforcements. He worked as a surveyor and military cartographer and was a member of the company's group of Sanskritists, which included such distinguished scholars as Sir William Jones and Charles Wilkins. However, Wilford is remembered for his eccentric theories of the Indian origins of the Bible and for being duped by an Indian pundit. He was so obsessed with finding an Indian account of the biblical flood narrative that one of the pundits in his employ forged one, called the Padmapurāṇa, *in which Noah (called Satyavrata in the text) has three sons: Jyapeti (= Japheth), Charma (= Ham), and Sharma (= Shem). Wilford initially championed the text as a great discovery in an article published in* Asiatick Researches, *from which the following passage about the Buddha is drawn. Here, Wilford argues, as Engelbert Kaempfer and Jones had before him, that the Buddha came from Africa. Wilford eventually learned of the forgery and recanted in print.*

————

Whether BUDDHA was a sage or a hero, the leader of a colony, or a whole colony personified, whether he was black or fair, whether his hair was curled or straight, if indeed he had any hair (which a commentator on the *Bhágavat* denies), whether he appeared then, or two hundred, or a thousand years, after CRISHNA, it is very certain that he was not of the true *Indian* race: in all his images, and in the statues of *Bauddhas*, male and female, which are to be seen in many parts of these provinces and in both peninsulas, there is an appearance of something *Egyptian* or *Ethiopian*; and both in features and dress, they differ widely from the ancient *Hindu* figures of heroes and demigods. SÁCYA has a resemblance in sound to SI-SAC, and we find CHÁNAC abbreviated from CHÁNACYA; so that SISAC and SES-ONCHOSIS may be corrupted from SÁCYASINHA, with a transposition of some letters, which we know to be frequent in proper names, as in the word *Banáres*. Many of his statues in *India* are colossal, nearly naked, and usually represented sitting in a contemplative attitude; nor am I disinclined to believe, that the famed statue of MEMNON, in *Egypt*, was erected in honour of MAHIMAN, which has MAHIMNÀ in one of its oblique cases, and the *Greeks* could hardly have pronounced that word otherwise than MAIMNA, or MEMNA: they certainly used *Mai* instead of *Mahà*, for HESYCHIUS expressly says, *Mai, μεγά. Ἰνδοί*; and *Mai* signifies *great* even in modern *Coptick*. We are told, that MAHIMAN, by his wife MAHÁMÁNYÀ, has a son named SHARMANA CARDAMA, who seems to be the SAMMANO CODOM of the *Bauddhas*, unless those last words be corrupted from SAMANTA GÓTAM, which are found in the *Amarcósh* among BUDDHA's names.[23]

◆   COLIN MACKENZIE (1753–1821)

Colin Mackenzie, born in the Outer Hebrides, sailed to India in 1783. Rising through the ranks from ensign to colonel, he served as a military engineer and surveyor for the East India Company. He was appointed surveyor general of India in 1817. In the course of his work, Mackenzie gathered thousands of inscriptions, tracts, and artifacts (many of which were sent to the British Museum). Like many other officers of the company, he became an amateur scholar of Indian religions, with a particular interest in Jainism. He published his findings in the leading orientalist journals of the day.

The passage below is drawn from an article Mackenzie wrote about Sri Lanka in 1796, when he held the rank of captain. However, the passage itself comes not from him but from John Herbert Harington (1764/5–1828), an administrator and judge for the East India Company, who provided an addendum to Mackenzie's essay.

As noted in chapter 3, Engelbert Kaempfer had attributed African origins to the Buddha, in part because of his curly hair—a point that would be repeated for more

than a century, including by Sir William Jones. Harington decided to ask some Bud-
dhist monks about it. Here, on a visit to the Buddhist "Temple at Oogulbodda" in Sri
Lanka on March 10, 1797, he describes "a colossal image of BUDDHA, *eighteen cubits*
in length, composed of earth and cement, in a sleeping posture; or rather reclining on
his lotos throne; his head resting on a pillow; and supported by the right arm, whilst
the left is extended on the thigh of the same side."

———

There are several other images of BUDDHA in this temple, which, having no peculiar characteristic, do not call for distinct notice. It may be of use to observe, however, that on my pointing out the uniformity of the head-dress, in respect to the
crisped hair; and asking whether it was meant to represent the hair of an *Abysin-*
nian; the priests, of whom four were present, answered in the negative, with apparent abhorrence; and the priest who had before attended me, repeating his previous information of BUDDHA's being the son of SUDODHANA rajah, and born in
Muggud deish (*Bahar*) added, in explanation of the hair being short and crisped,
that BUDDHA had on a certain occasion cut his hair with a golden sword, and its
appearance in consequence was meant to be represented on his images.[24]

◆   CAPTAIN MAHONY

By the end of the eighteenth century, we begin to find some positive representations
of the Buddha by Europeans, especially among officers of the East India Company.
An example is this excerpt from an article written in 1797 by one Captain Mahony.
It begins with a rather straightforward rendition of the traditional life of the Buddha,
followed by a positive valuation of his teachings. The term idol *does not appear.*

———

The word BHOODDHA, in the *Palee* and *Singhalai* languages, implies, *Universal*
Knowledge or Holiness; also *a Saint superior to all the Saints, even to the God* MAHA
BRACHMA; and is understood in these various senses by the natives of *Ceylon* . . . .

   BHOODDHA, before his appearance as man, was a God, and the Supreme of all
the Gods. At the solicitations of many of the Gods he descended on earth, and was
frequently born as a man, in which character he exercised every possible virtue, by
extraordinary instances of self-denial and piety. He was at length born* of MAHA-
MAYA DEVEE, after a pregnancy of 10 months, and had for father SOODDODÉNEH

———

* In the kingdom or country called *Dumba Deeva, Madda Dését*, and the city of *Kimbool wat-pooree.*

RAJA. He lived happily with his queen YASSODERA, and 40,000 concubines, for 31 years. The six next he passed in the midst of wildernesses, qualifying himself to be a BHOODDHA. At the close of this period, his calling became manifest to the world, and he exercised his functions as BHOODDHA for 45 years. He died in *Co-oseemarapooree*, at the Court of MALLELEH RAJA, Tuesday, the 15th of May; from which period the BHOODDHA WAROOSEH, or æra of BHOODDHA, is dated, which now (A. C. 1797) amounts to 2339 years.

BHOODDHA is not, properly speaking, considered as a God, but as having been born man, and in the end of time arrived at the dignity of a BHOODDHA, on account of his great virtues, and extraordinary good qualities. The title of BHOODDHA was not conferred on him by any Supreme Power; he adopted it by his own sovereign will, in the same manner as he became man, both of which events were predicted ages before. BHOODDHA, after his death, ascended to the Hall of Glory, called *Mooktzé*, otherwise *Nirgoowané*, which is a place above, and exceeding in magnificence, the 26th heaven; there he will live for ever, in happiness, and incorruptibility, never to be born again in the world; where his doctrine is at present extant, and will continue in all its splendour for 5000 years, according to his own prophecy. . . .

The religion of BHOODDHA, as far as I have had any insight into it, seems to be founded in a mild and simple morality. BHOODDHA has taken for his principles, Wisdom, Justice, and Benevolence;* from which principles emanate Ten Commandments, held by his followers as the true and only rule of their conduct. He places them under three heads; thought, word, and deed;† and it may be said, that the spirit of them is becoming, and well suited to him, whose mild nature was first shocked at the sacrifice of cattle. These Commandments comprise what is understood by the moral law, which has been generally preached by all the BHOODDHAS in different countries, but chiefly by the last, or GAUTEMEH BHOODDHA, in the empire of Raja GAHA NOOWEREH. They are contained in a Code of Laws written in the *Palee* language, called *Diksangeeyeh*.

The BHOODDHISTS have prayers adapted to circumstances, which are used privately in their houses, and publicly in presence of the congregation. They were first recorded by the King WATTEH GEMMOONOO ABEYENAJEH, as regularly handed down from BHOODDHA, in whose days the art of writing was not known. BHOODDHISTS are obliged to pray three times a day; about 5 o'clock in the morning, at

* *Singalese. Bhooddha, Dermah, Sangeh.*
† *Singalese. Hittenema, Keeyenema, Kerrenema.—Palee. Manneshet, Waak, Kayeh.*

noon, and towards the fall of night. Their devotions are addressed to BHOODDHA and his RAHATOONS (apostles), with a religious respect for his Code of Law, and the relicks, both of him, and the RAHATOONS. The respect afforded to the relics, is in memory of the characters to which they belonged, without ascribing to them a supernatural virtue. Four days in the month are dedicated to public worship, the four first days of the changes of the moon, when those who are able attend at the temples. There are no other public days of festival or thanksgiving: all are however at liberty to select such days for themselves, and this they particularize by acts of devotion, consisting in fasting, prayer, and forming resolutions for their future good conduct; all which devout acts are addressed to their *Saviour* BHOODDHA, &c.[25]

◆ MICHAEL SYMES (1761–1809)

A particularly learned British officer was the Irish major Michael Symes. He went to India at the age of nineteen as a cadet in the Bengal army of the East India Company. Rising through the ranks, he transferred into the 76th Regiment of the British army as a lieutenant in 1788, and was promoted to captain in 1793. In 1795, the Governor-General of India, Sir John Shore, had him lead an embassy to the court of King Bodawpaya of Burma in an effort to establish trade relations. Based on his seven months in Burma, in 1800 Symes published his five-hundred-page An Account of an Embassy to the Kingdom of Ava, Sent by the Governor-general of India, in the Year 1795.*

In the excerpt that follows, he demonstrates an impressive familiarity with the various positions of the day concerning the identity of the Buddha, drawing from works we have encountered earlier, such as those of Simon de la Loubére, who had been sent by Louis XIV to the court of Siam, and that of Guillaume le Gentil, the French astronomer. And he cogently disputes some of the more fanciful theories, politely expressing his disagreement with Sir William Jones's belief that the Buddha was the Norse god Oden.

AFTER what has been written, there can be little necessity to inform my readers that the Birmans are Hindoos: not votaries of Brahma, but sectaries of Boodh, which latter is admitted by Hindoos of all descriptions to be the ninth Avatar,* or descent of the deity in his capacity of preserver. He reformed the doctrines con-

---

* Sir William Jones, on the Gods of Greece, Italy, and India.

tained in the Vedas, and severely censured the sacrifice of cattle, or depriving any being of life: he is called the author of happiness: his place of residence was discovered at Gaya in Bengal, by the illustrious Amara,* renowned amongst men, "who caused an image of the supreme Boodh to be made, and he worshipped it: reverence be unto thee in the form of Boodh; reverence be unto thee, Lord of the Earth; reverence be unto thee, an incarnation of the deity, and, eternal one, reverence be unto thee, O God in the form of Mercy."

Gotma, or Goutum, according to the Hindoos of India, or Gaudma, among the inhabitants of the more eastern parts, is said† to have been a philosopher, and is by the Birmans believed to have flourished above 2300‡ years ago: he taught, in the Indian schools, the heterodox religion and philosophy of Boodh. The image that represents Boodh is called Gaudma, or Goutum, which is now a commonly received appellation of Boodh himself: this image is the primary object of worship in all countries situated between Bengal and China. The sectaries of Boodh contend with those of Brahma for the honour of antiquity, and are certainly far more numerous. The Cingaleze in Ceylon are Boodhists of the purest source, and the Birmans acknowledge to have originally received their religion from that island.§ It was brought, say the Rhahaans, first from Zehoo (Ceylon) to Arracan, and thence was introduced into Ava, and probably into China; for the Birmans assert with confidence that the Chinese are Boodhists.

This is a curious subject of investigation, and the concurrent testimony of circumstances, added to the opinions of the most intelligent writers, seem to leave little doubt of the fact. It cannot, however, be demonstrated beyond the possibility of dispute, till we shall have acquired a more perfect knowledge of Chinese letters, and a readier access to their repositories of learning. Little can at present be added to the lights cast on the subject by the late Sir William Jones, in his Discourse delivered to the Asiatic Society on the Chinese: that great man has expressed his conviction in positive terms, that "Boodh was unquestionably the Foe of China," and that he was also the god of Japan, and the Woden of the Goths, an opinion which corresponds with, and is perhaps grafted on, the information of the learned and

---

* See the translation of a Shanscrit inscription on a stone found in the temple of Boodh, at Gaya, by Mr. Wilkins. Asiat. Research. Vol. I. I am indebted for the annexed representation of the image of Boodh, at Gaya, to the kindness of Lord Teignmouth. The reader will observe the close resemblance it bears to that of the Birman Gaudma.

† Sir William Jones on the gods of Greece, Italy, and India.

‡ This agrees with the account of the Siamese computation given by Kaempfer.

§ The Birmans call Ceylon, Zehoo.

laborious Kæmpfer,* corroborated afterwards by his own researches. On whatever grounds the latter inference rests, it will not tend to weaken the belief of his
first position, when I observe that the Chinese deputies, on the occasion of our
introduction to the Seredaw or high priest of the Birman empire, prostrated themselves before him, and afterwards adored an image of Gaudma with more religious
fervour than mere politeness, or acquiescence to the customs of another nation,
would have excited: the Bonzes also of China, like the Rhahaans of Ava, wear yellow as the sacerdotal colour, and in many of their customs and ceremonies there
may be traced a striking similitude.

Whatever may be the antiquity of the worship of Boodh, the wide extent of its
reception cannot be doubted. The most authentic writer[†] on the eastern peninsula calls the image of Gaudma, as worshipped by the Siamese, Somona-codom:
being unacquainted with the language of Siam, which from so short a residence
as four months, it was impossible he could have acquired, he confounds two distinct words, Somona, and Codom, signifying Codom, or Gaudma, in his incarnate
state; the difference between the letters C and G may easily have arisen from the
mode of pronunciation in different countries; even in the Birman manner of uttering the word, the distinction between these letters is not very clear. The Boodh of
the Indians and the Birmans, is pronounced by the Siamese Pooth, or Pood, by the
vulgar, Poo; which, without any violence to probability, might be converted by the
Chinese into Foe;[‡] the Tamulic termination *en*, as Mr. Chambers remarks, creates
a striking resemblance between Pooden and the Woden of the Goths; every person
who has conversed with the natives of India knows that Boodh is the Dies Mercurii, the Wednesday, or Woden's day, of all Hindoos. Chronology, however, which
must always be accepted as a surer guide to truth, than inferences drawn from the
resemblance of words, and etymological reasoning, does not, to my mind, sufficiently establish that Boodh and Woden were the same. The period of the ninth

* Speaking of the Budz, or Seaka, of the Japanese, Kæmpfer says, "I have strong reasons to believe,
both from the affinity of the name, and the very nature of this religion, that its author and founder is
the very same person who the Bramins call Budha, and believe to be the essential spirit of Wishna, or
their deity, who made his ninth appearance in the world under this name: the Peguers call him Samana
Khutama." Hist. Japan, Book IV. ch. 6. Treating on the introduction of Boodh into China, the same author says, "About the year of Christ 518, one Darma, a great saint, and twenty-third successor on the
holy see of Seaka (Budha), came over into China from Seitenseku, as the Japanese writers explain it,
that is, from that part of the world which lies westward with regard to Japan, and laid, properly speaking, the first firm foundation of the Budsdoism in that mighty empire." Book. IV. ch. 6.

† Loubere.

‡ M. Gentil asserts that the Chinese admit, by their own accounts, that Foe, their object of worship,
was originally brought from India.

incarnation of Vishnu was long antecedent to the existence of the deified hero of Scandinavia. Sir William Jones determines the period when Boodh appeared on the earth to be 1014 years before the birth of Christ. Odin, or Woden, flourished at a period not very distant from our Saviour, and was, according to some, a contemporary of Pompey and of Julius Caesar. The author of the Northern Antiquities places him 70 years after the Christian era. Even the Birman Gaudma, conformably to their account, must have lived above 500 years before Woden. So immense a space can hardly be supposed to have been overlooked: but if the supposition refers, not to the warrior of the north, but to the original deity Odin, the attributes of the latter are as widely opposed to those of Boodh, who was himself only an incarnation of Vishnu, as the dates are incongruous. The deity, whose doctrines were introduced into Scandinavia, was a god of terror, and his votaries carried desolation and the sword throughout whole regions; but the Ninth Avatar* brought the peaceful olive, and came into the world for the sole purpose of preventing sanguinary acts. These apparent inconsistencies will naturally lead us to hesitate in acknowledging Boodh and Woden to be the same person: their doctrines are opposite, and their eras are widely remote.

Had that distinguished genius,[†] whose learning so lately illumined the East, been spared for the instruction and delight of mankind, he would probably have elucidated this obscurity, and have removed the dusky veil that still hangs over the religious legends of antiquity. The subject,[‡] as it now stands, affords an ample field for indulging in pleasing theories, and fanciful speculations; and as the probability increases of being able to trace all forms of divine worship to one sacred and primeval source, the inquiry in proportion becomes more interesting, and awakens a train of serious ideas in a reflecting mind.

It would be as unsatisfactory as tedious, to attempt leading my reader through the mazes of mythological fable, and extravagant allegory, in which the Hindoo religion, both Braminical and Boodhic, is enveloped and obscured; it may be sufficient to observe, that the Birmans believe in the Metempsychosis, and that, after having undergone a certain number of transmigrations, their souls will at last

---

* See the account of the Ninth Avatar, by the Rev. Mr. Maurice, in his History of Hindostan, Vol. II. Part 3.

† I need hardly observe that I mean Sir William Jones.

‡ General Vallancey, so justly celebrated for his knowledge of the antiquities of his country, has expressed his perfect conviction that the Hindoos have been in Britain and in Ireland. See Major Ouzeley's Oriental Collection, Vol. II. Much attention is certainly due to such respectable authority.

either be received into their Olympus on the mountain Meru,* or be sent to suffer torments in a place of divine punishments. Mercy they hold to be the first attribute of the divinity: "Reverence be to thee, O God, in the form of Mercy;" and they worship God by extending mercy unto all his creatures.[26]

◆ VINCENZO SANGERMANO (D. 1819)

Vincenzo (Vincentius) Sangermano was a Roman Catholic priest of the Barnabite order who spent the period from 1783 to 1806 as a missionary in Burma. His account of the Burmese empire was published in 1833, more than a decade after his death, as A Description of the Burmese Empire. *However, thirty-two years earlier, in 1801, Francis Buchanan of the East India Company had drawn heavily from information provided by Father Sangermano for his essay "On the Religion and Literature of the Burmas," published in* Asiatick Researches *(discussed in chapter 5).*

In the passage below, Sangermano says that in order to explain the religion of the Burmese, or "The Laws of Godama," as he calls it, he translated a short treatise that a celebrated Burmese monk, the tutor to the king, had written in 1763 at the request of a Roman Catholic bishop. Sangermano presumably translated the text for his bishop, and later gave a copy to Francis Hamilton, a Scottish surgeon and botanist who appears in the next chapter. We thus have a brief account of the life of the Buddha, in all its mythologized glory, as it was understood by a leading Burmese monk of the eighteenth century and prepared for a Roman Catholic bishop by an Italian Barnabite priest.

———

THE LAWS OF GODAMA

In order to fulfil this part of my undertaking, I think I cannot do better than present to the reader a short treatise on the religion of the Burmese, which a celebrated Talapoin, the tutor of the king, drew up at the request of one of our Bishops in the year 1763.

1. Four Gods have at different periods appeared in the present world, and have obtained the state of Niban, Chauchasan, Gonagon, Gaspà and Godoma. It is the law of the last mentioned that is at present obligatory among men.

---

* Meru properly denotes the pole, and, according to the learned Captain Wilford, it is the celestial north pole of the Hindoos, round which they place the garden of Indra, and describe it as the seat of delights.

He obtained the privilege of divinity at the age of thirty-five, when he began to promulgate his laws, in which employment he spent forty-five years. Having thus lived to the age of eighty in the practice of every good work, and having conferred salvation on every living creature, he was assumed into the state of Niban. From that time to the year 1763, there have passed 2306 years.

2. Godama spoke and taught as follows. "I a God, after having departed out of this world, will preserve my laws and my disciples in it for the space of 5000 years." Having likewise commanded that his statue and relics should be carefully kept and adored during this period, he thereby gave rise to the custom of adoring them. . . .

10. The Talapoin ends his summary by declaring, that out of the Burmese Empire and the island of Ceylon there are no true and legitimate priests of the laws of Godama, and by exhorting all strangers to embrace this law as alone containing the truth.

This treatise may give some idea of the laws of Godama regarding seculars; of those respecting the Talapoins, I shall speak further on. The sermons of Godoma, as they are called, are all contained in a great book called Sout, and it must be confessed that they inculcate some fine morality, of which I will give some specimens in the next chapter.

11. The books which contain the history of Godama represent him as a king who, having laid aside the ensigns of royalty, withdrew himself into a solitary place, put on the habit of a Talapoin, and gave himself up to the study and practice of virtue. But Godama had even before this acquired great merits. For he had already lived in 400,100,000 worlds, having begun as a little bird, and passed through 550 transmigrations, some happy, some unhappy, so as once even to have been an elephant. These former merits, united to his present generous abdication, procured for him at the age of thirty-five the gift of divine wisdom. This consists in seeing into the thoughts of all living beings: in the foreknowledge of all future events, however distant they may be: in the knowledge of the merits and demerits of all men: in the power of working miracles, particularly by causing fire and water to issue from his eyes at the same time, or fire from one eye and water from the other; and finally in a tender love towards all things living. Among other prodigies related of him, we may notice the one said to have happened at his birth; for he was no sooner born than he walked seven paces towards the north, exclaiming: "I am the noblest and greatest among men. This is the last time that I shall be born; never again shall I be conceived in the womb." In his stature also and the properties of his body there was something extraordinary. His height was more than nine cubits, his ears hung down to his shoulders, his tongue being thrust out of his

mouth reached even to his nose, and his hands, when he stood upright, touched his knees. In walking he always appeared elevated at least a cubit from the ground; his clothes did not touch his body, but were always a palm distant from it; and in the same manner, anything he took up remained always at a distance of a palm from his hands. During the forty-five years that he spent on earth after becoming a God, he was continually employed in the promulgation of his laws, and it was said that through his preaching 2,400,000,000 persons obtained the Niban. In the eightieth year of his age he died of dysentery, brought on by an excess in eating pork. Previous to his death he recommended that his statue and relics should be preserved and adored.

These have hence become objects of veneration to all the Burmese, wherever they are met with; but they are more particularly worshipped with greater pomp and by greater numbers in the Pagodas. These are pyramidal or conical buildings made of brick, painted and gilded on the outside. In these temples there is generally a niche in which is placed the statue of Godama; though in some both the niche and the statue are wanting. These are the public places of adoration for the Burmese, and are generally set apart from all other buildings, and surrounded by a wall of the same materials as the Pagoda itself.

12. Godama, upon his death, was immediately transported to the Niban, where he remains in a sort of ecstasy, without hearing, or seeing, or feeling, of having any sense of what goes on in the world, and in this state he will remain for eternity; and such will be the lot of all who have the good fortune to obtain this reward. But the laws of Godama will be observed upon earth for the space of 5000 years, reckoning from the day of his death, from which year, therefore, the Burmese begin their era. Of this period 2352 years have already elapsed. As soon as it is at an end, the laws of Godama will cease to be binding, another God must appear to promulgate a new code for the government of mankind.[27]

✦ JOSEPH ENDELIN DE JOINVILLE

Joseph Endelin de Joinville was a French naturalist who came to Sri Lanka in 1798 to work as surveyor general under Frederic North, the first governor of the British possessions on the island. In an 1801 essay entitled "On the Religion and Manners of the People of Ceylon," from which a passage appears below, de Joinville presents a thoughtful description of the Buddha based on what he learned about him in Sri Lanka. The essay is preceded by a letter from Frederic North to William Hunter, Secretary to the Society for Asiatic Researches, dated September 27, 1801. Sent from Colombo to Calcutta (known today as Kolkata), the letter states that Joinville's essay "was concluded before the arrival on this island of the embassy of Colonel SYMES, and of the accounts of the Religion and Customs of the Inhabitants of Bur-mah by Doctor BUCHANAN, contained in the sixth volume of the Researches of the Society."

We met Symes in the previous chapter and will meet Dr. Buchanan in this one, in two different selections.

⎯⎯⎯

It is generally known that the religion BOUDHOU is the religion of the people of *Ceylon*, but no one is acquainted with its form and precepts. I shall here relate what I have heard upon the subject, and I have the satisfaction to think, that though my information may not be altogether complete, yet it will serve as a clue for future and deeper researches. The first person who treats on such a subject, labours under disadvantages, which succeeding authors know how to turn to their own account, by finishing what a former hand had sketched, claiming the merit of the whole work. Regardless, however, of this consideration, I have the consolation to think I shall be useful to him who may next treat of the present subject.

If BOUDHOU be not an allegorical being, he is a man of genius, who has made laws and established a religion over a large tract of *Asia*. It is hard to say whether HE, or ZOROASTER, or BRAHMA were the most ancient. In fact, it would be necessary towards the decision of this question, first, to establish that these three legislators had really existed, or rather if these names are not merely attributes. ZOROASTER is the only one represented as a man, BRAHMA being always drawn as a part of and uniting the three supreme powers of Creator, preserver, and destroyer, in his own person. BOUDHOU is superior to all the gods; he is, however, not what we mean by a god, being inferior to them in some things, and above them in others. He is not purely a spirit, as he has a body: he over-runs the different worlds with rapidity, in the same manner as the geniuses in the Arabian Tales, well beloved by VISHNOU, and aided by his power. He governs the bad spirits, who have withdrawn their allegiance from the gods, and who are hurtful to men: yet he is the son of a king, a husband, a father, and a pilgrim. He is eighteen cubits in height, eats rice and vegetables, and has several of the attributes of humanity. He is called SAMAN the *Saint by Excellence*. I have made every inquiry, and have been informed that there is no etymology for the word BOUDHOU in the ancient languages of *Ceylon*. Whatever may be the opinion of the *Singhalese* respecting him, we shall consider him as a man. As BRAHMA is an idea, and not a being, there can be no question about whether BOUDHOU lived before or after what never existed as a being. But it would be well worth ascertaining which of the two religions, of BRAHMA or of BOUDHOU, is the more ancient. From the similarity of the two religions, there can be no doubt but that the one is the child of the other; but it is hard to know which is the mother. We find the religion of BOUDHOU in ancient times extending from the north of *Tartary* to *Ceylon*, and from the *Indus* to *Siam*, (I will not say as far as *China*, because I do not believe that FOE and BOUDHOU were the same person.) In the same manner we see that of BRAHMA followed in the same countries, and for as long a space of time. It is, therefore, not in history, but in the precepts of the two religions, that are to be found the *data* by which to decide this question. . . .

I am rather of opinion, upon a comparison of the two religions, that of BOUDHOU is the more ancient, for the following reasons—The religion of BOUDHOU having extended itself in very remote times, through every part of *India*, was in many respects monstrous and unformed. An uncreated world and mortal souls, are ideas to be held only in an infant state of society, and as society advances such ideas must vanish.—A fortiori, they cannot be established in opposition to a religion already prevailing in a country, the fundamental articles of which are the creation of the world and the immortality of the soul. Ideas in opposition to all religion cannot gain ground, at least cannot make head, when there is already an established faith; whence it is fair to infer, that if *Boudhism* could not have established itself among the *Brahmins*, and if it has been established in their country, that it must be the more ancient of the two. . . .

But to return to GAUTEME BOUDHOU: he is generally called SAMAN GAUTEME BOUDHOU VAHANSE; the Lord Saint GAUTEME BOUDHOU. It has been justly observed, that the SAMONOCODUM of the people of *Siam* is the same as the BOUDHOU of the *Singalese*. But I do not know that the analogy in the names has as yet been observed. We see now that SAMONO and SAMAN resemble each other; and that CODOM can be easily taken for GAUTEME. BOUDHOU, in one of his three voyages to *Lankadwipe*, the island of *Ceylon*, left on the top of *Jaman alé Sripade*, Adam's peak, the print of one of his feet; but though I have been at great pains to find it out, I have not as yet been able to ascertain whether it was his right or his left foot: and I am convinced that it must be, universally, a matter of doubt, for all the feet of BOUDHOU that I have seen in the temples are so awkwardly made, that there is no distinguishing the little toe from the great one. There is also a print of BOUDHOU's foot in *Siam*, but from the accounts of travellers, it is equally uncertain whether it is his right or his left; it suffices to know, that is the mark of BOUDHOU. This not being doubted by any of the *Singalese*, the very good christians excepted, to whom the *Portuguese* priests have clearly proved that this is the mark of ADAM's foot. The *Boudhists* of *Ceylon*, however, discredit the account of BOUDHOU having stridden from *Siam* to *Ceylon*, having one of his feet at each of these places at the same time. As BOUDHOU was but eighteen cubits high, it is a thing impossible according to their own tenets.

GAUTAME BOUDHOU was the son of a king of GIAMBU DWIPE, called SOUDODENE MAHA RAGIA, whose kingdom was one of these seven large stones that I have not been able to learn the names of; his mother was called MAYA, or rather *Maha* MAYA.—He was there known under the name of Prince SIDHARTE; he had a son by his wife JASSODERA DEVI, who was called RAHOULE, and who succeeded to the throne on the death of his father. Having in vain attempted, during four *asankes*, more than a hundred thousand *mahakalpes*, to become BOUDHOU, he at last made himself a pilgrim. At the end of six years pilgrimage, an account of which is given in a large volume, he became BOUDHOU; in forty-five years after, *Nivani*; having established an order of things in this *Mahakalpe*, which is to last for five thousand years; after which, there will be several changes in the present system; long wars and a successive diminution in the lives of men, till they are reduced so low as not to continue beyond five years; and every one will commit, during this short space of time, unheard crimes. A terrible rain will sweep from the face of the earth all except a small number of good people, who will receive timely notice of the evil, and will avoid it. All the wicked, after being drowned, will be changed into beasts, till at length MAITRI BOUDHOU will appear, and will establish a new order of things; he is now alive for the last time but one, and inhabits one of the superior heavens.[1]

◆ **FRANCIS HAMILTON (1762–1829)**

A particularly well-traveled scholar was the Scottish surgeon and botanist Francis Hamilton. A member of the Buchanan clan of Scotland, in 1818 he changed his surname to Buchanan; we thus find his earlier works under the name of Francis Hamilton and later ones under the name of Francis Buchanan.

After spending ten years as a ship's surgeon, in 1795 Hamilton was assigned to the first British mission to the kingdom of Ava (in modern Burma), during which he assembled a substantial herbarium of Burmese flora. It was during his time there that he met the Italian missionary Vincenzo Sangermano (whom we met in the previous chapter). Using materials given to him by the Catholic priest, in 1801 Hamilton published a long article in Asiatick Researches *entitled "On the Religion and Literature of the Burmas," which provided one of the most extensive descriptions of Buddhism to date. In 1802, Hamilton was posted to Kathmandu, where he collected Nepalese plants. However, he did not desist from his study of religion. In 1819, after his return to Scotland (and after changing his surname), he published* An Account of the Kingdom of Nepal *(see the excerpt later in this chapter), in which he compared the Buddhism he had observed in Burma with that of the Newar and Tibetan communities in Kathmandu.*

Throughout his travels, Dr. Hamilton seems to have kept abreast of the growing scholarship on Buddhism, which he surveys in the passage from "On the Religion and Literature of the Burmas" that appears below. As will be clear, despite his extended contact with Buddhist communities, he also held fast to the African hypothesis, although he parted company with Sir William Jones on the two-buddha theory. He

understood that Buddhism had once been widespread in India, and believed, as
many did, that it had been driven out by the Brahmins.

Much of "On the Religion and Literature of the Burmas" is taken up with the
translation of a summary of Buddhism written by a Burmese monk, which appears
in the previous chapter in the entry from Vincenzo Sangermano. However, Buchanan
precedes this with a long preface that provides an overview of the state of scholarship
on the Buddha in 1801, making mention of a number of the figures we have encoun-
tered thus far.

––––

HAVING now considered in a general manner the religion and science of the *Bur-*
mas, I must descend somewhat more to particulars: and in giving an account
of their faith, I cannot follow a better guide than the treatise of the ZARADO. It
will give the reader not only a faithful abridgment of the religious doctrine of the
Răhāns, but will also show him the progress made by the best informed priests of
the country in the art of composition and instruction.

BUT as a preface to this treatise, I must here insert some observations on the
history and name of the god.

THE author of the *Alphabetum Tibetanum* supposed BOUDDHA to have been
the same with the JESUS of the *Manichæans*; and father PAULINUS, in his triumph
over this absurdity, denies that any such person ever existed. Entirely neglecting
the authority of the numerous sects of BOUDDHA, who all suppose him to have
really lived, and to have been an *Indian* prince, the learned *Carmelite* from some
coincident attributes believes BOUDDHA and HERMES to have been the same. He
supposes them, as well as all the other gods of the *Greeks* and *Brahmens*, not to
have been real beings, but personifications of the elements and heavenly bodies.
In applying this supposition to BOUDDHA, as worshipped by the *Răhāns*, he quite
overlooks the essential difference of their making GODAMA an only God, and that
the doctrine of personification necessarily implies polytheism, a system of belief
held in abhorrence by these priests. I think it a more probable opinion, when the
Brahmens introduced their doctrine into *Hindustan*, that they could not venture
to deny the divinity of the god of the country; but on comparing his attributes
with those of their different gods, that they alleged him to be the same with their
TOTH; and by adopting him and his titles into the list of their deities, and many of
the prejudices of his followers into their capacious system, they greatly facilitated
the progress of their doctrine. It is true, that the various accounts of GODAMA,
said to be given in the legends of the different nations following his religion, agree
so little together, that they can hardly be made matter of historical evidence. But

many of these differences may have arisen from the mistakes of travellers; and it is only by procuring faithful translations of the different legends, that we can be enabled to determine what credit is due to their contents. In the mean time I must say, that I know of no plausible reason for believing that GODAMA did not exist, and was not an *Indian* prince, as his followers universally allege. The father, although a catholick, seems to found his objection on the supposition, that mankind could never be so absurd as for any length of time to worship a man. But the whole difficulty with PAULINUS is removed by the doctrine of GODAMA. His followers are, strictly speaking, atheists, as they suppose every thing to arise from fate: and their gods are merely men, who by their virtue acquire supreme happiness, and by their wisdom become entitled to impose a law on all living beings. If the BOUDDHA of the *Rāhāns* were merely the genius of the planet Mercury, as PAULINUS so violently urges, why do his followers place his abode or palace in the lowest habitation of *Nat*, among beings equally liable with mankind to old age, misery, change, and gravity? That the *Egyptian* religion was allegorical, I think, the learned father, with many other writers, have rendered extemely [*sic*] probable; and consequently I think that the doctrine of the *Brahmens* has in a considerable measure the same source: but I see no reason from thence to suppose, that BOUDDHA, RAMA, KISHEN, and other gods of *India*, may not have existed as men: for I have already stated it as probable, when the *Brahmens* arrived in *India*, that they adapted their own religious doctrine to the heroes and fabulous history of the country. Neither do I think it altogether impossible, that even in *Egypt* the priests, who at first introduced the worship of the elements and heavenly bodies, afterwards applied to these deities the names of such persons as were most celebrated among their countrymen, and intermingling the legendary tales concerning these personages with their own mystical philosophy, produced that absurd mass of theology, by which a great part of mankind have been so long subjugated.

DIFFERENT learned men have supposed BOUDDHA to have been the same with NOAH, MOSES, or SIPHOAS, thirty-fifth king of *Egypt*: but as I have not at present access to the works of HUET, VOSSIUS, or TOURMONT, I do not know on what reasons such suppositions have been formed. Sir W. Jones supposed BOUDDHA to have been the same with SESAC or SESOSTRIS, king of *Egypt*, "Who by conquest spread a new system of religion and philosophy, from the *Nile* to the *Ganges*, about 1,000 years before CHRIST." The affinity of the religion of *Egypt* with the present superstition of the *Hindustan*, and the fatal resemblance of the words SESAC and SAKYA, one of the names of GODAMA, seem to have given rise to this supposition. In my opinion, however, no two religions can be well more different, than that of the *Egyptian* polytheist, and that of the *Burma* unitarian. SESAC or SESOSTRIS is indeed placed by antiquarians at the time to which the learned judge alludes: but I shall hereafter have occasion to show, that, according to the most probable accounts, the origin of the religion of GODAMA ought to be referred to a much later period. That the religion of the *Brahmens* was introduced from *Egypt*, I have already mentioned as an opinion highly probable: but I suspect that this happened by no means so early as the time of SESOSTRIS, whose object in his military expeditions appears rather to have been plunder, and the captures of slaves, than the propagation of religion or philosophy. The persecution of the *Egyptian* priests by CAMBYSES is a more likely period for any very extensive emigration into *India*; at the same time it is not improbable, that the *Egyptians*, who before this traded to *India*, had previously communicated some knowledge of their science to the *Hindus*.

IT must be observed that the god, of whose doctrine we are now going to give an explanation, has a great variety of names, which are apt to produce much confusion. GODAMA or KODAMA is the most common appellation among his worshippers in *India* beyond the *Ganges*. It seems also to be common among the *Hindus*, and by Sir WILLIAM JONES copying I suppose from the *Sanscrit*, it is written GOTAMAS. This name PAULINUS informs us may be written GODAMA or GAUDAMA, and literally signifies cow-herd, but metaphorically king. It has however been mentioned to me, on the authority of a pundit belonging to our supreme native court in *Bengal*, that the meaning of GODAMA is eminently wise, a sage. SOMONA, the name prefixed to this appellation by M. DE LA LOUBERE, signifies that he had adopted the dress of a *Răhăn*, as I was informed by MUE-DAUNG SEIT-AGIO, an intelligent *Siammese* painter at *Amarapura*. The same circumstance is implied by BURA-ZAYNDU, one of the most common titles bestowed on him in the *Burma* empire: for his images are almost always in the dress of a *Răhăn*. Many other appellations are given to GODAMA from the postures in which he is represented in his various images. Thus a famous image at *Pougan* is named ANANDA, which signifies plenty, from its supposed efficacy in producing that blessing.

In the *Pali* language, and among the *Cingalese*, a common name for this divinity is BOUDDHA. This Mr. CHAMBERS writes BUDDOU, PAULINUS BUDHA, and from these two authors I have collected the following corruptions of that name. BUDDA, or BUTTA, of BEAUSOBRE and BOCHART, BOD of the *Arabians*, BODDA of EDRISI, *Boutta* of CLEMENS ALEXANDRINUS, and BAOUTH of M. GENTIL. This name is said to be an appellation expressive of wisdom. I can readily agree with these two learned men, that the POUT of the *Siamese*, POUT, POTT, POTI, POT of the natives of *Thibet*, and the BUT of the *Cochinchinese*, may also be corruptions of BOUD-DHA. The *Siammese* painter told me, that the most common name for GODAMA among his countrymen is POUTTEE SAT, which he interpreted into BURALOUN, a common appellation among the *Burmas*. Among these indeed I very rarely heard BOUDDHA used, probably because BURALOUN has the same meaning. Mr. CHAM-BERS, following M. GENTIL, and followed by PAULINUS, conceives the FO or FOHI of the *Chinese* to be also a corruption of BOUDDAH. The etymology is here so forced, that I do not think it merits great attention: yet I allow it to be a probable opinion, although not completely established, that FO and BOUDDHA are the same god. The derivation of TAAUTOS, TOTH, or TOUTH, the *Egyptian* name from HER-MES, from the same word BOUDDHA, seems to me perfectly fanciful: and I must entirely dissent even from the rational Mr. CHAMBERS, when he supposed BOUD-DHA to be the same with the WODEN of the *Scandinavians*. No two religions surely can be more different; nor can I conceive it to be a sufficient proof of a common origin, that the same day of the week is called after the two gods. No circumstance indeed seems to have occasioned more mistakes among the antiquarians, than from one or two coincident attributes to suppose two divinities of different nations to be the same: an error adopted by all the *Greeks* and *Romans*, whether from re-spect to their gods, or from national vanity.

A CONSIDERABLE degree of confusion is to be found in the various accounts of the religions of the *Chinese*. GROSIER, the latest author on the subject, with whom I have met, seems by no means to have had good information. I know well that some of the *Brahmenical* gods are worshipped in *China*, having seen their images in that great temple opposite to *Canton*, which was the palace of the last native princes of the *Chinese* empire. I have lately seen some elegant drawings of the *Chinese* gods, belonging to the Reverend Mr. BROWN, of *Calcutta*: and as far as I can trust my own memory, they appear to be very exact representations. Al-though the *Chinese* have given to these idols their own features, and dress, with new names, yet there can be no doubt of their being the same with the gods of the *Brahmens*. Among them YOU-LOE-FAT, the god of wisdom, has a very strong re-semblance to the images of GODAMA; and perhaps the *Chinese* ambassadors, and their suite, whom I saw at *Amarapura* worshipping the images of BOUDDHA, con-ceived the two deities to be the same. When in the first century of the *Christian* æra the superstition of a *Chinese* monarch had introduced into his dominions the religion of the *Brahmens*, his successors were too just to hinder their subjects from worshipping what gods they thought proper; but they were too wise to admit the *Brahmens* as priests, or to tolerate their intriguing spirit, or their detestable system of government; a conduct entirely similar to that wisely adopted towards the *Jesuits* by the late emperor YONG-TCHING. On the whole I am inclined to believe, that the religion most commonly professed by the vulgar *Chinese*, has nearly the same affinity to that of the *Brahmens*, which the sect of quakers has to our established church. It is true, that they have *Bonzes*, or regular priests: but these are neither *Brahmens*, nor are they acknowledged by the *Răhāns* to be legitimate priests of BOUDDHA. But the worship of these *Brahmenical* gods, as communicated to the *Chinese*, is quite distinct from that of GODAMA. Whether the god FO be one of these gods of the *Brahmens*, or whether he be SHAKA, or whether all the three be distinct, I will not presume, for want of sufficient information, to assert; but there is a great probability, that a very considerable sect among the *Chinese* worship GODAMA under the name of SHAKA, or, as the *Portuguese* write it, XACA.

THE sect of the BOUDDHA is said by some to have been introduced into *China* in the year of our æra 63. Others allege, that this even did not happen till the year 519: and that the apostle was a certain DARMA, third son of an *Indian* king, the twenty-eighth in descent from SHAKA, or as, the *Dutch* write, SJAKA. The name SHAKA Sir WILLIAM JONES wrote SAKYA, and PAULINUS SHAKYA. It signifies, according to that learned etymologist, the cunning, the god of good and bad fortune. From *China* the religion of SHAKA seems to have spread to *Japan, Tonquin, Cochinchina*, and the most remote parts of *Tartary*.

IT must however be observed, that the religion of *Cochinchina*, described by BOIRET as that of BUT, THAT-DALNA, NHIN-NHUC or THICA MAUNI-PHUT, and alleged to have been introduced from *Ceylon* in the reign of the *Chinese* emperor MINH-DE, seems to differ in many essential circumstances from the doctrine of the *Burma Răhāns*. The *Cochinchinese* are alleged to suppose, that BUT created the heavens, the earth, and indeed the whole universe: and from BOIRET's mentioning that they adore BUT as the principal deity, we may infer, that they allow of other gods. The priests of the *Cochinchinese* are alleged to be pretenders to the arts of magic, enchantment and necromancy, and to implore the divinity to assist them in such deceptions. In these circumstances the worship of BUT in *Cochinchina* differs from that of BOUDDHA in *Ava*; and I suspect, that there, as well as in *China*, the prevailing vulgar religion is the worship of the gods of the *Brahmens* freed from the doctrine of cast; and that BOUDDHA is with them the favourite god, as different members of the *Egyptian* theocracy in different places met with very different degrees of respect. Still however the accounts I have seen of the vulgar religion in these eastern regions are very unsatisfactory; and the hints given us by ALEXANDER of *Rhodes*, concerning the doctrine of THICCA in *Tonkin* and *Co-*

chinchina, bear a much stronger resemblance to the worship of the *Răhāns*, than the accounts of BOIRET.

THESE various names applied to the god, of whom I am treating, are all appellatives, expressing his various attributes, as we use the terms, almighty, the most high, and other familiar phrases, to denote the Creator of the universe. Many other appellations of BOUDDHA may be seen in PAULINUS, who copies them from the *Amarasinha*, a work of the *Hindus*; but as I do not know, that these titles are ever bestowed on GODAMA by those who worship him as the only god, I shall forbear to enumerate them.

THE name by which this divinity was called on earth, was probably DHERMA or DHARMA rajah; although it must be observed, that among the *Hindus* it has never been customary to call any prince by his proper name. This custom has been communicated to the *Burmas* with such strength, that it is almost impossible to learn the name of any prince during his reign. His titles can only lawfully be mentioned; and the law is enforced with such rigour, that *Burmas*, even in *Calcutta*, shudder when requested to mention the dreadful name; nor am I satisfied, that either Captain SYMES, or I, could ever procure the real name of the reigning monarch. DHERMA rajah signifies, according to PAULINUS, the virtuous or beneficent king, and may be only a title bestowed on that prince, whose real name, as his reign still continues, it may not be lawful to mention. This etymologist also alleges, that the name HERMES must be derived from the *Sanscrit* word *Dherma*, signifying virtue or beneficence: although interpreter was imagined to be the meaning of this word by the *Greeks*, as the father probably would say, owing to their ignorance of the *Samfordam*, as he has chosen to name the language of the *Hindus*. His opinion however is supported with ingenuity; and the word *Turm*, which WINCKELMANN luckily found upon two old pots in *Italy*, is by no means a weak support to an etymological reasoner. Having thus endeavoured to collect the various appellations bestowed on the god of the *Burmas*, I proceed with the translation of "A Short View of the Religion of Godama."[2]

✦ ALEXANDER HAMILTON (1762–1824)

The Edinburgh Review, *founded in 1802, would become one of the most influential British periodicals of the nineteenth century. In 1806, it carried a review of the seventh volume of* Asiatick Researches. *Although articles in this scholarly journal were anonymous, there is good reason to believe that the review, excerpted below, is by Lieutenant Alexander Hamilton, a former officer of the East India Company whose love of classical Indian literature was so great that he was known as "Sanscrit Hamilton." He is remembered today for giving Sanskrit lessons in Paris while under house arrest after the Treaty of Amiens was broken by Napoleon.*

The passage below is concerned with an article excerpted in chapter 4, "On Sin-ghala, or Ceylon, and the Doctrines of Bhooddha, from the Books of the Singhalais" by Captain Mahony. The reviewer concludes, mistakenly, that Mahony's essay holds an importance of which its author was unaware: it demonstrates that Buddhists wor-ship Vishnu.

———

The writer of this article pretends no acquaintance with the sacred language of Ceylon. The fruits of his inquiries are given without pretension to erudition, and evidently without suspecting the important consequences deducible from the in-formation he has furnished. But that information leads to results so singularly in-teresting, though unforeseen by the author, that his dissertation proves infinitely more curious in the volume before us, and will demand from us rather an ample commentary than a succinct statement.

The religion of Buddha seems, at one period, to have been prevalent over great part of Hindûstan; but though now nearly extinct in that country, his doctrines may still vie, in point of extensive domination, with those of Mohamed. The rich and populous plains of Siam, Pegu, and Ava; the whole Chinese empire and its tributary kingdoms; the theocratic states of Budtan and Tibet; all the Tartar tribes, excepting the few who have embraced Islamism; the inhabitants of Ceylon, and most of the eastern isles, follow the tenets, and celebrate the rites prescribed by the system of faith distinguished by that appellation. These tenets, indeed, have never been satisfactorily explained. Some information may be collected on the subject, from a memoir of M. de Guignes, extracted from Chinese documents. M. de la Loubera furnishes some popular legends in his instructive account of Siam: the celebrated Pallas presents a variety of facts in his account of the Monghols: but these combined sources afford very imperfect information, and the *desiderata* are ill supplied by the reveries of Georgi, seduced, by some fancied analogies with the Christian religion, to imagine that this ancient superstition was only a modern perversion of its sacred truths. Our own travellers, Symes and Turner, occupied with more important researches during the brief period of their respective excur-sions, have neglected, or despised, inquiries into religious opinions. Hence, we are still ignorant whether the doctrines of Buddha, universally admitted to be a native of India, bear any, and what, affinity, with the religion of Brahma. By some they are considered as totally different, and of higher antiquity; whilst the Brahmans themselves class Buddha among their Avatára, of whom they consider him as the last.

Many circumstances, indeed, had induced us to imagine, that the Buddhists were a sect whose opinions were not materially different from those of other Hindus. Pallas had exhibited the cosmography of the Monghols, abounding in Sanscrit terms, and, in many particulars, similar to that given by Dr. Buchanan of the Burmans, which we have shown to be borrowed from the Bhuvana cosa, a geographical treatise found in greater or less detail in all the Puránâ. Colonel Symes makes mention of a dramatic entertainment, of which he was a spectator, in Pegu, founded on the history of Ráma the 7th Avatára; and Turner describes a monument at Tasisudon, on which the Hindu goddess Cáli was represented; and speaks of the celebration of the festival of Durgá, at the same place. These coincidences excited our suspicions that the two systems would be found, upon further examination, to be more nearly connected than was imagined. The paper before us, composed by an officer who has no hypothesis to support, and is probably little conversant with Hindu mythology, completely confirms the justice of our conjectures, and proves that, notwithstanding their rejection of the Vedá, the Buddhists are genuine Vaïsnava, or adorers of Visnu.

After mentioning the periodical destructions and renovations of the world, which forms a distinguishing feature in both systems, Captain Mahony adds, "For the government of the world at those different periods, there were twenty-two Buddhas, a proportionate number of whom belonged to each period." This number of *twenty-two* is too remarkable to be overlooked; and we find in the Bhagavat Purana, that the descents of Visnu upon earth were also twenty-two, though the ten called Avatára were the most remarkable. But as, in a discovery calculated to excite public curiosity, our authority may be called in question, we take leave to subjoin an abridged translation of the third chapter of the Bhágavat, of which two copies are deposited in the Imperial library of Paris.[3]

◆   EDWARD MOOR (1771–1848)

Edward Moor sailed for India as a cadet of the East India Company in 1783, when he was eleven years of age. In 1790, he commanded a grenadier company in the First Anglo-Maratha War, serving gallantly at the Siege of Dharwar, and was wounded in a battle in Bangalore. He later sustained two more wounds to his knee and was forced to return to England to convalesce, during which time he wrote a lengthy account of the war. Because he was permanently disabled by his wounds, when he returned to India in 1796, Moor was appointed garrison storekeeper in Bombay (known today as Mumbai). In 1800, at the request of the Governor of Bombay, he wrote Digest of the Military Orders and Regulations of the Bombay Army.

It was upon his permanent return to England that Moor wrote the book for which he is most famous, the lavishly illustrated Hindu Pantheon, *published in 1810. For each deity there was an engraving and a description, compiled by Moor from published works and from his correspondence with the Sanskrit scholars of the East India Company. The following is drawn from his description of the Buddha. Moor begins by explaining why the Brahmin priests of Hinduism did not like the Buddha. We see here also that more than a century after Dr. Kaempfer's claim, the African hypothesis lives on.*

———

SUCH *Hindus* as admit BUDDHA to be an incarnation of VISHNU, agree in his being the last important appearance of the deity on earth; but many among the *Brahmans*, and other tribes, deny their identity; and the *Buddhists*, countenanced by the *Rahans*, their priests, do, in general, likewise assert the independent existence, and of course paramount character, of the deity of their exclusive worship. As most of VISHNU's *Avataras* were apparently destined for the accomplishment of some especial object, so this of BUDDHA seems to have been for the purpose of reclaiming the *Hindus* from their proneness to animal sacrifice, and their prodigality even of human blood. A people having once satisfied themselves, that the fat of bulls, and kids and goats, is acceptable to their deities, and a priesthood having gained such a triumph as to persuade their deluded flock into a belief of the meritorious immolation of their brethren or themselves, cannot but with great difficulty be diverted from practices, and divested of feelings, so repugnant to humanity; their continued existence evincing their strength and tenacity. The mild heresy preached by BUDDHA, a leading tenet of which is the *sin of depriving any animal of life*, would naturally alarm the orthodox priesthood, whose coffers overflowed from the donations of affrighted sinners, and whose hierarchy was threated by the dawn of reason and the diffusion of philosophy. It cannot therefore be supposed, that such an innovation, condemning the prescribed doctrines of their most sacred books, and the practices founded on them of the most sacred sect, in its consequences deeply involving the supposed sanctity of both, could be contemplated by the *Brahmans* without considerable jealousy, or its progress witnessed without opposition. And we are accordingly informed, the *Buddhism* having in time so encroached on the respect antecedently shown to the *Brahmans*, and caused a great diminution of their flock, that latter were roused, not only to the exercise of legitimate and reasonable means of resistance, but at length to the excesses of invective, and the terrible resource of civil and religious persecution. Whatever rivalrous enmity might anciently have been excited, it seems now happily extinct: rivalry is no longer, and enmity died with it. The orthodox supremacy of the *Brahmans*, in almost all parts of the hither peninsula, views with piety, and perhaps with contempt, the heretical insignificance of the fallen *Rahans*, or priests of BUDDHA.

I am not sufficiently informed of the tenets or usages of the *Buddhists*, to say in what particulars especially consist the difference between them and the tenets and usages of the *Brahmans*. A continuance of many centuries will perhaps have widened those sectarial differences; but whatever they may now be, a very great dissonance in doctrine and superstition is not, I think, discoverable in times remote. . . .

Some statues of BUDDHA certainly exhibit thick *Ethiopian* lips; but all, with wooly hair: there is something mysterious, and still unexplained, connected with the hair of this, and only of this, *Indian* deity. The fact of so many different tales having been invented to account for his crisped woolly head, is alone sufficient to excite suspicion that there is something to conceal—something to be ashamed of; more exists than meets the eye. One authority asserts that he was born without hair: this is not peculiar, and, unless something extraordinary was connected with the hair of BUDDHA, need not to have been noticed.[4]

◆   FRANCIS WILFORD (1761–1822)

We first encountered Francis Wilford, remembered for his eccentric theories of the Indian origins of the Bible and for being duped by an Indian pundit, in chapter 4. Among his beliefs was that elements of early Christianity could be found in India; he discerned these, for example, in the dispute between the Buddha and the crucified Devadatta. Over one hundred years after Guy Tachard had dismissed the association of Devadatta with Jesus, Captain Wilford revives it here.

———

ESSAY V: *ORIGIN AND DECLINE OF THE*
CHRISTIAN RELIGION *IN* INDIA.

IV. The followers of BUDD'HA, in *Siam* and the *Burman Empire*, mention the wars of their legislator with DÉVE-TÁT, who, they say, is the legislator of the *Christians*. He is the same who is called a *Tacshaca* also by the *Hindus*, and who manifested himself in the first year of the *Christian Era*. They say that he was either a brother, or a relation of BUDD'HA; or in other words, he was a collateral form of BUDD'HA. They acknowledge some conformity between his doctrine and theirs; because, as they say, his disciples borrowed many things from BUDD'HA. He allowed them, however, to kill and eat all sorts of animals, and seduced very many of the disciples of BUDD'HA; and, aspiring to sovereignty, he waged war against SAMAŃA-GAUTAMA. He appeared at the head of a new sect, and engaged several kings and nations to join him. He had the gift of miracles, and asserted that he was a god. DÉVE-TÁT being several times worsted in this war, made overtures of peace, and SAMAŃA-GAUTAMA consented, on condition that he would subscribe to three articles which he was going to propose. These were to worship, first, God; then his word; and thirdly, the person who imitates the divine perfection, or, in other words, to worship BUDD'HA. This last article was rejected by DÉVE-TÁT or his disciples, and they went to war again, when DÉVE-TÁT was defeated in the forest of *Sálatúyah* in the *Peninsula*. He was taken prisoner, and empaled alive, with his limbs trussed up, upon a double cross; and in that state hurled into the infernal regions. 'SAMAŃA-GAUTAMA, however, foretold, that in the end he would really become a god. BUDD'HA, or GAUTAMA is also represented waging war with PRA-ÀRIA-SERIA, for PRA-ÀRYYÁ-'SIRA, the venerable chief, or Sire of the *Àrryás* or *Christians*; and another chief of them, called PRA-SWANE, or PRA-'SWANA, from his loudly preaching against the doctrine of GAUTAMA. BUDD'HA and DÉVA-TWASHŤÁ are made contemporaries in this romance: but this can be no objection; for it is only in allusion to the wars of their followers in subsequent times. The learned are very well acquainted, that this mode of writing history once prevailed in the west at a very early period.[5]

◆   WILLIAM ERSKINE (1773–1852)

William Erskine traveled to India in 1804 at the invitation of his fellow Scotsman Sir James Mackintosh, eventually securing a position as clerk to the small-cause court in Bombay (known today as Mumbai). An amateur scholar, he assisted Mackintosh in founding the Literary Society of Bombay that same year.

Erskine taught himself Persian and devoted great efforts to translating the memoirs of Babur (1483–1531), the first Mughal emperor of India. He also developed an interest in the Buddhist, Jain, and Hindu temples in the region, including a remarkable group of caves filled with Hindu and Buddhist statues on Elephanta Island in Bombay Harbor. On November 2, 1813, he read a paper to the Literary Society of Bombay entitled

"Account of the Cave-Temple of Elephanta with a Plan of the Drawings of the Principal Figures." In the following passage taken from this paper, Erskine draws conclusions about Hinduism and Buddhism based on the statues he encountered.

———

When the Brahmins are taxed with idolatry, they always excuse themselves, as has been already remarked, by alleging the necessity of making an impression on rude minds by means of some intelligible symbols, on which the ignorant may fix their thoughts, and to which they may look for reward and punishment.

As in many of their incarnations the gods are supposed to have appeared with several heads, with the heads of animals, with a number of hands, and other singularities; their images in the temples correctly represent all these peculiarities.

All Brahmanical excavations that I have observed are flat-roofed within, and most of them incline to a square, though they frequently have an oblong figure.

The religion of the Bouddhists differs very greatly from that of the Brahmins; as in the latter, God is introduced everywhere,—in the former, he is introduced no where. The gods of the Brahmins pervade and animate all nature; the god of the Bouddhists, like the god of the Epicureans, remains in repose, quite unconcerned about human affairs, and therefore is not the object of worship. With them there is no intelligent divine being who judges of human actions as good or bad, and rewards or punishes that as such;—this indeed is practically the same as having no God. Good and ill, according to their creed, are however supposed to spring invariably from virtue and vice; there being as they believe an inseparable and necessary connexion between virtue and prosperity, vice and misfortune. Yet, as the mind of man must have some object of confidence on which to rest its hopes and to which to direct its supplication and prayer, they teach that from time to time men of surpassing piety and self-denial have appeared on the earth, and from their singular worth have after death been transferred to a state of superior bliss; which state, however, they say that we can only intimate by describing it as an absence of all pain, as we can only define health as an absence of all disease. These saints or prophets, after reforming the world in their lifetime, and by their superior sanctity attaining the power of performing miracles, are still imagined after death to have certain powers of influencing us. It is these men transferred by death to bliss who are the object of Bouddhist worship. This worship assumes different forms in different countries, and is by some supposed to be more widely diffused than any other religion. In Siam it is chiefly paid to Godoma or Sommona-Codom: but it is worthy of remark, that wherever this form of religion prevails in its original state, the relics of these holy men or saints are the object of worship. The largest temples are often in the form of a pyramid or of the section of a globe, and are supposed to contain a tooth, hair, or other relic of a saint. The forms of these holy places have been adopted from the custom prevalent in these countries of depositing the ashes of the deceased under a pyramid or globular mound: the pyramids are often of great size, and on their summits are umbrellas which are frequently adorned with bells; sometimes this pyramid is gilded over. Other temples of nearly similar construction, but hollow within, contain images to which adoration is directed. The images of these saints have different attitudes, sometimes sitting cross-legged in a meditative posture, sometimes standing upright.

As all the ideas of this religion relate to men, and as no incarnations or transformations of superior beings are recorded, it is obvious that in their temples we can expect to find no unnatural images, no figures compounded of man and beast, no monsters with many hands or many heads.

As the priests and scholars of the Bouddhists live in a sort of collegiate establishment near some great temples, we shall find a multitude of such cells around the excavation in their cave-temples; and while all such cells are flat-roofed, the great temple is supported on two rows of pillars with aisles, and is uniformly vaulted and oblong.[6]

◆ GEORGE STANLEY FABER (1773–1854)

The remarkable Anglican cleric and biblical scholar George Stanley Faber first gained notoriety in 1799, when he preached sermons at Oxford in which he connected five of the seven vials of wrath mentioned in Revelation 16—"And I heard a great voice out of the temple saying to the seven angels, Go your ways, and pour out the vials of the wrath of God upon the earth"—with recent events. He would later identify the pouring of the fifth vial—"And the fifth angel poured out his vial upon the seat of the beast; and his kingdom was full of darkness"—with Napoleon's escape from Elba in 1815. In the following year, Faber published the three-volume Origin of Pagan Idolatry Ascertained from Historical Testimony and Circumstantial Evidence, *from which an excerpt follows.*

Like Sir William Jones before him, Faber placed great stock in the existence of flood stories in the myths of many nations, seeing them as confirmation of the flood account in Genesis. All humanity thus has descended from the three sons of Noah: Ham, Shem, and Japheth. According to Genesis 11, their offspring, that is, all mankind, assembled into a single community that spoke a single language. They gathered on a plain in the land of Shinar and began building a tower—what would come to

be known as the Tower of Babel—that would reach up to heaven. God, fearing that
they would be able to do whatever they imagined, "confounded their language," and
scattered them across the face of the earth.

Reading extensively in the scholarly journals of the day such as Asiatick Researches, *Faber discerned sets of three in the various forms of idolatry of the world*
and ascribed this to the origin of humanity in the three sons of Noah. Because all hu-
manity once spoke a single language before God's intervention, he also placed great
stock in (false) cognates.

——————

Brahmenism may be prior to Buddhism, or Buddhism may be prior to Brahmenism, in the *particular* country of Hindostan: but this will not establish the superior
antiquity of either, so far as its *primeval* origin is concerned. Without attempting
to determine the question of *local* priority, the settling of which is no way necessary to my present plan, I certainly think it manifest, that each system is *as old* as
the dispersion from Babel: and I think it equally manifest, both for reasons which
will hereafter appear, and because Buddhism is on the whole more simple than
Brahmenism, that Buddhism is the more ancient system of the two, having been
struck out even prior to the building of the tower. . . .

The identity of Thoth and Buddha cannot be doubted: and, when their history
is inquired into, it can be as little doubted, that they are severally the great father,
who is primarily Adam and secondarily Noah. But the character of these deities
runs into that of Idris and Edris: and as they appear no less than he to be the patri-
arch Enoch, so he no less than they will prove also to be the great father who was
manifested at the commencement of both worlds.

In allusion to the triple offspring of Adam and Noah, the oriental Buddha was
believed to have triplicated himself, and is pronounced to be the same as the triad
springing from unity. Much the same idea seems to have been entertained of Thoth
or Hermes, as we may collect from the title of *Thrice-greatest* which was bestowed
upon him: for, as his identity with Buddha may be distinctly proved from other
considerations, and as Buddha was esteemed as a triple deity, the descriptive title
of Thoth must obviously be understood as relating to his supposed triplication.[7]

✦ MICHEL-JEAN FRANÇOIS OZERAY (1764–1859)

In 1817, the French scholar Michel-Jean François Ozeray published a small book en-
titled Recherches sur Buddou ou Bouddou. *The full English title would be* Research
on Buddou or Bouddou, Religious Founder of East Asia; Preceded by General

Considerations on the First Worship Rendered to the Creator, on the Corruption of Religion, the Establishment of Cults of the Sun, Moon, Planets, Sky, Earth, Mountains, Waters, Forests, Humans, and Animals. *Ozeray was not an officer of the East India Company, nor, it seems, was he someone with a particular interest in Asia. His other books are histories of France and regions of France, along with a history of the cathedral at Chartres.*

In his discussion of the Buddha, Ozeray concludes that all the figures known by those many names are undeniably the same person; "in order to be convinced, it would be enough, in the absence of other evidence, to cast a glance upon the principal statues that one sees in the temples raised in his honor: they are presented, apart from some slight differences, in the same principal aspect. Its attitude announces meditation; the body is dressed in a great robe; the head covered with a cap, which varies according to localities; the eyes fixed upon the ground and motionless, the legs crossed, the hands joined or supported in such and such a manner on the knees." (He mistakes the Buddha's hair for a cap.)

What is noteworthy about Ozeray's discussion, excerpted below, is that he sees the Buddha above all as a philosopher. He is flawed, because his religion does not reject polytheism, and yet his teaching of morality should be praised for countering coarse error and superstitition. Ozeray is familiar with the accounts of the life of the Buddha from the eighteenth century and draws from them. In a sense, he seeks to demythologize the Buddha, while conceding that the Buddha is deified in Asia. At the end of the book he lists the countries, along with population figures, where "the doctrine and fable of the Buddha triumphed over ancient superstitions."

———

It is an undeniable fact; Boudou is a famous personage; he was not wrested from oblivion through the pains of a hardworking annalist or a skilful antiquarian. It is neither to an inscription nor to a medallion that he owes a new existence; he is known by his life and his morals. Descended from the altar where blindness and superstition had placed him, Boudou is a distinguished philosopher, a sage born for the happiness of his fellow creatures and for the good of humanity.

Divinized man, he is the foremost of the religious legislators of East Asia. His doctrine, though of the second wave of error, while destroying coarse superstitions, still preserves the vice of its origin: it is infected with polytheism. As for morality, the author presents, but often exaggerates the duties of man, seduced by the desire to make him love them more.

His influence has not been the same everywhere. Here Bouddism triumphs over beliefs that cannot be understood, short-lived unwritten traditions, about local divinities worshipped with the most passionate devotion in times of prosperity, objects of contempt and hatred in a moment of despair. There it opposes its false wisdom to authorized errors, to a glimmer of philosophy, to the seduction of the example, to the sway of usage, to the force of habit.[8]

◆   ROBERT FELLOWES (1770–1847)

Robert Fellowes was an Anglican clergyman and philanthropist who wrote extensively on a range of topics, with a special interest in religion. A liberal with deist views, he is the author of The Religion of the Universe: With Consolatory Views of a Future State, and Suggestions on the Most Beneficial Topics of Theological Instruction.

In 1817, under the pseudonym Philalethes, Fellowes published a history of Ceylon, which had recently come under British control. In the passages from that history which appear below, he presents two lengthy versions of the life of the Buddha, complete with footnotes where he discusses his sources, which include François Valentijn's Oud en Nieuw Oost-Indiën *(Old and New East Indies), excerpted in chapter 4. In his notes he also comments on various points of scholarly inquiry, such as the place of origin of the Buddha and whether Buddhism or Brahmanism came first. The first selection covers the Buddha's entire life; the second dwells at length on the period from his birth to his enlightenment. Although Fellowes generally refrains from editorial comment, he declares at one point, "Truth is uniform and consistent, but fiction is variable and incongruous; and therefore it is no wonder that the accounts of Boodh, which are a tissue of fables, should be very dissimilar and inconsistent."*

———

CHAP. XXX.

Worship of Boodh; fabulous Account of his Nativity. His early
Achievements; his Marriage. He retires into a Wood; a magnificent
Seat dropped from Heaven. Hostility of the Devils to his Worship; their
desperate Attack upon Boodh; their total Discomfiture. Boodh sheltered
in a violent Storm by the flat Head of a huge Serpent. The Devils tempt
Boodh in the Form of Women. He enters a Tower of Rubies; sees a Host
of Angels; teaches his Doctrine at Sewetnure; retires to another Town,
where he dies in a Fruit Garden. His disciples comforted for his Loss.
Inconsistency in the Accounts of Boodh. Saints or Deities subordinate to
Boodh; Modes of Worship.

THE present worship* of the Singalese owes its origin to Boodh, who appeared in the island 623 years before the birth of Christ. The priests of the country assert that Boodh, whose footstep is still to be seen on the top of Adam's Peak, came to this island from the east, and left his laws for their instruction on tables of stone. His height was twelve feet, and each foot equal to two of ordinary mortals. They say that this Boodh, before he came into the world, had his abode in the third heaven, where he ruled over millions of angels. He found that men were living in a sort of moral anarchy, without laws or institutions; and were plunged in an abyss of ignorance and misery. He accordingly ordered it so, that he should come into the world from the maternal bosom† of the Queen or Empress Mahamajedewi, and he first opened his eyes upon the light of this sublunary sphere, in a pleasure garden of the King or Emperor Zuddodene Raja. On his first appearance he seemed to be seven years of age. He made seven steps to the east, seven to the west, seven to the south, seven to the north, where, lifting up his right hand, in a posture of supplication, and invoking God, he sunk into a cradle and assumed the form of a new-born child. The king indulged in a transport of joy at the birth of this marvellous child, had him brought to his court, and called him by the name of Ziddatare Cumanca, or the prince who hopes to do whatever he desires.

He performed many wonderful feats before his sixteenth year, when the Emperor of Candy resolved to marry him to the Princess Jasodera, who had been born on the same day with Boodh. This princess was the daughter of the King Andusaek Raja, and the Queen Ammitanam Bisso, whose family was as ancient as that of the emperor and empress. After the celebration of his marriage, Boodh and his wife lived together for thirteen years, and had one son, to whom they gave the name of

---

* Valentyn has remarked, that the Singalese, in one part of the island, agree in the names of their deities and in their religious rites, with those of the people on the coast of Malabar; and, in another, with those of the Siamese. The places, in which they were formerly wont to celebrate their religious worship, were denominated pagodas. The antient kings of Ceylon had erected in the neighbourhood of Trincomalée a pagoda, which was celebrated through India for its great extent and magnificence, but which was demolished by the Portuguese in 1622, when the stones were used in the construction of a fort.

Valentyn mentions, that there was a very antient prophecy respecting this pagoda, current among the Singalese. This prophecy, which was originally discovered on an old stone, had deen [sic] decyphered by some of the sages of Ceylon, and was found to signify that Manica Raja had erected this pagoda to the honour of the god Videmal, in the year 1300 before the Nativity, but that a certain people, denominated Franks, should come and destroy the same, and that another king should afterwards restore the sacred edifice to its original magnificence.

† "Hy quam," says the Dutchman, "uit het midden van haare borsten." His conception is said to have taken place on the full moon in the month of July, 622 years before the birth of Christ, and he was born on the full moon in the May of the following year.

Rahule Cumane. Boodh, finding that, if he took proper care of this child, he should not have sufficient time to devote to the instruction of mankind, determined to abandon his family and to retire into a wood, where he spent six years in a state of great indigence and distress. Whilst he was in this lonely situation, a magnificent stool, covered with a blaze of diamonds, fell from heaven under a white tree, named Zeremabod. The prophet sat down upon this sumptuous seat, and then went again out of the wood. On this occasion he assumed the name of Boodh.

Boodh had with him for a guard Thiakre Aramma Vishnu and Maheeschweere. They had each a dagger in their hand. The devils remarked that, after this none of their attempts upon mankind were successful; and that their power declined under the ascendant of Boodh. They accordingly resolved with their chief Wasse Mantimanda, to make a violent attack upon the author of this new sect, which threatened to cause a general apostacy from the worship of demons, and to become the universal faith.

The devils accordingly made their appearance like an embattled host, when they attacked Boodh with impetuous violence. But Boodh met them with a much more powerful army, whilst every blade of grass, tree, branch and leaf, converted into a shower of arms, assisted in the conflict. The devils could not long resist this accumulation of hostility. They vanished into smoke. After this victory, Boodh, in the joy of his triumph, assumed for a week the name of Gauteme Boodh, in order to denote that he had vanquished his enemies.

In the following week it began to rain violently, when the devils were very busy, although they did not dare to approach Boodh, whose prowess they had so lately experienced. But they saw, to their utter astonishment, that a snake of immense size had laid the flat part of its head on the head of Boodh, in order to protect him from the rain.

In the third week, the devils again showed themselves in the form of women, and practised all their wiles, in order to ensnare the affections of Boodh; but they were soon vanquished as before, and obliged hastily to retire.

In the fourth week, Boodh paid peculiar honours to the tree under which he sat.

In the fifth week, a tower of rubies descended from heaven, into which he entered, in order to receive the homage of his votaries.

In the sixth week, he left this tower, and retired under a tree, named Kiripallununge, where he beheld a multitude of angels in the air, in whose presence he glorified God in the language of love and praise.

In the seventh week he withdrew to a town called Sewetnure, where the Emperor Cosele Maha Raja had a place prepared for his reception. Here he taught his doctrines to kings, princes, and subjects. He now added five apostles to his mission, two of whom he placed on his right hand, and two on his left, whilst the fifth was appointed to minister to his necessities. Besides these he had 500 disciples, whom he employed to announce his mission, to diffuse his doctrines over the whole world, and to eradicate the heresies of other sects. He also composed different books, which were designed to preserve his doctrine, and to furnish precepts for the regulation of conduct. Here he remained occupied for forty-five years, till he went into the town of Cussirana Nure, in the province of Mallewe, when he retired into a fruit-garden belonging to the king, where reclining on a couch, which had been prepared to receive him, he expired in the same place, the same month, and the same hour, in which he was born.

His disciples were disconsolate for his loss; but they heard the admonitions of his spirit, saying, Do not lament because my time is come to depart out of the world. Burn my body, and lay my bones in the grave: but, above all, be diligent in maintaining the doctrine I have taught. He ordered that Ceylon, Siam, and Arracan, should particularly engage their attention, as the sovereignty of these countries was vested in the descendants of the emperor, Zuddodene Raja.

Truth is uniform and consistent, but fiction is variable and incongruous; and therefore it is no wonder that the accounts* of Boodh, which are a tissue of fables, should be very dissimilar and inconsistent.

* "Hy is elf maanden in de buik van zyn moeder geweest." Valentyn, p. 369. Undecim menses in utero matris fuit; and all this time his brightness rendered him as visible as a silken thread, which is run through a chrystal. In their accounts of Boodh, or Buddha, learned men differ about the age in which he lived, and the country in which his religious doctrines were first promulgated. It seems, however, to be highly probable, that the system which he inculcated was anterior to that of the Brahmins, by which it had begun to be superseded about the commencement of the Christian æra, though it maintained its ground in some parts of the peninsula of India till a later period. It is at this day diffused over the empire of the Birmans, and the kingdom of Siam and Cambodia. But in those countries, in which the votaries of Boodh were extirpated by those of Brahma, the latter adopted many of the notions of their predecessors, and the two religions have thus been in some degree amalgamated. They both prevail in Ceylon, rather in a state of amicable union than hostile separation. If the Island of Ceylon did not form the first cradle in which the religion of Boodh was fondled into life, nurtured in its growth, and matured in its strength, it seems certain, that it was introduced into this country from the continent of India soon after its commencement. Sir William Jones supposes Boodh, or Buddha, to have been the same with Sesostris, who, about ten centuries before the Christian æra, rendered his conquests subservient to the extension of a new religion from the Nile to the Ganges. But if Boodh and Sesostris were two names for the same individual, the mighty conqueror must have wreathed his sword in the olive branch when he promulgated his doctrine in the East; for the religion of Boodh is essentially a religion of peace; and conquerors are not very likely to inculcate truths that represent their greatest achievements as vile and contemptible, exciting the displeasure of God, and meriting the abhorrence of mankind. According to the Hindoos, Boodh was the ninth avatar, or descent of the Deity in the char-

The Singalese say that Boodh always wore a yellow dress, as a similar colour is still worn by his priests. They have also a tradition that he passed most of his time on Adam's Peak, where he resided at his death. They add, that he ascended to heaven from this spot; and they seem to have borrowed this circumstance of his history from some account which they had heard of the ascension of Christ.

In addition to Boodh, the religious calendar of the Singalese is distinguished by seven other saints or subordinate deities, to each of whom they ascribe peculiar powers and authorities. Of these they exhibit different external representations. One is seen in the shape of an elephant, another in that of the priapus of the ancients; one is figured as an ape, another as a beautiful horse: and all of them have the care of the water tanks.

They worship the images of all these saints; but this worship consists only in the form of placing their clasped hands upon the top of their heads, prostrating themselves three times upon the earth, and uttering this brief invocation: "Budhum Sarnaa Gochal;" O Boodh, think on me! This they never omit in their pagodas, but they practise no other forms of supplication; though, once in their lives, they pronounce three or four thousand prayers. But this solemnity they defer till they are very old; and it more especially belongs to a particular class of persons amongst them, who begin to accommodate themselves to the practice from early youth.

CHAP. XXXI.

Another Account of the Birth of Boodh, with a Variety of Mythological Details.

TWENTY-SIX Boodhs,* according to the traditions of the Singalese, preceded the birth of Gautama Boodh, whose doctrine was in a very remote period diffused

---

acter of preserver, or the ninth incarnation of Vishnu: and Sir William Jones asserts that the Boodh, or Buddha of the Hindoos, is the Fo, or Foe of the Chinese. Gaduma, Gautuma, or Gauda, is one of the appellations by which Boodh is often designated in the East. Kæmpfer, in his History of Japan, says, that a great saint, called Durma, and a twenty-third successor in the holy see of Seaka, Boodh, or Buddha, came over into China from Seilenseku, or from that part of the world which was westward with respect to Japan, and laid the first firm foundation of Boodhism in that populous empire. Though the worship of Brahma is a competitor for the palm of antiquity with that of Boodh, yet the priority of the latter appears to be the most credible, as the oldest books of the Brahmins make mention of Boodh, and so far establish the remote antiquity of his worship. A strong line of distinction is drawn between the Brahmins and the priests of Boodh by these peculiarities, that in the latter the priesthood is not indelible, that it does not constitute a caste, and that those who belong to it may eat flesh, though they may not put the animal to death.

   * The names of these twenty-six Boodhs, or sages, were Tanhankere, Metankere, Saranankere, Dipankare, Condanje, Mangela, Sumana, Reewette, Soobiette, Anomadasja, Paduma, Naradde, Som-

over a large part of the East. Gautama Boodh was born in heaven, under the name of Santusitte, but not till his birth had received the permission of the preceding Boodhs.

The sovereign of heaven, on this occasion, said to Santusitte—You have now received permission to become a Boodh: now therefore is the time appointed for you to appear in the world under that character. He was accordingly conceived in the womb of Mahamajadevi, the Queen of King Suddenam Raddure. His mother was surprised by the pains of labour, as she was proceeding on an excursion of pleasure to a garden in the neighbourhood; and the birth of her infant took place under a tree named Halgas. As soon as he was born, Brahma brought some cloth of gold from heaven, in which he wrapped the child, he was to grow up a holy man, and without sin. Brahma, then taking up the infant, saluted the queen, as the glorious mother of a Boodh. But the mother survived her delivery only seven days, when she passed into heaven, which is the destiny of all the mothers of the Boodhs, on account of their immaculate purity.

After this four heavenly beings appeared, named Pattenasto, Wirudde, Wirubaiksa, Waiissere Wema. They brought with them the skin of a tiger, which had been prepared in heaven, on which they laid the child, and fondled it in their arms; as did all the nobles of his father. After this the child raised himself up from the earth, and on whatever spot he set his right foot, there sprung up a red rose-tree, full of leaves and flowers.

The young prince fixing his feet on the ground, looked towards the east, when all the people and nobles shouted—There is no one so great and glorious as the being whom ye see: the same exclamation was heard when he turned himself to the other three quarters of the world. Upon this the young prince, who appears to have had very little modesty for one so recently born, said to all the people, There is none so great as I am. He then declared, that he was the master, or teacher of all men; and that no instruction in wisdom was to be had except from him. Again he said—That no man was greater than he; and that all were his inferiors. A fourth time he exclaimed—There is none so great as I; when, advancing his foot seven steps, seven rose-trees instantly appeared, and the same thing happened throughout his whole life; so that wherever he set his foot roses grew. When Boodh had proceeded these seven steps, his father came and took him away, and he appeared as a new-born child.

---

mede, Sujaetje, Piadasse, Attodasse, Dammadasse, Siddatta, Tissa, Pussa, Wipassa, Seeki, Wessaboo, Kakalauda, Konagamme, Kaeikgramma.

The young prince was brought into the palace in a great state, and much merriment ensued. There was, at that time, a celebrated priest, who frequently ascended into heaven, and was a constant visitor in the palace of the king. This priest, in one of his recent celestial excursions, having observed more than usual rejoicing in heaven, enquired the reason, when he was told that the Queen Mahamajadevi had been delivered of a son, who was destined to become a Boodh.

The priest proceeded with the intelligence he had obtained to the palace of Suddenam Raddure, when he asked the king about the birth of the young prince, whom he desired to behold. All men who were sinners used to testify profound reverence to this priest; but this holy child shewed no signs of homage, but put his feet upon the priest's head. The priest was greatly rejoiced, and, taking the prince in his arms, discovered in his hands and feet 216 tokens by which the Boodhs were always distinguished, along with thirty-two larger and eighty smaller marks in his body. The priest was greatly rejoiced at having thus verified the Booddhism of the child.

On another occasion, the king, having noticed some wonderful works which his son performed, called together forty-six of the most learned people in his dominions, out of whom he selected eight more learned that the rest; and of these he inquired whether this child would be a Boodh or a Brahmin. Seven of them, examining two of his fingers, said that he would become either a Boodh or a king; but the eighth, on looking at the forehead of the prince, saw a twisted hair, which, whenever it was touched, became as long as a man's arm, and then again curled up into its former state. By this sign it was determined that he would certainly become a Boodh.

When the prince was sixteen years old, his father resolved to procure him a wife; and he was to have a choice of wives such as no prince ever had before; for the king assembled no less than 40,000 princesses for the purpose. But multiplicity often makes preference difficult; and this appears to have been the case in the present instance; for the princess whom the prince took for his bride was not one of these 40,000, but a lady named Jasundere Devi, of extraordinary beauty and exalted family. She was the daughter of King Sopperabaedi.

Three palaces were erected for the prince and his consort; one for his residence during the hot season, another during the cold, and another during that of the rains. The king also had a delicious garden made for the recreation of the pair: and a large train of domestics was appointed to minister to their luxury and magnificence.

The king now consulted the wise men about the time when his son would become a Boodh; and they informed him, that it would take place when his son met an old man; secondly, a sick man; thirdly, a dead man; and fourthly, a sangatar, or priest, with a bald head.

The king, who had been apprised that if his son became a Boodh, a potent devil, named Wassawarti Marua, with many other confederate demons, would attempt his destruction, was anxious to delay or to avert the period of his inauguration; and he accordingly ordered the place where he resided to be surrounded by a wall with four gates, where a strict watch was to be kept, and no ingress to be given to any persons like those who have been described.

The prince, who had attained the age of thirty years, was one day proceeding to the garden which the king had provided for his recreation, when one of the heavenly devetas, who were anxious that he should become a Boodh, and who knew that the appointed period was at hand, descended from the celestial regions, and appeared before the prince in the form of an old man. The prince, who was in his carriage, observing this old man, asked one of his attendants if the person he beheld was born in that state, or had become so by gradual decay.

The attendant, who did not at the time think of the prohibition, which he had received, not to reveal such a circumstance to the prince, or to let him fix his eyes on such a form, said that it was an old man; and, when the prince proceeded to inquire whether he also should grow old, the attendant said, that all who were born, and lived, just one day become old. The prince said, if I am one day to exhibit such a picture of decrepitude and deformity as I have just beheld, what pleasure can I any longer derive from all the grandeur with which I am surrounded; and from all the means of gratification I possess? He accordingly ordered the driver not to proceed to the garden, but to return back to the palace.

The father remarking that his son had suddenly come back, without taking his usual recreation, asked the reason of his attendants, when he was told that the prince had met an old man, which had caused him to return. The king accordingly directed, that a watch of a thousand men should be posted at each gate, who were strictly enjoined not to suffer any persons of a particular description to have admission into the royal residence. At the same time, in order to dispel the melancholy, which had seized the mind of the prince, he directed that music and dancing should be provided as a remedy.

After an interval had elapsed, the prince, thinking no more of the above-mentioned occurrence, prepared for another excursion to the garden of delight. The devetas then dispatched one of their number in the form of a sick man, the sight of which caused the prince to make inquiries similar to those he had done before, when he again desisted from his purpose, and returned to the palace. His father now ordered 2000 watchmen to be placed at each gate, and the music and dancing to be renewed.

After some days, the prince met a dead body in a state of putrefaction, which the devetas exhibited to his view. On making inquiry respecting the loathsome spectacle, the prince was told, that his body would one day assume the same appearance, when he again returned, with grief and melancholy as before. His father again commanded that the watch should be increased, and that the expedient of music and dancing should again be tried upon the prince's mind.

The next time that the prince attempted to visit the garden of pleasure, he met one of the devetas in the form of a Sangatar on the way. He was told that this was an auspicious appearance, and a portent of good. The prince, delighted with this intelligence, continued his journey to the garden, full of hope and joy, to which he had long been a stranger. Whilst the prince was in this situation, his wife Jasundera Devi was delivered of a prince. His grandfather, having searched the planets and prefigured his future fortunes, made his son, who was still in the garden, acquainted with the result.

The prince, having seen the child, gave him the name of Rakulo, and said to his attendants—"What, though I have a son born, a magnificent court, and a large establishment, they cannot be supported without great exactions on the industry of my subjects, which must often be attended with injustice and oppression. The birth of a prince, therefore, is no just ground for the congratulations of the people."

When the prince returned from the garden, his attendants described to the king, the form which his son had seen on the way, and the joy it had produced. The king again ordered the dancing to be renewed in the palace, but the prince refused to be present at the festive scene; and, occupied with the thought of becoming a Boodh, retired to his chamber for meditation and repose. But his father said to the dancers, That as his son was sorrowful, they must exhilarate his spirits, and not depart till the effect had been produced.

The prince, however, persisted in refusing to admit the dancers to his presence, and they accordingly retired to a place of rest. The prince rose at midnight; and, whilst the whole palace was resplendent with torches, he beheld the musicians and dancers merged in profound sleep. Some of them were slavering at the mouth, others were lying in a state of perfect nudity; others were talking in their sleep. The prince contemplating this scene, said within himself, "I must exhibit a spectacle, not less humiliating than this, when I fall asleep; and therefore, it is better for me to be released from this tenement of flesh."

The prince now prepared to leave the palace unobserved; but, as he was proceeding to open the door, he was accosted by one of the nobles, or officers of the court, to whom the prince said, that the period for his becoming a Boodh was at hand, and that he must fetch his horse Cantecanam. The prince mounted the horse, and ordered the officer to get up behind him.

Before they left the court, the horse neighed so loud, that the devetas, in order to prevent it from awakening the people in the palace, came and led it out of the gate. The gate was 100 feet high, and the door made of stone, to open which required the united efforts of 1000 men. But the devetas opened it so softly, that the prince departed unperceived by the watch.

The above-mentioned devil having noticed these proceedings, thought that it would be a great diminution of his dignity if the prince should become a Boodh. In order to prevent this from taking place, the devil appeared to the prince in a blaze of light, and said, That in seven days he should be exalted to the monarchy of the whole world, if he would abandon the attempt to become a Boodh. This assurance was repeated three times.

The prince asked the spectre who it was? When it replied, "I am Wassawarti Marua, the chief of all the devils." The prince said, "I have devoted my kingdom, my wife, my child, my eyes, and my flesh to the relief and solace of the poor; nor will I receive at your hands all the kingdoms in the world; and, though you and a thousand more should tempt me with this prospect of grandeur, you should not induce me to desist from the design of becoming a Boodh." Before the devil departed, he warned him not to make the attempt, and menaced the most dreadful vengeance if an opportunity offered.

The prince now travelled 120 miles till he came to the river Anomanam, which was a quarter of a mile broad. His horse sprung with him over the stream, and alighted on a bed of fine sand on the opposite side. The prince now thought, that if he were to become a Boodh, he must cut off his hair, which he proceeded to do without further delay. Taking the hair in his hand, he said, The hair of a Boodh, instead of falling to the earth, will mount to the sky. He accordingly threw it out of his hand, when it rose aloft, and a deveta or angel appeared, who conveyed it to heaven in a case of gold.

The prince then thought that his royal dress was not such as became a Boodh. This suggestion no sooner occurred, than Brahma brought him from heaven a yellow, or saffron robe, like what the Boodh are wont to wear. The prince then threw off his royal apparel and put on the saffron dress, which had been so miraculously communicated. The suit which the prince had ceased to wear Mahobramma inclosed in a box of gold, and conveyed to heaven.

The prince now committed his horse to the care of his attendant, to conduct back to the palace; but the generous steed, unwilling to quit his master, sprung into the river and died.

The prince then wandered for six years through numerous regions, and traversed various wilds, without eating any thing, and experiencing every species of distress. The above-mentioned devil kept continually pursuing his footsteps, in order to watch an opportunity of vengeance, but none appears to have occurred. At the end of the sixth year, and at the period of the full moon in the fifteenth day of the month, the prince said, "Now shall I become a Boodh, and obtain a delicious repast, as all the Boodhs have done."

There was a town named Barnasnuru, in which a princess resided, who was wont, on this occasion, to provide a repast for the Boodh. This princess had 1000 cows, which were kept where the sweetest herbage grew. She took the milk of these 1000 cows, and gave it to 500 to drink. She afterwards gave the milk of these 500 cows to 250; of these 250 to 125; of these 125 to sixty-four; of these sixty-four to thirty-two; of these thirty-two to sixteen; and of these sixteen to eight. In the milk of these eight cows she boiled some rice; and she sent one of her maidens, named Fourre, to make preparations for the reception of the Boodh, under a tree called Nugagas. Whilst the maiden was thus employed, the Boodh appeared, when she went to inform the princess, who sent her back with the rice which she had cooked in a magnificent golden bowl. The Boodh took the bowl and proceeded to the river Neranjanam Ganga, where it is requisite on this solemnity for all those who become Boodh to keep their feast. Of the rice which was in the bowl the prince made forty-nine cakes, which he put one after another in his mouth. After emptying the bowl he threw it into the river, when it rose to the top of the water, and floated to the point where the bowls of the other Boodhs lay. It then sunk to the bottom; and such a noise was made by the collision of the different bowls, that it was heard not only by the other Boodhs, but by Mahahella Naja Radjura, who was a king in Nagalove, or the world under the earth.

This subterraneous king, on hearing the clang of the bowls said, "Kakasomda has been a Boodh for some days; Kamagamma has been a Boodh for some days; this is the day in which Gautama is become a Boodh—we must go and celebrate the festival." He accordingly departed with 40,000 dancers, whilst the Boodh, leaving the place where he had thrown the bowl, had retired under the Bogas, or sacred tree. The Boodh was placed on a raised seat reclining against the tree, when the above-mentioned monarch made his appearance with his 40,000 attendants, who began to weave the dance. The devetas also came with dancers and musicians; and a Sakkrea, who was four miles high, brought a train of 10,000 dependants playing upon pipes which were fourteen cubits long. Brahma came also with 10,000 men, bearing white umbrellas. He himself held an umbrella over the Boodh, and the others stood round about him; after which other celestial forms appeared with flutes and a diversity of musical instruments. Whilst they were celebrating the festival, the rejoicing, with which it was accompanied, was heard by the devil Wassawarti Marua, who had so long in vain persecuted the prince, and who thought, that if he could not succeed in effecting his vengeance on this solemn occasion, the opportunity would be lost for ever. He accordingly ordered his drum, called Wassawarti Goza, to be beat, which uttered such a stunning sound, that it made the ears bleed of all his subordinate fiends. They all assembled, and asked why he had called them together, and if he wanted their services in any impending war. He replied, that they must exert themselves to do all possible injury to the new-made Boodh. They accordingly transformed themselves into snakes, crows, and other shapes, and departed to act against the Boodh. Wassawarti himself had 1000 hands and 500 heads; and in each of his hands he held arms of different kinds, whilst he sat upon an elephant, named Girinucalla, on which he led his host of devils.

This assemblage of fiends surrounded those who were celebrating the feast, who, being greatly alarmed, threw away their musical instruments and umbrellas, and fled with precipitation, leaving Boodh alone. The devils now hemmed him in on all sides: but, though deserted by all his friends, he felt assured, that the alms which he had given would stand him in good stead, and keep him from all harm.

Wassawarti now called for a raging tempest, in order to tear up the tree by the roots on which Boodh reclined, and to carry both him and it into other realms; but, though all the neighbouring trees were beat down and dispersed by the wind, not a leaf of the Bogas was shaken. The devil had now recourse to an impetuous torrent of water, in order to effect his vindictive purpose, and next to a raging fire; but all these elements of destruction were employed in vain, as well as other expedients which his rage led him to try. He now made furious attacks upon Boodh with one of his arms, which was more powerful than the rest, and of a round form; but, instead of wounding the holy man, it remained suspended like an umbrella over his head.

Wassawarti, finding that all his attempts proved abortive, now claimed the seat on which the Boodh sat under the Bogas as his own, and called his devils to attest his right, which they proclaimed with a terrible cry. But the Boodh said that the earth should be his witness; and immediately a female form rose half above the surface, and declared the right of Boodh to the seat with such an appalling voice, that Wassawarti, with all his assembled fiends, instantly fled. The Boodh now remained here seven days without rising from his seat; but on the seventh day he arose, when he stood for seven days, looking up to the Bogas. Near this tree was a house of diamonds and rubies, in which he remained for seven days, meditating his law. He next went for seven days to a water-tank, which was frequented by a snake, named Musselindenam Nagea. Boodh now stood for seven days under the flat head of the serpent, which he employed as a protection from the rain. Hence he went under another tree, called Keripallugas, where he continued seven days; and next he proceeded to a tree named Halgas, under which he passed fourteen days.

The devil Wassawarti had three sisters, who, having heard that their brother had failed in all his attempts upon the Boodh, visited him with a company of 600 captivating females, who employed every feminine artifice to fascinate his affections and make him their slave. But he remained invincible even to all this variety of blandishments. Having passed through this terrible ordeal, he became established as a Boodh, and assembled his company of priests.[9]

◆ FRANCIS (HAMILTON) BUCHANAN (1762–1829)

Earlier in this chapter, we read an excerpt from Francis Hamilton's 1801 essay "On the Religion and Literature of the Burmas." A year later, Dr. Hamilton was posted to Nepal and wrote a book about the country, which was published in 1819 (by which time he had changed his surname to Buchanan).

In the following passage from this book, Hamilton attempts to describe the Tibetan view of the Buddha. Admittedly, it is a complicated topic, and he provides a confused description. Reading in Peter Simon Pallas's account that the Mongolians believe that Dschakshimuni (Śākyamuni) was the fifth buddha, and knowing that the Burmese consider Gotama the fourth, Hamilton concludes that Gautama and Sakya (he also calls him Sakya Singha) are different, and that the Burmese reject Sakya as a heretic. The Tibetans, however, worship Sakya, who came to their country at the time of Christ, and still lives in Lhasa "in perpetual youth" (presumably a reference to the Dalai Lama). Yet Hamilton also is aware of the institution of the incarnate lama— the identification of a deceased master's next incarnation—mentioning, for example, the "Tishu Lama," otherwise known as the Tashi Lama or Panchen Lama.

The Lamas are the priests of the sect of Bouddh, in Thibet and the adjacent territories, and are monks, who have nominally at least forsaken the pleasures of the world. They totally reject the doctrine of cast, and a person of any nation may be admitted into the order. The whole, at least of those at a distance, consider themselves as under the authority of Sakya Gomba, who came from India about the time of Jesus Christ, and has ever since resided at Lassa, where he remains in perpetual youth. On this account he is not considered as an incarnation (Avatar). There are, however, many personages of this sect who are considered as incarnations of different Budhs, or persons who have obtained divinity. These enter into the bodies of children, and inspire them through life; and when the body dies, the deity enters into another. Of this nature is the Dharma Raja, or spiritual chief of what we call Bhotan; and still more celebrated is the Tishu Lama, who resides at Degarchi, and is the spiritual guide of the Chinese emperors. This class of supposed deities seems to be pretty numerous, as, in the territory of the Lapcha and Kirats, their number would appear to have been at least twelve, as so many were known to my informant, who was only well acquainted with the former territory. The ordinary lamas pretend only to be saints. The best account I have seen of their doctrine is that given by the learned Pallas, which is much more complete than any I could procure in Nepal. The followers of Buddh have had five great lawgivers, and a sixth is daily expected. As each of these is supposed to have been an incarnation of a Buddh or Bourkan, and as all have been usually taken as one person, we may readily account for the difference that prevails in the opinions concerning the era when this sect arose. Gautama is the fourth of these lawgivers, and his doctrine alone is received by the priests of Ava, who reject the fifth as a heretic; but by the Bouddhists of Nepal, Thibet, Tartary, and China, he is named Sakya. Gautama, according to the best authorities, lived in the sixth century before the Christian era, and Sakya in the first century after the birth of our Lord.

Although there is no distinction of cast among the Sayn or Bhotiyas, yet they are not without differences in religious opinions; for some of them in Nepal worship at Swayambhunath, while others prefer a temple of Bouddhama, which is situated near Pasupanath. The doctrine of Sakya Singha differs most essentially from that of Gautama. The Bhotiyas, following the former, worship all the spirits, that by the Burmas are called Nat, a practice which is held in abhorrence by the Rahans of Ava. They also consider the Buddhs as emanations from a supreme deity, view many of their Lamas as incarnations of a Buddh, and accordingly worship them as living Gods, although they do not consider them as equal to Sakya, who is the Lama of Lassa. There is among the Lamas no prohibition against the laity from studying any character or any book; but they must have wonderfully degraded the human understanding, when they can induce the people to swallow the belief in the deities living among them. It is true, that these are in all probability very much secluded, and rarely shown to the vulgar, except at a very great distance, and in obscurity; but still this seems to be nearly the utmost height of human imbecility.

The belief of Sakya having lived among them since about the commencement of the Christian era, is probably confined to Nepal, and other remote parts, where no means of knowing the contrary exists. Such an absurdity could scarcely pass among actual observers, however degraded in understanding, and in Thibet the Lama of Lassa is probably considered as merely an incarnation of Sakya.[10]

◆   R. N. GOLOWNIN (1776–1831)

The Russian ship captain R. N. Golownin served as a volunteer in the British navy during the Napoleonic Wars. After his return to Russia, he was given command of the sloop of war Diana, *which set sail from Kamchatka in May 1811 on a surveying expedition. When Captain Golownin and six of his crew disembarked at Kunashiri Island in Japan, they were invited into a fort and then arrested, apparently in retaliation for a Russian raid on the island of Saghalien. They were then taken to Hakodate in Hokkaido and then to Matsumae, where they were imprisoned. Although they escaped on one occasion, they were recaptured and held captive until October 1813, when the Russians negotiated their release.*

Golownin's movements during that time were obviously limited, but he sought as much information about the country as he could through conversations with guards, interpreters, and the many curious Japanese who questioned him. After his release, he published Recollections of Japan, Comprising a Particular Account of the Religion, Language, Government, Laws and Manners of the People. *In it, Golownin has little to say about Buddhism. The following is a long footnote added by the editor of his memoir.*

———

* These facts, connected with this religion, manifest in a most extraordinary degree the rapid spreading of the knowledge, though corrupted, of the Christian religion to the eastward of Judea. About the year A.D. 55, the Chinese emperor, Mimti, heard of a sect in India called the sect of *Xaca*, and he was so much pleased with their tenets, as to send special messengers thither, with order to acquire a perfect knowledge of their forms and opinions. About the year A.D. 62, these messengers,

returning by way of Japan, found the tenets of Xaca already introduced there,—a brief sketch of which will suffice to prove the fact in question. Some of these were that there are future recompenses established for virtue, and punishment for vice: that good men after death are received into a place of happiness where all desires are fulfilled, but the wicked shut up in a place of torment; that Xaca is the saviour of mankind; that he was born of a female in order that he might recal [*sic*] man to the way of salvation from whence he had previously seen that they had strayed; that he came to expiate the sins of the world, in order that, after death, they might acquire a happy resurrection; and that the godhead consists of three persons in unity—a coincidence in chronology and doctrine which strikes at the very root of those assertions of infidelity, that would look for the origin of the Christian gospel, in the corrupted traditions of the East, supported by the unfounded assertions of anterior antiquity. (*See Charlevoix.*)

The limits of a note do not admit of further detail; but the subject is well worthy the attention of Christian Divines, anxious to overturn the strong hold of modern scepticism.

It is a remarkable fact, that the followers of this religion worship an image with three heads and forty hands, as a symbol of a Trinity of persons in the godhead, and of the universality of the divine operations. They believe also that, whatever crimes may have been committed, the sinner may expect salvation if he dies invoking the Deity, whom they represent as having undergone a most severe penance, in order to wash away the sins of mankind. They also believe that this god is invisible, and of a nature quite distinct from the elements of matter; that he existed before the creation of heaven and earth; that he had no beginning, and will have no end; that all things were created by him; that his essence is spread through the heavens, upon the earth, and beyond it; that he is present every where; that he governs and preserves all things; that he is immovable, immaterial, and ought to be reverenced as the inexhaustible source of all good.—ED.[11]

◆ JOHN CRAWFURD (1783–1868)

John Crawfurd was born in the Inner Hebrides. After studying medicine at Edinburgh, he went to India in 1803, where he served as an army surgeon. He would go on to become one of the East India Company's leading diplomats and administrators, in what are today Malaysia, Indonesia, Thailand, Vietnam, Singapore, and Burma.

In 1811, Crawfurd participated in the British expedition to seize Java from the Dutch. He would spend five years there (also visiting Bali and Sulawesi). Based on his studies there, he published his three-volume History of the Indian Archipelago *in 1820.*

In the passage below, Crawfurd seeks to determine whether the Buddha had ever been worshipped in Java, and what can be concluded from the presence or absence of such worship. He speculates (incorrectly) that the hundreds of statues of the Buddha at Borobudur do not represent a deified person named Buddha but instead depict Hindu priests who came to Java to reform the worship of Śiva, "the destroying power." Based on this inference, Crawfurd concludes that Buddhism is not a separate religion but in fact a modification of Brahmanism. Therefore, the forms of Buddhism found elsewhere in Southeast Asia are corruptions of "genuine Buddhism."

———

The word Buddha, or Buda, is never to be discovered in any modern or ancient Javanese manuscript that I have heard of, as applicable to a deified person of this name; and there is no evidence from such a source of any worship to such a personage. The names and attributes of the principal gods of the Hindu pantheon are quite familiar to every Javanese scholar, but of the names of Buddha they are wholly ignorant. The *images* of the Hindu deities they cannot, indeed, in general, particularize by name, but they recognize them to be such, while those of Buddha they denominate *Pandita Sabrang*, or foreign Pundits or Brahmins.

On the strength of these *data*, I may repeat, that the Buddhism of the Javanese was not the worship of a deified person of the name of Buddha, but a modification of the worship of the destroying power [Śiva]; and that the images of Buddha, so abundantly scattered over the island, represent the sages who brought about the reform. When Buddha is represented on the sculptures of Boro Budur receiving gifts of fruits and flowers, I conclude that he represents a priest receiving charity or donations from his disciples or followers, and not a divinity receiving offerings from his votaries, because this last practice is no part of the Hindu form of worship.

IF these inferences be just, the religion which is pourtrayed in the relics of Hinduism in the principal temples of Java, may be looked upon as a genuine example of the reform ascribed to Buddha, and the testimony which they afford will be considered as a proof that the religions of Brama and Buddha are essentially the same, the one being, as for some time suspected by oriental scholars, nothing but a modification of the other. If this reasoning be admitted as conclusive, we shall be compelled to consider the religion of the Burmans, Siamese, and Cingalese, as corruptions of genuine Buddhism, most probably superinduced by local causes and superstitions, which, operating upon the original system, produced, in the course of ages, a form of worship differing essentially from its purest form.[12]

◆ JOHN DAVY (1790–1868)

The British physician John Davy—younger brother of the famous chemist Sir Hum-phry Davy, inventor of the miners' Davy lamp—served as Inspector General of Hos-pitals for the British army. In this capacity, he was posted throughout the empire, including at the colony of Ceylon. Based on his time there, in 1821 he published An Account of the Interior of Ceylon, and of its Inhabitants, *which included a chapter entitled "Doubtful Points of The Religion of Boodhoo."*

Here, Dr. Davy, a good scientist, uses his powers of observation to address the question of the Buddha's origins, surveying a range of opinions on the topic.

————

Is Boodhoo an incarnation of Visnu? Is the religion of Boodhoo grafted on, and a heresy of the Brahminical? Several oriental scholars of eminence maintain the af-firmative. The Boodhists themselves are positive in holding the negative. Where all is probably fiction, one assertion may be opposed to another. The Boodhists con-tend, that the last Boodhoo was never Visnu; but that their present Visnu is fated to become a Boodhoo. In respect to the second question,—the mythological por-tion of the Boodhaical system in Ceylon does appear to be a graft of the Brahmini-cal; but that which is purely Boodhaical seems to have had an independent origin: it is different in principle; it is as directly opposite as the doctrines of the Saddu-cees to the Pharisees, and surely cannot with propriety be considered a heresy.

The question in what part of the world this religion first appeared is still in-volved in considerable obscurity. The majority of oriental scholars are in favour of its western origin, and maintain that it is derived from some part of Africa,—probably Ethiopia. A very few hold the contrary opinion, that the north of Asia was its birth-place and cradle.

The principal argument of those who maintain the first opinion, is derived from the appearance of some of the images of Boodhoo. It is said, they show that Boodhoo was an African, having marked on them the short woolly hair, the flat dilated nostrils, the thick fleshy lip, and indeed every feature of the African coun-tenance. If this be generally so, it certainly is strong evidence. I have paid par-ticular attention to innumerable figures of Boodhoo, made in Ceylon; I have seen several from Ava and Siam; two or three of Foh, from China; one of Mahamoonie, and of a Lama, and a Dalai Lama, from Tibet; and the result of my observations is the persuasion, that the asserted resemblance is either accidental or fanciful. The features of the Tibetian, Burman, and Chinese images, are more or less Tartar; and those of the Ceylon figures, Singalese:—and, it is worthy of remark, that the more carefully and ably the figures are made, the more complete is the copying of the national features. The argument, therefore, from the African countenance, appears to me untenable; and I know no other of force in favour of African origin, which the Boodhists themselves will not patiently listen to, considering even the supposition a species of insult,—their ideas of the African (of the Kaffer) being very low, and full of contempt, as is evident, from their giving him the office of tormentor in the infernal regions, in common with dogs and crows. If questioned respecting the hair of Boodhoo, they say it was like their own, and that the object of artists is not to represent curly, woolly hair, but hair cut short, as Boodhoo's was when he became priest; and, to prove this, they observe, that one long hair or lock was left uncut on his forehead, which is represented as a circle or curl, in all images that are correctly executed.

The opinion, that the religion of Boodhoo had its origin in the north-east part of Asia, has been advanced by Dr. Hamilton, in his valuable paper on the religion and literature of the Burmas. It is the opinion of the Boodhists themselves. To my enquiries respecting Kosol-rattè where Boodhoo is said to have resided, and from whence he is supposed to have propagated his religion, a learned native replied,— "It is to the eastward of Ceylon, and further northward." He arrived at this conclusion, from circumstances mentioned in religious books. From these books it appears, that there was frequent intercourse between Kosol and Ava, and Bengal. Whence it may be inferred, that the former country could not be very remote from the two latter. In the same books certain directions of Boodhoo are preserved respecting woollen robes, and the times of bathing: in Kosol, he allowed his disciples to bathe only once in fifteen days; but in hot countries, once daily,—a most convincing proof that the climate of Kosol must have been at least cool, and not tropical. Were stronger evidence required, the same source affords it:—according to a passage in these works, in Kosol, in the month of September, at noon precisely, when the sun is at its greatest altitude, the shadow of a man was six times the length of his foot. Hence, it is evident that Kosol was pretty far north; in confirmation of which, allusions are made in these works to snow and ice.

The extent of country over which the Boodhaical system has spread is immense: even now, variously modified, it is perhaps more widely extended than any other religion. It appears to be the religion of the whole of Tartary, of China, of Japan, and their dependencies, and of all the countries between China and the Burrampooter.

What its exact modifications are in all these countries, in a great measure, still remains to be ascertained. There is some reason to believe, that in Ava and Siam the system is least contaminated and of the greatest purity, and that in China, it has undergone the greatest adulteration. In the former countries, there are no temples erected to the gods, and no worship permitted excepting of Boodhoo; and, it may be added there are no distinctions of caste. It has been supposed, that the system in general is equally pure, that the worship of Boodhoo and the gods could not come in contact, and that caste is unknown to Booddhists. That this supposition is not quite correct, is evident from the state of religion in Ceylon, where the worship of Boodhoo is connected with that of the gods, and associated with caste; and, I suspect that Ceylon is not, or at least was not a solitary example of the kind. It is highly probable that a similar combination of worship formerly existed on the continent of India, wherever the Boodhaical system prevailed. On such an idea may be explained, in a satisfactory manner, "the singular fact," as Mr. Erskine expresses it, and to which he has called the attention of enquirers, "of the existence of temples of opposite characters and of different and hostile religions, only a few miles from each other, and in some instances, as at Ellora, even united in the same range." By the analogy of Ceylon, the fact is explained, with the rejection of the inference of the hostility of the two establishments, on which its apparent singularity depends.

The extension of the religion of Boodhoo to the most eastern parts of Asia is more than probable: how far it has ever extended in an opposite direction is not perhaps an easy question to determine. I am not aware that it has been traced, in a satisfactory manner much to the westward of the Indian Caucasus.

What are we to think of the opinions of those eminent men, who have imagined its extension over all Europe as well as Asia, and have identified Boodhoo with Fro, Thor, and Odin, the gods of the Scandinavians? What analogies are there between the Boodhaical and the Scandinavian systems? The points of resemblance, if any, are certainly very few, whilst those of dissimilitude are innumerable. What two beings can be more different in character than Boodhoo and Odin: the one subduing his passions, and resigning a princely vest for a priest's robe; the other a conqueror and founder of a kingdom: the one teaching the annihilation of existence, as the final reward of virtue; the other inculcating the immortality of the soul: the one living a life of the greatest abstinence, exhorting his followers to imitate his example, and forbidding them the use of fermented liquors; the other, in Valhalla, leading a life the most jovial, drinking wine himself and regaling his companions, the Einheriar, (the ghosts of the brave slain in battle,) with mede and beer, which they drank out of human skulls after feasting on pork: the one prohibiting the killing of any animal, even the minutest, and on this principle straining the water he drank, to save the lives of the animalcules, he might otherwise swallow,—inculcating humanity and mercy, and accepting no offerings but flowers; the other, the god of war, delighting in bloodshed, esteeming valour the first virtue, and gratified with no offering so much as that of human sacrifices:—the contrast might be carried farther, were it necessary;—even the periods of their existence do not agree; Boodhoo having flourished little more than a century after the founding of Rome; whilst Odin, according to his historian, did not emigrate from the east with his family and people, till the time of Pompey. Were there any similarity of system, both might have had a similar origin; but where no similarity appears, but total difference, is it reasonable to suppose that the two sprang from the same root? Dr. Hamilton, from such considerations, has already opposed the notion, that our ancestors were Boodhists; and, I cannot help thinking, that every one who will give the subject a careful consideration, unbiassed by hypothesis, will adopt his conclusion. The argument from the name of a day, on which the analogy between Boodhoo and Odin or Woden is chiefly founded, is hardly worth noticing: I may remark cursorily, that Wednesday, (Woden's day,) in Ceylon, is generally called Sawummia-dinna, wind-day, on the idea that wind was created on that day; if it is ever called Boodhoo's day, I believe it to be not in reference to the being worshipped, but to Boodahoo, the mild god or planet, who is supposed to preside over Wednesday.[13]

✦   JULIUS HEINRICH KLAPROTH (1783–1835)

Julius Heinrich Klaproth was born in Berlin, the son of the famous chemist (and discoverer of uranium) Martin Heinrich Klaproth (1743–1817). As a young man, he became fascinated with Chinese, teaching himself the language at the Berlin Royal Library from a Spanish–Chinese dictionary compiled by a Roman Catholic missionary. Eventually, he would also learn Manchu, Mongolian, Sanskrit, Turkish, Arabian, and Persian.

Klaproth attracted the attention of Count Jan Potocki, a Polish nobleman who invited him to join a Russian embassy to China in 1805. When the embassy was unable to reach Peking, Klaproth returned to St. Petersburg, where he continued his studies of Chinese and Manchu at the Academy of Sciences before returning to Berlin. By 1816, he had concluded that the leading center in Europe for Oriental studies was Paris. Supported by a stipend from the Prussian government (provided at the urging of Alexander and Wilhelm von Humboldt), he would spend the rest of his life there, making important contributions to lexicography and writing scathing reviews of works by those whose linguistic skills did not match his own.

In 1824, Klaproth published a life of the Buddha, drawn from Mongolian sources, in Journal Asiatique. *The following passage, which opens the article, demonstrates the positive attitude of French savants toward the Buddha in the decades after the Revolution.*

———

No other religion, other than that of Jesus Christ, has contributed as much to the betterment of men as that of *Bouddha*. Originating in Hindustan, it is spread throughout most of Asia. Its domination extends from the sources of the Indus to the Pacific Ocean and even to Japan. The fierce nomads of Central Asia were changed by it into soft and virtuous men, and its beneficent influence is felt as far as southern Siberia.

Like all the beliefs that originate from India, Bouddhisme is founded on a great principle, "that the universe is animated by the same spirit, individualized under innumerable forms by matter, which is only an illusion."

The Buddha appeared as a reformer of the dominant religion of India. He rejected the Vedas, blood sacrifice, and the distinction of castes. Otherwise, the philosophical principles of his doctrine are the same as those found in the other branches of the religion of the Hindus.[14]

✦ THOMAS ABERCROMBIE TRANT (1805–1832)

Thomas Abercrombie Trant was the son of Major General Nicholas Trant, the British army officer and veteran of the Napoleonic Wars. He served with distinction in the First Anglo-Burmese War (1824–26), and upon his return to England in 1827, he published an account of his experiences. As his various compatriots were contributing increasingly detailed accounts of the life of the Buddha, Captain Trant of the 38th Foot provided something more succinct.

———

The Burmahs, like the Cingalese, are Buddhists, and devoted to the worship of Boodh Buddha, or Gaudma, who, in the Hindoo mythology, figures as the ninth Avatar or incarnation of the deity upon earth. He was the son of Mahadavee and Shooddhōduum, and, when young, went to school, taking with him ten thousand other boys. On his arrival there, he began to instruct his master, who, unable to answer his questions, and astonished at his knowledge, ran and hid himself among the boys. Boodhu then commenced teaching his doctrines, and married no less than eighty-four thousand wives. The rest of his life was passed on earth in prayers and meditations; and before he left the world, the gods came down and worshipped him.[15]

Samuel Davis was a career officer of the East India Company, arriving in Madras in 1780. He became a close friend of William Jones, the cofounder and an important member of the Asiatick Society (renamed the Asiatic Society of Bengal in 1832). He is remembered as the leading British expert of his day on classical Indian astronomy, though he began his work in India as a surveyor and draftsman.

In 1783, Warren Hastings, the Governor-General of Bengal, appointed Davis to join Hastings's cousin Lieutenant Samuel Turner on a mission to Tibet. However, when the party reached the Tibetan-Bhutanese border, the Tibetans refused to let the entire party enter, and Davis was left behind in Bhutan. He used his time to create watercolors and pencil sketches of the Bhutanese landscape and architecture. He also kept a journal, which was read to the Asiatic Society on February 20, 1830 (eleven years after his death), and published as "Remarks on the Religious and Social Institutions of the Bouteas, or Inhabitants of Boutan."

In the passage below, Davis turns his artist's eye to statues of the Buddha.

————

MANY principles and forms of the religion of the Lamas are evidently borrowed from that of the Hindoos. They have similar ceremonies performed on the banks of rivers, and the Ganges is held in equal veneration. A little of its water is a most valuable acquisition to one of their faquires or pilgrims, who carries it in a small brass or silver bottle, carefully corked, and tied to his girdle. Their supreme deity, called indiscriminately by the name Sijamony, Mahamony, and Sejatoba, is said to have been brought many ages ago by one of the superior Lamas from Benares, and others of them must have been of foreign extraction; for although plainly drawn and carved as females, the priests would not allow them of that sex; and often, as they think, decide the distinction with a pair of whiskers, when the turn of the features and swell of bosom shew whiskers to be misapplied.[16]

◆ HORACE HAYMAN WILSON (1786–1860)

In a previous section in this chapter, we read the remarks of John Crawfurd concerning Buddhism in Java. A well-traveled British diplomat, Crawfurd later published Journal of an Embassy from the Governor-General of India to the Courts of Siam and Cochin China; Exhibiting a View of the Actual State of Those Kingdoms. *In this work, he devotes a long section to the views of Buddhism of H. H. (for Horace Hayman) Wilson, one of the great Sanskrit scholars of the nineteenth century.*

As a young man in England, Wilson spent school holidays with an uncle who worked as an assayer in the Royal Mint, calculating the quantities of particular metals in coins. At the age of eighteen, he began training as a surgeon and in 1808 was appointed assistant surgeon to the East India Company, arriving in Calcutta (spelled today as Kolkata) the following year. However, upon his arrival, the assay master of the Calcutta mint learned of Wilson's metallurgical skills and recruited him to work there. In 1816, Wilson was promoted to assay master, and continued in that position until his departure from India in 1833.

In addition to acting in the Calcutta theatre, Wilson developed a strong interest in Indian languages, especially Sanskrit. His first translation, in 1813, was of the famous lyric poem The Cloud Messenger *(Meghadūta), by Kālidāsa. In 1819, he published his well-regarded* Sanskrit-English Dictionary. *Then in 1833, Wilson returned to Britain to assume the Boden Professorship in Sanskrit at Oxford, established by Joseph Boden to aid in the transmission of the Gospel to the Indian intelligentsia—though his election had been opposed by some because of his close ties to the Hindu literati, his indulgence of "concubinage" during his time in India, and his irregular church attendance. In addition to holding the Boden chair, Wilson also served as librarian of East India House in London, the headquarters of the East India Company.*

Wilson apparently provided Crawfurd with some notes on Buddhism while he was still in India, which Crawfurd presents here.

The history of Buddhism, one of the forms of worship which has produced the longest and the most extensive influence upon the destinies and opinions of mankind, has justly excited much interest and curiosity; and I shall therefore relate, in some detail, the few facts in regard to it, which fell under my observation in Siam; premising, that in order to prepare myself for any favourable opportunities of inquiry which might arise, I had been furnished by Mr. Horace Wilson, the enlightened and accomplished Secretary of the Asiatic Society of Calcutta, with a series of learned notes. The reader will be enabled to judge how far the hints which I have collected tend to confirm or correct the opinions of Mr. Wilson; and to put it in his power to come to a fair judgment, I shall begin by transcribing the most material portion of the notes in question.

"The original *Buddha,*" says Mr. Wilson, "seems to have been of Scythian or Tartar extraction, and to have existed above one thousand years before Christ. The records of China, as mentioned by M. de Guigne, assign about this date, and call Cashmir the seat of his nativity. The Raja Tarinjini, however, or History of Cashmir, which may, by reasonable inferences, be made to agree tolerably well with the

Chinese statement of the date, does not mention where he was born, and connects the prevalence of his religion in Cashmir, with a Tartar, or *Tarushca*, a Turk, or Scythian subjugation of the country. The existence of the Bauddhaic creed in Tartary, may be traced from a very early period to the present day, and is a corroborative proof of its indigenous origin.

"Although, however, the Northern origin of *Buddha* might be easily made out more satisfactorily, the fact is scarcely worth investigating with reference to the present condition of the Buddha faith; there is merely a nominal connexion between them,—the real founder being *Gautama*, the son of *Sudhodana*, a prince of *Magadha*, or Behar, who flourished in the sixth century before Christ, or 542. This personage might have borrowed the anti-vedaic notions of the elder *Buddha*, and the tenderness for animal life; he was probably, however, instigated very much by animosity towards the Brahmans, as it is a curious part of the history of a religious innovator in India, that he should be a *Chetriya*, or of the military caste.

"Very great confusion has been occasioned in all discussions relating to *Buddha*, by identifying these two persons,—an error originating with the Hindoos themselves, and easily accounted for; the Puranas, the earliest authorities for the accounts of Buddha, being unquestionably some centuries later than *Gautama*. With his history, therefore, their authors were familiar, whilst a faint and imperfect tradition kept alive some recollection of his predecessor. They consequently mixed up the two, and blended, obviously, in a very awkward manner, the *Buddha*, the ninth Avatar of Vishnu, who appeared shortly after CRISHNA, with the Prince of Magadha, the son of *Sudhodan* and *Máyá Devi*.

"For the names and birth-place of *Gautama* we have the authority of all the Hindoo accounts, and their *Magadha* is manifestly the *Mokito* of the Chinese, the Mokokf of the Japanese, and the Macadesa of the Singalese; for the date, we must be content with the foreign notions, the Siamese placing Gautama's birth 544 years before Christ; the Singalese 542; and the Burmans 546; Indian history so far confirming this, as to place the family of Gautama on the throne of *Magadha* from the seventh century to the third of Christ.

"A very common name of *Gautama* is *Sácya*, *Sácya Muni*, or *Sácya Sinha*, the *Xakia* of the Archipelago. It generally occurs as a synonyme of *Gautama*. Whether it properly belongs to him may be doubtful. The term *Buddha* is a generic one—it might have been a proper name once, but it has since become an epithet; and instead of calling Gautama Buddha, we should be quite right in calling him *a* Buddha. A *Prácrit* vocabulary, brought by a Burman priest to Calcutta, and which seems to be little more than a translation of the *Amera Cosha*, opens with a string of thirty generic names, the first of which is *Buddha*. Several others are familiar, as *Sugata, Dhermarája, Magavar, Na'th*, &c. They might be rendered,—The Wise—The Virtuous—The King of Justice—The Lord—The Master. Then come the synonymes of *the* Buddha, commencing oddly enough with *Jina*; the rest are *Sácya, Siddhanta, Saudhodini, Gautama, Sácya Sinha, Sácya Muni*, and *Aditya Bandhu*. They certainly are all applied to one person. But there were more than one preeminent Buddhas; the Singalese enumerate five, of whom the fifth, Maitréya, is yet to come. The vocabulary or *Hémachandra* names seven—*Vipaswi, Sic'hi, Viswabhu, Cratuch handa, Canchana, Cásyapa*; and the seventh, as usual, *Sácyasinha*, &c. The Burman priest alluded to above, asserted there were twenty-eight Buddhas. Hamilton, in his Nepal, separates *Gautama* from *Sácyasinha*, calling the former the fourth, the latter the fifth *Buddha*, and stating this last to have lived in the first century of the Christian era. There is so far particular reason to think this not impossible, that there seems to have been a new source of confusion introduced into the history of *Buddha*, by blending him again with a different person, or with *Sálivahana*, as in the *Aji Saka* of the Japanese; and the stories of Devatat and Devadatta, the enemy of *Sácya*, or *Sálivahana*.—Now, quere, whether this confusion may not all be resolved into the various senses of the word *Sácya*, which is a regular derivative from *Sáca*, meaning a *pot-herb* or an *era*; or from *Sáca*, a native of a country, the position of which is unknown, but identified etymologically with that of the *Sacæ*, or Scythians? Now the Sanscrit etymologists have abandoned the explanation of the term *Sácya*, merely making it a grammatical formative from the root *Sac*, to be able or powerful. As there was no authority for its import, conjecture was at liberty to explain it, and hence the confusion. *Sácya* may therefore be applicable to any *Buddha*, as to one who confines himself to vegetable food. It is applicable to *Salivahana*, the institutor of the era, the Saca still in use; whilst as a specific term it seems to be a foreign one, and to confirm my view of the Scythian origin of the faith. There being no satisfactory Sanscrit explanation of it, except as an attribute, is rather in favour of this notion. The addition of *Sinha* and *Muni* only imply preeminence. Hence *Sacya sinha* is explained by Sanscrit writers to be the chief of the *Sacyas*; but they do not tell us, at least satisfactorily, who the *Sacyas* were. I am rather disposed to think that the name is the lawful property of the first *Buddha*, erroneously given to *Gautama*: it may also belong to *Salivahana*, but in a sense quite unconnected with the Buddha religion."[17]

◆   KARL FRIEDRICH NEUMANN (1793–1870)

The German scholar Karl Friedrich Neumann traveled to China in 1829. During his two-year stay there, he collected some twelve thousand Chinese texts, which he sent back to the royal library in Munich. Neumann published on a wide range of topics, including Armenian literature, American history, the history of the Sino-British wars, and the pirates of the China Sea. He also wrote a book about Chinese Buddhism, excerpted below, where he expressed his low opinion of the Buddha.

———

It has for some time past been the fashion of learned men to praise greatly the doctrine of Shakiamuny; but it seems that this praise is very much overrated. It is true that Buddhism blunted the edge of the barbarian ferocity of the Mongolians; but what positive advantages have resulted from this doctrine in Tartary? Is the state of society much better than it was in the time Chingize? There are thousands of idle people whose business it is to do *Nothing*, to think on *Nothing*, and to live as much as possible upon *Nothing*. A wise legislation works against the slothfulness of human nature, and Buddha seemed to have adored this indolent goddess. . . . But this we know, man is born to act and to suffer, and not to spend his life in worthless speculations and monkish idleness; he is not born to thwart all his affections, but to enjoy the world. The low state of half the human kind, the mean oppression of the weaker sex in every country where Buddhism prevails, would alone speak volumes against this doctrine. . . .

Buddhism is a reform of the old Hindoo orthodox church; it is a new building on the same ground, and with the same materials, but without that most cruel and abominable invention of the human mind—the infamous system of castes. All the outworks of Hindooism remain; the whole legion of gods and goddesses, of spirits and demons, together with all the fabulous mountains and seas, with their monstrous inhabitants. In a word, Buddhism is the Lutheranism of the Hindoo church; and the Brahmans were not less cruel than the priesthood of the Catholic church; the reformers of the East were extirpated by fire and sword, like the reformers in the West.[18]

◆   CHARLES COLEMAN

One of the great debates of the early nineteenth century was, which came first, Hinduism or Buddhism? Arguments for both sides are set here by Charles Coleman from the chapter entitled "Buddha" in his 1832 work, The Mythology of the Hindus.

The conflicting opinions which have prevailed among the most intelligent Oriental writers respecting the origin and antiquity of this and the Jaina sects, and the little historical light that has yet been afforded to disperse the darkness that ages has spread over them, leave us, at the end of many learned disquisitions, involved in almost as many doubts as when we commenced upon them. By some, the extensive sect of Buddha is supposed to have derived its origin from, and to have been identified with, the ninth *avatar*, or the last appearance of Vishnu upon earth; when he is said to have appeared to reclaim the Hindus from numerous abominations into which they had fallen, and to teach them more benevolent forms of worship than those which, through the means of human and animal sacrifices, they then practised. These mild doctrines were too simple, and interfered too strongly with the privileges of the Brahminical priests to be long tolerated by them. A religious war, in consequence, ensued between the old and the new sects, and that of Buddha was ultimately expelled from the hither peninsula of India.

In noticing this most beneficent of the explanations of Vishnu's ninth incarnation, we are left in considerable perplexity to account for the apparently inadequate manifestation of his power to punish the sacrilegious Brahminical opponents of his divine will: and this will lead to the observation, that the Buddhas wholly, and the Brahmans partially, disavow this incarnation of Vishnu; the former insisting that the worship of Buddha possesses a far higher claim to antiquity than that of the deities of the Brahmans, who, they maintain, came from other countries, and established their own religion, mainly by the power of the sword, on the ruins of the more ancient one of Buddha, which had for ages prevailed. This point will be noticed again presently. . . .

As in most cases where much obscurity prevails, conjecture is correspondingly active, numerous arguments have been adduced by European writers in support of the claims of those two sects. By some it has been urged, in favour of the Buddhas, that, as man in a primitive state of society would be more likely to entertain a belief that the universe was the effect of chance, or of some natural operation, rather than the creation of a divine power, it will follow, that such being the creed of the Buddhas, that portion of the people of India who had adopted the Brahminical faith must have done so, and have departed from an earlier belief, in consequence of an advance of knowledge among them, which other parts of the same country did not experience; and that, therefore, while the Brahmans, who first among them acknowledged and worshipped a supreme Being, were departing afterwards from that unity of worship, and erecting idols as symbols of his power and attributes, the Buddhas remained stedfast in their disbelief of a first divine cause, and in their adoration only of virtue and goodness, as exemplified by their learned and pious sages, whom they in consequence raised to a state of beatitude and worshipped. The religion of Buddha must then, they say, be the most ancient. Others, adopting an opposite reasoning, have argued that the Brahmans, when they arrived in India from some other country, found the worship of Buddha to be then established, and, in compliance with the feelings of the aboriginal inhabitants, engrafted it on their own polytheism.

Others again, the advocates of the priority of the Brahmans, either urge the ninth *avatar* of Vishnu, or allege that the sect of Buddha has been founded by good and virtuous men, who were disgusted at, and dissatisfied with the idol worship of the Brahmans, and who, running into contrary extremes, introduced, in opposition thereto, and to its attendant sanguinary sacrifices, as a *summum bonum* of earthly consideration, a love and adoration of virtue and justice, and a benevolent regard towards the most minute of sentient animals. The major part of these learned theorists have, however, concurred in making Egypt the fountain-head from which one of these sectarial streams first issued, but they have not agreed on the main point—which of them had that honour; as it is by one given to the Buddha atheist, and by the other to the Brahminical polytheist. . . .

Leaving this doubtful point of antiquity to the judgment of the reader, I will proceed to describe, as briefly as I can, the very extensive sect (perhaps the most extensive that is known) of Buddha, whose doctrines are now acknowledged in Ceylon, some parts of Hindustan, Nepal, Thibet, some of the provinces of Tartary, the empires and their dependencies of China and Japan, the kingdoms of Ava and Siam, and most of the various countries which are situated on the shores of the China Sea.

In this vast extent of country Buddha is known under numerous names, and has been identified by learned European writers, alike with the patriarchs of our own sacred history, the sovereigns of Egypt, and the princes of Hindustan. Some have supposed him to have been Noah, Moses, &c.; others Sesac or Sesostris of Egypt. While others, again, have imagined him to have been the same with Woden, the god of the Scandinavians, whose worship extended during the barbarous ages over the various kingdoms of the west. It will be unnecessary to discuss these theories, as it is my object to describe the practices and creeds of the Hindu religions, as far as I can comprehend them, as they actually prevail, rather than to enter upon abstruse arguments, which, after all, would be only heaping another conjecture upon the unstable pile that has already preceded it.[19]

✦ EDWARD UPHAM (1776–1834)

Edward Upham, the eccentric mayor of Exeter, was yet another amateur orientalist who never set foot in Asia. He wrote novels about Persia and ancient Egypt, includ-ing the three-volume Rameses: An Egyptian Tale *(1824), as well as a two-volume history of the Ottoman Empire. In addition, he is the author of the first English-language book with Buddhism in its title:* The History and Doctrine of Budhism, Popularly Illustrated: With Notices of the Kappooism or Demon Worship and of the Bali or Planetary Incantations of Ceylon, embellished with 43 lithographic prints from the original singalese designs, *published in London in 1829.*

Four years later, Upham published unreliable translations (by others) of three im-portant Sri Lankan chronicles, including the Mahāvaṃsa, *the "Great Chronicle." In the passage below, he observes that in these texts we find only fragments of the Bud-dha's true teaching, and he laments the loss of the "more ancient and purer doctrine" of the Buddha.*

––––––

While these volumes principally unfold the historic annals of Buddhism, together with the faith and doctrines of Guadma as established in Ceylon, their earlier rec-ords excite in numerous passages the deepest regret, as they impress upon us the conviction that we have in them but the relics and fragments of a far more refined and intellectual code, which passages manifest a system of ethics so much supe-rior to the modern dogmata of the Buddha Guadma, that we cannot help lament-ing the cause which has annihilated the evidences of their more intimate connex-ion, and only allowed us to surmise, from very insufficient guides, what that more ancient and purer doctrine really was. Where, indeed, can we at present look for the solution of this interesting problem? Where are we able clearly to trace the sovereign supremacy of this system, and the origin and progress of those sangui-nary struggles in which its professors were engaged with those of a rival and more imposing form of faith? We can only conjecture that such was the case, and that the retreat of the persecuted votaries of Buddhism peopled and civilised the Indo-Chinese countries, and even spread their tenets among the barbarous communities of the Eastern Archipelago, while its influence was also acknowledged by the vast countries around the base of the "snowy Himaláya;" thus exercising a powerful sway over more than a hundred and eighty millions of the human race, in whose varied annals we may trace in this respect a corroborative uniformity of era.

Of the points which require elucidation in reference to Eastern antiquities, and on which we may hope to receive very material assistance from Buddhist writings, as it is to them that we must look eventually for a satisfactory solution, the following are not of the least striking interest: the priority of the comparative antiquity of the two great systems in India, the Brahmanical and the Buddhist; the epoch at which the seeds were sown of that bitter and inveterate hatred which the votaries of the respective creeds have borne from time immemorial, and do still bear towards each other; a classification of the names and characters occurring in the Buddhist writings, so as to explain which are purely mythological and which are historical, and on what data the Chinese ground their era of 1043 B.C.; thus placing the introduction of Buddhism into China five centuries anterior to the period stated by the Indo-Chinese and Singhalese,—these and many other questions of importance to our acquaintance with the genuine history of Buddhism, are as yet, and it is much to be feared are likely to remain for some time, among the desiderata of Oriental literature.

As it is admitted that the present volumes do not throw much light on the *esoteric* system of the Buddhist lawgivers, it is questionable how far the editor is called on to explain here his views on that part of the subject; yet, if these sacred annals of the Singhalese fail to exhibit the purer philosophy and ethics of Buddhism, they at least shew the practical effect of these doctrines, as adapted to a particular race of people, and modified to suit their cherished prejudices. They open also a curious and novel line of history, exemplified in the actions and characters of individuals respecting whom we previously knew nothing, and even now have no other sources of information. It is by thus tracing, however indistinctly, the chain of influence, from the practical results up to the system by which they are produced, that we can hope to form an approximate idea of the claims of the Buddhist doctrine, and may expect in time to unfold more clearly and satisfactorily the arcana of its profound and mysterious scheme. That it deserves such examination, the fact of its extensive adoption proves unhesitatingly; and it will be matter of no small congratulation when the research shall have been accomplished.[20]

◆ JEAN-PIERRE ABEL-RÉMUSAT (1788–1832)

In 1814, the French Sinologist Jean-Pierre Abel-Rémusat was appointed to hold the newly established chair in Chinese at the Collège de France. A physician, he had taught himself Chinese in order to read a text about the medicinal qualities of various plants. His most important contribution to European views of the Buddha was the Foe koue ki, *whose full title is* Foĕ Kouĕ Ki ou Relation des royaumes bouddhiques: Voyage dans la Tartarie, dans l'Afghanistan et dans l'Inde, exécuté à la fin du IVe

siècle, par Chỹ Fǎ Hian (Fo guo ji or Account of the Buddhist Kingdoms: Travels in Tartary, in Afghanistan, and in India at the end of the Fourth Century, by Shi Faxian) *published in Paris in 1836. This was Abel-Rémusat's translation of the* Record of Buddhist Kingdoms (Fo guo ji), *the travel journals of the Chinese monk Faxian (ca. 337–ca. 422), which provides an invaluable description of Buddhism in India and Sri Lanka at the beginning of the fifth century; Faxian set out for India in 399, returning to China in 412.*

The Chinese text is relatively short, only about fifty pages in translation, but Abel-Rémusat provided detailed notes and footnotes, in which he sought to identify and explain the many Buddhist persons, places, and doctrines that occur in Faxian's work. In producing these annotations, he made use of other Chinese sources as well as the available scholarship of the day.

Abel-Rémusat died in the cholera epidemic of 1832, when the book was only half finished. Julius Heinrich Klaproth took over the project until his own death three years later. It was completed by Ernest-Augustin Xavier Clerc de Landresse and published in 1836. An English-language edition, without the footnotes and without Landresse's substantial introduction, appeared in 1848.

Abel-Rémusat's work is remarkable in many ways, including its incorporation of Chinese, Sanskrit, Mongolian, and Tibetan terms in their original scripts. For the European view of the life of the Buddha, it was the first concerted attempt to identify the places in the Buddha's biography with actual locations in India. Because Faxian's text is organized according to his itinerary, the events of the life of the Buddha are recounted out of sequence. However, if those elements were extracted and placed in biographical order, Abel-Rémusat's work represents the most detailed life of the Buddha to appear in Europe up to that time, consisting of translations from Chinese Buddhist texts.

Two famous events are presented here: Prince Siddhārtha's first encounter with death and his attainment of enlightenment.

———

Shortly afterwards, he would go forth again. The king issued an edict to the effect that when the prince should go abroad, the ground should be cleared and no impurity should come near his route. He issued by the western gate of the town. The god transformed himself in a corpse which they were carrying out of the town. The relatives of the deceased followed the vehicle sobbing and weeping, complaining to heaven of their loss and eternal separation. The prince asked, "What is this?" They replied. "It is a corpse." The former again asked, "And what is that?" The attendants replied. "It is the end. The soul hath departed. The four elements are now about to dissipate. The sensitive soul and the spirit, being no longer in equilibrium, the air passes away and entirely ceases, the fire is extinguished, and the body becomes cold. Air having departed first, and afterwards fire, the soul and the understanding disappear. The members elongate and stiffen. There is nothing more to recognise. At the end of ten days the flesh decays, the blood flows, the belly swells, putrefies, and becomes fetid; there is nothing there to take. The body is filled with worms which devour it. The nerves and the veins are destroyed by putrefaction; the articulations are disjointed and the bones dispersed. The skull goes one way, the spine, the ribs, the arms, the legs, the feet and hands, each another. The birds that fly, the beasts that walk, assemble to devour them. Gods, dragons, demons, genii, emperors and kings, people, the poor, the rich, the noble, the plebeian,— none are exempt from this calamity." The prince gave a long sigh, and said in verse, "When I contemplate old age, sickness and death, I groan over human life and its instability! It is even so in my own person. This body is a perishable thing; but the soul hath no form. Under the false semblance of death, it is re-born! Its crimes and its good work are not dispersed. It is not a single generation that comprises its beginning or its end. Its duration is prolonged by ignorance and lust. It is thence that it obtains grief and joy. Though the body die, the soul perisheth not. It is not ether, it is not in the sea, it entereth not into mountains and rocks. There is no place in the world where there is exemption from death." Thereupon the prince turned his chariot and proceeded back to the palace, pondering sadly how all living beings are subject to old age, sickness, and death. He was so distressed that he eat none. The king enquired if the prince had been cheerful during his excursion. They answered that he fell in with a funeral and hath laid up sadness for several years.[21]

He then advanced once more, and beheld the hill *Sou lin*. The country was flat and regular, and on every side clear and delightful. It produced delicate and beautiful plants. Sweet rivulets flowed in abundance. The perfume of flowers was delicious and pure. In the midst there was a lofty and handsome tree, all the branches of which were disposed with regularity the one above the other: all the leaves were adjoined to each other, and the flowers thickly locked together as the ornament of the gods. A pennon was at the top of the tree. It was the king of all the forest, and of original happiness. Then (Buddha) advancing a little, beheld a man mowing grass. The Bodhisattwa asked, "What is now thy name?" "My name is 'Happy Omen,' and I now cut the *grass of happy omen*." "If thou give me of that grass, then shall the ten parts of the world possess a happy omen." Then *Happy Omen* pronounced the following gátha: "He hath rejected the dignity of Holy King, the seven treasures, the damsel of jasper for a spouse, beds of gold and of silver, carpets, broidered and many coloured stuffs, the plaintive voice of the bird *Kan than*, the harmony of the eight concords, and his superiority over the God Brahma, and now he provides himself with grass." The Bodhisattwa replied with this gátha: "I have made a vow during an *asankya*: it is to save men of the five conditions. I now proceed to fulfil this vow. It is on this account that I desired that the mower of grass should give me a handful of the grass, that holding it out towards the king of the trees, worldly thoughts might be wholly dispersed. Now must I carry out these purposes." The mower then presented him with the grass, and spread it upon the ground as had been told him. The Bodhisattwa sat down, and received the present. The Bodhisattwa performed the three things necessary to be seated, and having come before the tree, said, "If I can obtain the doctrine, I shall not evade the three oaths; my sides shall dry up and become immobile. If it be so that I attain complete Buddhahood, and obtain the doctrine, every hour shall produce its thought." Thereupon the Bodhisattwa sat down, and entered ecstasy. He cast away sorrow and the idea of joy; without either sadness or the thoughts of pleasure, his heart neither rested upon good, nor directed itself to evil. He was truly in the mean. Like a man who bathes, and, purified, covers himself with white felt; without, he was all purity, within, a spotless augury. Annihilated in repose, he completed without change the four contemplations; and after finishing these, he obtained determinate thought without abating his great compassion; by his knowledge and procedure, he penetrated the prime wonders, and comprehended the operation of the thirty-seven classes of the doctrine. And what are the thirty-seven classes? They are, first, the four stases of ideas of the *mens*; secondly, the four interruptions of the *mens*; thirdly, the four spiritual sufficiencies; fourthly, the five roots; fifthly, the five forces; sixthly, the seven intelligent *mens*; seventhly, the eight right actions. After the having run these over, he recommenced the void of pain. Extraordinarily without form, without wish or *ego*, he thought of the world which, by avarice, love, gluttony, lust, falls into the pains of life and death. How few understand how to know themselves, all deriving their origin from the twelve *nidánas*! What are these twelve? Their origin is ignorance; ignorance in action produces knowledge; knowledge in action produces name and title; title in action produces the six entrances; the six entrances in action produce desire; desire in action produces love; love in action produces *caption*; caption in action produces possession; possession in action produces birth; birth in action produces old age and death, pain and compassion, sorrow and suffering, which are the pains of the heart and the instrument, of great calamity. When the soul has fallen into the vicissitude of life and death, if it would obtain the doctrine, it must interrupt love, and extinguish and suppress passion and lust. When quietude comes, then is ignorance extinct; ignorance being extinct, then is action extinct; action becoming extinct, then is knowledge extinct; knowledge being extinct, then are name and title extinct; name and title extinct, then are the six entrances extinct; the six entrances extinct, then is renewed pleasure extinct; renewed pleasure extinct, then is desire extinct; desire extinct, then is love extinct; love extinct, caption is extinct; caption extinct, then is possession extinct; possession extinct, then is birth extinct; birth extinct, then are ended old age and death, sadness, compassion, pain and sorrow, the afflictions of the heart and all great calamities; and by this is meant to *have the doctrine.*[22]

◆ GEORGE TURNOUR (1799–1843)

George Turnour was born in Sri Lanka, the son of a British civil servant. After being educated in England, he returned to his birthplace to spend most of his brief career there, studying Singhala and Pāli literature. In the Ceylon Almanack *of 1833 and 1834, he published "Epitome of the History of Ceylon, and the Historical Inscriptions," republished in a single volume in 1836 as* The First Twenty Chapters of the Maha-wanso and a Preparatory Essay on Pali Buddhistical Literature. *This text contains a translation of "the first twenty chapters of the Mahawanso and a prefatory essay on Pali Buddhistical literature." The* Mahāvaṃsa, *the "Great Chronicle" of Sri Lanka, recounts the (legendary) visits of the Buddha to Sri Lanka and the history of the subsequent transmission of the dharma from India to Sri Lanka. Turnour did not complete his study of the text before his untimely death.*

Turnour was particularly interested in what historical information might be gleaned from Buddhist texts. In the passage below, he considers the question of the prehistoric buddhas (according to different schema, Śākyamuni was the fourth, seventh, or twenty-fifth), each preceding his successor by billions of years. Turnour considers this preposterous, and speculates as to when this idea began and who "the first disturber of Buddhistical chronology" was.

————

I profess not to be able to show, either the age in which the *first* systematic perversion of the Buddhistical records took place, or how often that mystification was repeated; but self-condemnatory evidence more convincing than that which the *Piṭakattayaṅ* and the *Aṭṭhakathá* themselves contain, that such a mystification was adopted at the advent of SÁKYA cannot, I conceive, be reasonably expected to exist. In those authorities, (both which are still held by the Buddhists to be inspired writings,) you are, as one of their cardinal points of faith, required to believe, moreover, that a revolution of human affairs, in all respects similar to the one that took place at the advent of SÁKYA, occurred at the manifestation of every preceding BUDDHO. The question, therefore, as to whether SÁKYA was or was not the first disturber of Buddhistical chronology, is dependent on the establishment of the still more important historical fact of whether the preceding BUDDHÁ had any existence but in his pretended revelation. For impartial evidence on this interesting question, we must not, of course, search Buddhistical writings; and it is not my design to enter into any speculative discussion at present.

It is, however, not unworthy of general remark that, as far as the surviving records of antiquity will admit of a judgment being formed, the learned consider it to be established that the Egyptians and the Hindus, the two nations who earliest attained an advanced condition of civilization, both preserved their chronology underanged, till about the age in which Buddhism acquired its greatest spread over the civilized regions of Asia; and that it was only then that the propounders of religious mysteries in Egypt and in those regions attempted to remodel their historical data, attributing to their respective nations a greater antiquity than that previously claimed by them.[23]

✦ ALEXANDER CSOMA DE KŐRÖS (1784–1842)

In 1819, the young Transylvanian scholar Alexander Csoma de Kőrös set out to "discover the obscure origins of our homeland"—that is, of the Hungarians and the Hungarian language. Magyar, the Hungarian language, is not Indo-European and thus does not belong to the Germanic, Slavic, or Romance families. His travels took him to Turkey and Egypt, and Baghdad, Tehran, and Kabul. Then in 1822, Csoma arrived in the Himalayan region of Kashmir. Searching in vain for a caravan that he could join for the journey to the oasis city of Yarkand in China, he spent the next year traveling back and forth—between Srinagar, the capital of Kashmir, and Leh, the capital of Ladakh, the westernmost region of the Tibetan cultural domain—hoping to meet one. On one of these trips, he instead encountered an Englishman, traveling alone in the opposite direction. This was the veterinarian William Moorcroft (1767–1825), who persuaded Csoma to postpone his search for the source of the Hungarian language in order to learn Tibetan.

Csoma agreed. He settled in Ladakh in June 1823, and arranged to study Tibetan language and literature under the tutelage of a lama named Sangye Phuntsok. Csoma studied diligently for the next seven years in a variety of locations along the southwestern borders of Tibet, sometimes with a British stipend, sometimes without resources. During this time, he produced a Tibetan–English dictionary, a grammar of the Tibetan language, and an English translation of the great ninth-century compendium of Buddhist terminology, the Mahāvyutpatti. In 1830, Csoma departed the Tibetan borderlands for Calcutta, the headquarters of the East India Company, where he worked in the library of the Asiatic Society. In 1842, he set off from Calcutta to travel to Sikkim, planning then to proceed through Lhasa to his long-postponed destination, the Tarim Basin. But disease, which he had successfully outrun years before, caught him in Darjeeling, where he died of malaria.

During his time in Calcutta, Csoma published numerous articles on Tibetan Buddhist literature under the auspices of the Asiatic Society of Bengal. Among these was an article in its journal, Asiatic Researches, which appeared in 1839 and was entitled "Notices on the Life of Shakya, Extracted from the Tibetan Authorities." Thirty-two pages in length, including extensive notes, it is one of the most detailed and accurate (in terms of its representation of the tradition) biographies of the Buddha to appear in a Western language. Rather than translating a single text, Csoma produced a synthetic biography, drawing from two famous Sanskrit lives of the Buddha, which he read in Tibetan translation: the Lalitavistara and the Abhiniṣkramaṇa. He supplemented the biography with numerous translations of relevant passages, including a lengthy extract on the funeral of the Buddha.

Csoma organized the biography around the famous "twelve deeds" that all buddhas are said to perform. They are, in his rendition: (1) he descended from among the gods; (2) he entered into the womb, or was incarnated; (3) he was born; (4) he displayed all sorts of arts; (5) he was married or enjoyed the pleasures of the conjugal state; (6) he left his house and took the religious character; (7) he performed penances; (8) he overcame the devil, or the god of pleasures, Káma Déva; (9) he arrived at supreme perfection, or became Buddha; (10) he turned the wheel of the law or published his doctrine; (11) he was delivered from pain, or died; (12) his relics were deposited. The second through sixth of Csoma's descriptions of these deeds are presented here.

———

II.—HE ENTERED INTO THE WOMB,
OR WAS INCARNATED.

There was a consultation again among the gods in what form *Bodhisatwa* should enter into the womb or body of the woman whom he had chosen to be his mother. A young elephant with six adorned horned trunks, such as being proper in brahmanical works, was preferred. He, therefore, leaving *Tushita*, descends, and, in the form of an elephant, enters by the right side, into the womb or cavity of the body of MÁYA DEVÍ (Tib. *Lhamó-sgyu-phrul-má*), the wife of SHUDHODANA. She never felt such a pleasure as at that moment. Next morning she tells the king the dream she had respecting that elephant. The Brahmans and the interpreters of dreams being called by the king, they propound that the queen shall be delivered of a son, who will become either an universal monarch or a *Buddha*. The king greatly rejoicing upon hearing these predictions, orders alms to be distributed, and offerings or sacrifices to be made to the gods for the safety and happy delivery of MÁYA DEVÍ, and for the prosperity of the child that was to be born: and he himself is very solicitous to do every thing according to her pleasure. The gods render her every service, and all nature is favourably disposed on account of *Bodhisatwa*, or the incarnated saint.

III — HE WAS BORN.

MÁYA DEVÍ was delivered of *Bodhisatwa* or the child, on the fifteenth day of the 4th moon of the Wood-Rat year; when she was in the garden of grove *Lumbini* whither she had gone with great procession for her recreation. The child (SHÁKYA) came out by her right side, she being in the standing posture, and holding fast the branch of a tree, INDRA, and other gods, assisted her. Soon after his birth, SHÁKYA walked seven paces towards each of the four cardinal points, and uttered the name of each of them, telling what he was about to do with respect to them. Several miracles happened at his birth: for instance the whole world was illuminated with great light or brightness; the earth quaked, or trembled several times; the blind saw, &c., &c.

There was born at the same time with SHÁKYA, the sons of four kings in central or Gangetic India. At *Rájagriha* in *Magadha*; at *Shravasti* in *Kosala*; at *Kaushambhi*, and at *Ujjayaní* (as VIMBASARA or SHRENIKA, PRASENAJIT, &c., &c.)

Likewise, at *Capilavastu*, there were born to the *Kshetriya* tribe 500 male and 500 female children; 500 male and female servants; 500 young elephants, 500 horses and colts, 500 treasures also opened; all the wishes of SHUDODHANA being thus fulfilled, he gave his son the name *Siddhártha* or "*Surva Siddhártha*" (Tib. *Don-grub* or *Don-thams-chad-grub'pa*).

Seven days after the birth of SHÁKYA, his mother dies, and is born again among the gods, in the *Traya-strimsha* (33) heaven.

From *Lumbini* SHÁKYA is carried with great solemnity to *Capilavastu*, is taken to the temple of a particular god of the Shakyas to salute him; but it is the god who shows reverence to him. Hence, one of the many names of SHAKYA is *Dévata Déva*, Tib. *Lhahi Lha*: god of gods. He is entrusted to GAUTAMÍ (his aunt), who together with 32 nurses, takes care of him. On a certain occasion it was found that the strength of SHÁKYA, (when yet a child) equaled that of a thousand elephants.

The Brahmans and other diviners observing the characteristic signs on the body of SHÁKYA, foretell that he shall become an universal monarch, if he remains at home; or a *Buddha*, if he leaves his houses and assumes the religious character.

An Hermit or Sage, called NAG-PO (or according to others *Nyon-mongs-med*) admonished by the great illumination of the world, together with his nephew MIS-BYIN (*S. Narada*) goes to *Capilavastu*, to salute the new born child. He has a long conversation with SHUDHODANA, and foretells to him that his son shall not become an universal monarch (*Chakravarti*) as some foretold of him, but a *Buddha*. He laments that being too old, he cannot reach the time, in which he shall teach his doctrine. He recommends to NARADA to become his disciple.

IV.—*HE DISPLAYED ALL SORTS OF ARTS.*

On a lucky or auspicious day (according to the observations of the Astrologers) SHUDHODANA intending to send his son (SHAKYA) unto a school to learn his letters, ordered the city to be cleansed and decorated; offerings or sacrifices to be made to the gods, and alms to be distributed. But, when brought to the school-master, he shews that, without being instructed, he knows every kind of letter shown by the school-master. And he himself encounters 64 different alphabets (among which are mentioned those of *Yavana* and *Huna* also; but they are mostly fanciful names) and shews their figures. The Master is astonished at his wisdom, and utters several *slokas* expressive of his praise. Likewise, in Arithmetic and Astronomy, he is more expert than all others. He is acquainted with the art of subduing, or breaking in, an elephant, and with all the 64 mechanical arts, with military weapons and machines. He excels all other young Shakyas in the gymnastic exercises; as, in wrestling, leaping, swimming, archery, throwing the discus, &c. He clears the roads from an immense tree that had fallen down.

V.—*HE WAS MARRIED OR ENJOYED THE*
PLEASURES OF THE CONJUGAL STATE.

Afterwards, when grown up, SHAKYA, being desired by his father to marry expresses in writing the requisite qualities of a woman, whom he would be willing to take for his wife, if there be found any such. The King orders his ministers to seek for such a damsel. They find one (S. GOPÁ; Tib: *Sa-htsho-ma*) the daughter of

SHAKYA PE-CHON-CHAN, but he declines to give his daughter except the young Prince be acquainted with the practice of every mechanical art. SHAKYA therefore exhibits his skill in all sorts of mechanical arts, and by this means he obtains GOPÁ, who is described as the model of prudent and virtuous women. He marries afterwards YASHODHARÁ (Tib: GRAGS-HDSIN-MA) and another of the name of RI-LAGS-SKYES (Deer-born.) The first two are much celebrated. But it seems that frequently both the names are attributed to the same person. By YASHODHARÁ, SHÁKYA had one son named RAHULA (Tib. SGRA-GCHAN-HDSIN.)

VI.—HE LEFT HIS HOUSE AND TOOK THE RELIGIOUS CHARACTER.

SHÁKYA is stated to have passed 29 years in the court of SHUDHODANA his father, enjoying during that time all worldly pleasures. Afterwards the following circumstances determine him to take the religious character.

Riding in a carriage to the grove for his recreation, he observes at different occasions—an old man;—a sick person;—a corpse, and lastly a man in a religious garb. He talks with his groom about those persons, and turns back at each occasion, and gives himself to meditation, on old age, sickness, death, and on the religious state. He visits a village of the agriculturists, observes their wretched condition, meditates in the shade of a *Jambu* tree. That shade out of respect for him, ceases to change with the progress of the sun. On his way home, many hoarded treasures open and offer themselves to him. He rejects them.

Notwithstanding all the vigilance of his father and of his relations to prevent him from leaving the court, (since according to the predictions regarding him they hope, that he shall become an universal monarch) he finds means for leaving the royal residence. At midnight mounting his horse called the "Praiseworthy" (Tib. *Bsnags-ldan*) he rides for six miles; then, dismounting, he sends back, by the servant, the horse and all the ornaments he had: and directs him to tell his father and his relations not to be grieved on his departure; for when he shall have found the supreme wisdom he will return and console them. Upon the servant's return there was great lamentation in the court of SHUDHODANA.

With his own sword, SHÁKYA cuts off the hair on his head; he then changes his fine linen clothes for a common garment of dark-red colour, presented by INDRA in disguise of a hunter. He commences his peregrination, and successively goes to *Rájagriha* in *Magadha*. The King VIMBASÁRA or SHRENIKA (in Tib. *Gsugs-chan-snying-po*) having seen him from his palace is much pleased with his manners. Afterwards being informed of him by his domestics, visits him; has a long conversation with him, and offers him means for living according to his pleasure. He will not accept of any thing. On the request of the King, he relates that he is of the *Shakya* race that inhabit *Capilavastu* in *Kosala*, on the bank of the *Bhagirathi* river in the vicinity of the Himalaya. He is of the royal family, the son of SHUDHODANA (Tib. *Zas Gtsang*) and that he has renounced the world, and now seeks only to find supreme wisdom.[24]

◆   EUGÈNE BURNOUF (1801–1852)

On or around April 20, 1837, twenty-four Sanskrit manuscripts of Buddhist texts arrived in Paris, sent by Brian Houghton Hodgson, Assistant British Resident to the court of Nepal, seven months earlier. Two French Sanskritists were assigned the task of going through the texts. One of them, Eugène Burnouf, selected the Lotus Sūtra, *and began reading. Before long, he had produced an entire translation of the text but felt that before it was published, "I would like to give an introduction to this bizarre work." In 1844, he published* Introduction à l'histoire du Buddhisme indien, *the single most influential work on Buddhism to be published in the nineteenth century. The first European monograph devoted to Indian Buddhism, it was written by a scholar who read Sanskrit well. Up until that point, Sanskrit Buddhist texts, that is, Buddhist texts originating from India, were unknown. Burnouf thus faced a major challenge, which he describes in the first passage below; he alludes to the many odd theories about the Buddha that were circulating at the time.*

In his Introduction, *Burnouf seeks to present the human Buddha, the teacher of morality who fought against the corruption of the Brahmin priests, who set forth the dharma to all who would listen, regardless of caste or class. It is this Buddha whom Burnouf characterizes in the second passage below. The Buddha had never been described in quite these terms by a European—or by an Asian, for that matter. Our image of the Buddha derives above all from Burnouf's book.*

———

It is time to pass on to the examination of some of the volumes of the collection of Nepal to which we have access, in order to discover there, if this is possible, the main features of the history of Indian Buddhism.

I say if this is possible, not with the puerile desire to exaggerate the difficulties of this research, but with the just sentiment of diffidence that I feel in undertaking it. It is not a question here of concentrating on an obscure but isolated text the strength that the rigorous and patient use of analysis gives to the mind, even less to draw from monuments already well known consequences that are new and worthy to take their place in history. The task I impose upon myself, although different, is equally arduous. It is necessary to browse through almost one hundred volumes, all manuscripts, written in four languages still little known, for whose study we have only lexicons, I could say of imperfect vocabularies, one of which has given birth to popular dialects even whose names are almost unknown. To these difficulties of form, add those of content: an entirely new subject, innumerable schools, an immense metaphysical apparatus, a mythology without boundaries; everywhere disorder and a dispiriting vagueness on questions of time and place; then, outside and among the small number of scholars whom a laudable curiosity attracts towards the results promised to this research, ready-made solutions, opinions that are immovable and ready to resist the authority of the texts, because they pride themselves in resting on an authority superior to all others, that of common sense. Do I need to recall that, for some people, all the questions related to Buddhism were already decided, when no one had read a single line of the books I shall analyze shortly, when the existence of these books was not even suspected by anyone? For some, Buddhism was a venerable cult born in Central Asia, and whose origin was lost in the mists of time; for others it was a miserable counterfeit of Nestorianism; Buddha has been made a Negro, because he had frizzy hair; a Mongol, because he had slanted eyes; a Scythe, because he was called Śākya. He has even been made a planet; and I do not know whether some scholars do not still delight today in recognizing this peaceful sage in the traits of the bellicose Odin. Certainly, it is permissible to hesitate, when to such vast solutions one promises only to substitute doubts, or only explanations that are simple and almost vulgar. The hesitation can even lead to discouragement, when one retraces one's steps and compares the results obtained to the time they have cost. I would like, nevertheless, to rely on the indulgence of serious persons to whom these studies are addressed; and while they leave me with the feeling of my insufficiency, with which I am affected more than ever, the hope for their benevolent consideration has given me the courage to produce these rough drafts, destined to open the way to research, which, while still not having a numerous public, is nonetheless in itself of incontestable value for the history of the human spirit.[25]

It is into the milieu of a society so constituted that was born, in a family of kṣatriyas, that of the Śākyas of Kapilavastu, who claimed descent from the ancient solar race of India, a young prince who, renouncing the world at the age of twenty-nine, became a monk under the name of Śākyamuni or also śramaṇa Gautama. His doctrine, which according to the sūtras was more moral than metaphysical, at least in its principle, rested on an opinion accepted as a fact and on a hope presented as a certitude. This opinion is that the visible world is in perpetual change; that death succeeds life and life death; that man, like all that surrounds him, revolves in the eternal circle of transmigration; that he successively passes through all forms of life from the most elementary to the most perfect; that the place he occupies on the vast scale of living beings depends upon the merit of the actions he performs in this world; and thus the virtuous man must, after this life, be reborn with a divine body, and the guilty with a body of the damned; that the rewards of heaven and the punishments of hell have only a limited duration, like everything in the world; that time exhausts the merit of virtuous actions as it effaces the faults of evil actions; and that the fatal law of change brings the god as well as the damned back to earth, in order to again put both to the test and make them pass through a new series of transformations. The hope that Śākyamuni brought to humanity was the possibility to escape from the law of transmigration, entering what he calls *nirvāṇa*, that is to say, annihilation. The definitive sign of this annihilation was death; but a precursory sign in this life announced the man predestined for this supreme liberation; it was the possession of an unlimited science, which gave him a clear view of the world as it is, that is to say, the knowledge of physical and moral laws; and in short, it was the practice of the six transcendent perfections: that of alms-giving, morality, science, energy, patience, and charity. The authority on which the monk of the Śākya race supported his teaching was entirely personal; it was formed of two elements, one real and the other ideal. The first was the consistency and the saintliness of his conduct, of which chastity, patience, and charity formed the principal features. The second was the claim he made to be buddha, that is to say, enlightened, and as such to possess superhuman science and power. With his power, he performed miracles; with his science, he perceived, in a form clear and complete, the past and the future. Thereby, he could recount everything that each man had done in his previous existences; and so he asserted that an infinite number of beings had long ago attained like him, through the practice of the same virtues, the dignity of buddha, before entering into complete annihilation. In the end, he presented himself to humanity as its saviour, and he promised that his death would not annihilate his doctrine; but that this doctrine would endure for a great number of centuries after him, and that when his salutary action ceased, there would come into the world a new buddha, whom he announced by name and whom, before descending to earth, the legends say, he himself had crowned in heaven, with the title of *future buddha*.[26]

INTRODUCTION

1. Urs App has discovered perhaps the first European to conclude that the inhabitants of China, Japan, and Pegu (in modern Burma) worshipped the same idol. He is the Jesuit Belchior Nunes Barreto, who in a letter of January 13, 1558, stated, describing Zen Buddhism, "This is the pseudo-theology of Xaqua [that is, Śākyamuni] and Amida [Amitābha], which also reigns over China and Pegu where this pest, to the best of my knowledge, came from." See Urs App, *The Cult of Emptiness: The Western Discovery of Buddhist Thought and the Invention of Oriental Philosophy* (Rorschach, Switzerland: UniversityMedia, 2012), p. 42.

2. Athansius Kircher, SJ, *China Illustrata*, trans. Charles D. Van Tuyl (Bloomington, IN: Indiana University Research Institute, 1987), p. 141.

3. Father Fernaõ de Queyroz, SJ, *The Temporal and Spiritual Conquest of Ceylon*, trans. Father S. G. Perera [1688] (Colombo, Sri Lanka: Government Printer, 1930), p. 120.

4. Engelbert Kaempfer, *The History of Japan, Giving an Account of the Ancient and Present STATE and GOVERNMENT of that EMPIRE; Of Its Temples, Palaces, Castles and other Buildings; Of Its Metals, Minerals, Trees, Plants, Animals, Birds and Fishes; Of the Chronology and Succession of the EMPERORS, Ecclesiastical and Secular; Of the Original Descent, Religions, Customs, and Manufactures of the natives, and of their Trade and Commerce with the Dutch and the Chinese. Together with a Description of the Kingdom of Siam. Written in High-Dutch by Engelbertus Kæmp-*

fer, M. D. Physician to the Dutch embassy to the Emperor's Court; and translated from his Original Manuscript, never before printed by and translated by J. G. SCHEUCHZER, F. R. S. and a Member of the College of Physicians, London. With the Life of the Author, and an Introduction. ILLUSTRATED with many COPPER PLATES, vol. 1 (London: Printed for the TRANSLATOR, 1727), p. 36.

5. William and Robert Chambers, eds., *Chambers's Information for the People*, new ed., vol. 2 (London: W. and R. Chambers, 1857), s.v. "Buddhism," pp. 443–44.

6. Eugène Burnouf, "De la langue et de la littérature sanscrite. Discours d'ouverture, prononcé au Collège de France," *Revue des deux mondes*, vol. 1, 2nd ser. (Février, 1833), 273.

7. Eugène Burnouf, *Introduction to the History of Indian Buddhism*, trans. Katia Buffetrille and Donald S. Lopez Jr. (Chicago: University of Chicago Press, 2010), p. 329.

8. Ibid., p. 337.

9. In Léon Feer, comp., *Papiers d'Eugène Burnouf conservés à la Bibliothèque Nationale* (Paris: H. Champion, 1899), p. 156. Translated from the French by Donald Lopez.

10. Burnouf, *Introduction to the History of Indian Buddhism*, p. 328.

CHAPTER ONE

1. Clement of Alexandria, *Stromata*, bk. 1, chap. 15. (Text within quotation marks is from Megasthenes' *Indica*.)

2. *Adversus Jovinianum* is one of the works that comprises *The Book of Wikked Wives*, which the clerk Jankyn, the fifth and final husband of the Wife of Bath, reads aloud to her in "The Wife of Bath's Prologue" in Chaucer's *Canterbury Tales*. See Ralph Hanna III and Traugott Lawler, eds., *Jankyn's Book of Wikked Wives*, Chaucer Library (Athens, GA: University of Georgia Press, 1997), pp. 166–67.

3. Socrates of Constantinople, *Historia Ecclesiastica*, in *A Select Library of Nicene and Post-Nicene Fathers of the Christian Church*, ed. Philip Schaff and Henry Wace, 2nd ser., vol. 2, *Socrates, Sozomenus: Church Histories* (New York: Christian Literature Company, 1890), p. 25. For a study of references to the Buddha in the early church, especially in connection with Manichaeism, see Timothy Pettipiece, "The Buddha in Early Christian Literature," *Millennium: Jahrbuch zu Kultur und Geschichte des ersten Jahrtausends n. Chr., Yearbook on the Culture and History of the First Millennium C. E.* 6 (2009): 133–43.

4. From Daniel Gimaret, *Le livre de Bilawhar et Būdāsf selon la version arabe ismaélienne* (Geneva: Droz, 1971), pp. 208–15. Translated from the French by Peggy McCracken.

5. From St. John Damascene, *Barlaam and Ioasaph*, trans. G. R. Woodward and H. Mattingly, Loeb Classical Library (Cambridge, MA: Harvard University Press, 1983), pp. 55–61.

6. See John Andrew Boyle, "The Journey of Het'um I, King of Little Armenia to the Great Khan Möngke," *Central Asiatic Journal* 9 (1964): 188–89.

7. *The Book of Ser Marco Polo the Venetian Concerning the Kingdoms and Marvels of the East*, trans. and ed. Sir Henry Yule, 2 vols.; 3rd ed., rev. Henri Cordier (London: Murray, 1926; reprint, New York: AMS, 1986), 2:316–19. See also the extensive notes of Yule and Cordier, pp. 320–30.

8. From Rashīd al-Dīn, *Compendium of Chronicles*, in Karl Jahn, *Rashīd al-Dīn's "History of India": Collected Essays with Facsimiles and Indices*, Central Asiatic Studies (The Hague: Mouton, 1965), pp. xlviii–xlix.

9. From Odoric of Pordenone, *The Travels of Sir John Mandeville with Three Narratives in Illustration of It: The Voyages of Johannes de Plano Capri, The Journal of Friar William de Rubruquis, The Journal of Friar Odoric* (New York: Dover, 1964), pp. 344–46.

CHAPTER TWO

1. See Georg Schurhammer, SJ, *Francis Xavier: His Life, His Times*, vol. 3, *Indonesia and India, 1545–1549*, trans. M. Jospeh Costelloe, SJ (Rome: Jesuit Historical Institute, 1980), pp. 484–85, 574.

2. Francis Xavier, letter "To His Companions in Europe" from Cochin [Kochi], January 29, 1552, in *The Letters and Instructions of Francis Xavier*, translated and introduced by M. Joseph Costelloe, SJ (St. Louis: Institute of Jesuit Sources, 1992), pp. 336–37.

3. Guillaume Postel, *Des merveilles du monde, et principalemét [sic] des admirables choses des Indes, & du nouveau monde: histoire extraicte des escriptz tresdignes de foy, tant de ceulx qui encores sont a present audict pays, come de ceulx qui encores vivantz peu paravat en sont retournez* (Paris, 1553), pp. 20–23. Translated from the French by Peggy McCracken.

4. Martín de Rada, OESA, *Relación verdadera de las cosas del reyno de Taibin, por otro nombre China, y del viage que a él hizo el muy reverendo padre fray Martin de Rada, provincial que fué del orden de St. Augustin, que lo vio y anduvo en la provincia de Hocquien año de 1575 hecha por el mismo*; translated in *South China in the Sixteenth Century, Being the Narratives of Galeote Pereira, Fr. Gaspar da Cruz, O. P., Fr. Martín da Rada, O. E. S. A. (1550–1575)*, ed. C. R. Boxer (London: Hakluyt Society, 1953), pp. 307–8, 309.

5. *A discourse of the nauigation which the Portugales doe make to the realmes and prouinces of the east partes of the worlde and of the knowledge that growes by them of the great things, which are in the dominions of China*. Written by Barnardine of Escalanta, of the realme of Galisia priest. Translated out of Spanish into English, by Iohn Frampton (London, 1579), p. 45.

6. Juan Gonzáles de Mendoza, OESA, *The historie of the great and mightie kingdome of China, and the situation thereof togither with the great riches, huge citties, politike gouernement, and rare inuentions in the same* (London: Printed by I. Wolfe for Edward White, 1588), pp. 28–29.

7. William Adams, from "The Kingdom of Japonia"; see Thomas Rundall, ed., *Memorials of the Empire of Japon: In the XVI and XVII Centuries* (London: Hakluyt Society, 1850), p. 12.

8. Cesar Fredericke, in Robert Kerr, *A General History and Collection of Voyages and Travels*, vol. 7 (Edinburgh: George Ramsey and Company, 1812), pp. 191–92.

CHAPTER THREE

1. Matteo Ricci, SJ, *The True Meaning of the Lord of Heaven (T'ien-chu Shih-i)*, trans. Douglas Lancashire and Peter Hu Kuo-chen, SJ (St. Louis: Institute of Jesuit Sources, 1985), pp. 453, 455.

2. Ibid., p. 241.

3. Samuel Purchas, *Purchas his Pilgrimage. Or Relations of the World and the Religions Observed in All Ages and Places discovered, from the Creation unto this Present. In foure Parts, This First Containeth a Theologicall and Geographicall Historie of Asia, Africa, and America, with the Islands Adiacent. Declaring the Ancient Religions before the Floud, the Heathnish, Jewish, and Saracenicall in all Ages since, in those parts professed, with their several Opinions, Idols, Oracles, Temples, Priestes, Fasts, Feasts, Sacrifices, and Rites Religious: Their beginnings, Proceedings, Alterations, Sects, Orders and Successions. With briefe Descriptions of the Countries, Nations, States, Discoveries, Private and Publike Customes, and the most Remarkable Rarities of Nature, or Humane Industrie, in the same*, vol. 1 (London: William Stansby, 1613), p. 398.

4. Nicholas Trigault, SJ, *The Christian Expedition among the Chinese undertaken by the Society of Jesus from the commentaries of Father Matteo Ricci of the same Society . . . in which the customs, laws, and principles of the Chinese kingdom and the most difficult first beginnings of the new Church there are accurately and with great fidelity described*, in *The China That Was: China as Discovered by the Jesuits at the Close of the Sixteenth Century*, trans. L. J. Gallagher, SJ (Milwaukee: Bruce, 1942), pp. 164–65. See also Matteo Ricci, *China in the Sixteenth Century: The Journals of Matthew Ricci; 1583–1610*, trans. from the Latin by Louis J. Gallagher, SJ (New York: Random House, 1953), pp. 98–99.

5. Roberto de Nobili, SJ, *Report Concerning Certain Customs of the Indian Nation* (composed in 1613), in *Preaching Wisdom to the Wise: Three Treatises by Roberto de Nobili, S.J., Missionary and Scholar in 17ᵗʰ Century India*, translated and introduced by Anand Amaladass, SJ, and Francis X. Clooney, SJ (St. Louis: Institute of Jesuit Sources, 2000), pp. 86, 93.

6. Richard Cocks, *Diary Kept by the Head of the English Factory in Japan*, vol. 1, *June 1, 1615–December 31, 1616* (Tokyo: Historiographical Institute, University of Tokyo, 1978), pp. 336–38.

7. Christopher (Cristoforo) Borri, SJ, "An Account of Cochin-China in Two Parts. The First Treats of the Temporal State of that Kingdom; The Second, of What Concerns the Spiritual," in John Pinkerton, *A General Collection of the Best and Most Interesting Voyages and Travels in All Parts of the World; Many of Which Are Now First Translated into English. Digested on a New Plan*, vol. 9 (London, 1811), pp. 820–22.

8. Álvaro Semedo, SJ, *The history of that great and renowned monarchy of China wherein all the particular provinces are accurately described, as also the dispositions, manners, learning, lawes, militia, government, and religion of the people: together with the traffick and commodities of that countrey* (London: Printed by E. Tyler for Iohn Crook, 1655), pp. 89–90.

9. Athansius Kircher, SJ, *China Illustrata*, trans. Charles D. Van Tuyl (Bloomington: Indiana University Research Institute, 1987), pp. 141–42.

10. Jean-Baptiste Tavernier, *A Collection of Several Relations and Treatises Singular and Curious of John Baptista Tavernier, Baron of Aubonne, Not Printed Among his First Six Voyages* (London, 1680), pp. 49–50.

11. Robert Knox, *An Historical Relation of the Island Ceylon in the East-Indies; Together, With an Account of the Detaining in Captivity the Author and divers other Englishmen now Living there, and of the Author's Miraculous Escape* (London, 1681), pp. 80–82. For a modern edition see Robert Knox, *An Historical Relation of Ceylon* (Glasgow: James MacLehose and Sons, 1911).

12. Abbé de Choisy, *Journal of a Voyage to Siam, 1685–1686*, translated and introduced by Michael Smithies (Kuala Lumpur, Malaysia: Oxford University Press, 1993), pp. 175–76.

13. Alexandre, Chevalier de Chaumont, *A relation of the late embassy of Monsr. de Chaumont, Knt. to the court of the King of Siam with an account of the government, state, manners, religion and commerce of that kingdom* (London, 1687), pp. 88–91.

14. Father Fernaõ de Queyroz, SJ, *The Temporal and Spiritual Conquest of Ceylon*, trans. Father S. G. Perera [1688] (Colombo, Sri Lanka: government printer, 1930), pp. 118–20.

15. See ibid., p. 122. Rui Magone speculates that the text is the four-volume *Shishi yuanliu yinghua shiji* (*The Origins, Transformations and Deeds of Buddha*) published in 1486, itself a version of the *Shijia rulai yinghua lu* (*Record of the Teachings of the Tathāgata Śākyamuni Buddha*) by Baocheng, a Buddhist of the Ming dynasty (1368–1643). See Rui Magone, "The Fô and the Xekiâ: Tomás Pereira's Critical Description of Chinese Buddhism," in *In the Light and Shadow of an Emperor: Tomás Pereira, SJ (1645–1708), the Kangzi Emperor and the Jesuit Mission in China*, ed. Artur K. Wardega, SJ, and António Vasconcelos de Saldanha (Newcastle upon Tyne, England: Cambridge Scholars Publishing, 2012): 252–74.

16. Queyroz, *The Temporal and Spiritual Conquest of Ceylon*, pp. 122–41.

17. Guy Tachard, SJ, *A relation of the voyage to Siam: performed by six Jesuits, sent by the French King, to the Indies and China, in the year, 1685: with their astrological observations, and their remarks of natural philosophy, geography, hydrography, and history / published in the original, by the express orders of His Most Christian Majesty; and now made English, and illustrated with sculptures* (London: 1688), pp. 275–78.

18. Ibid., pp. 289–92.

19. Ibid., pp. 295–99.

20. Nicolas Gervaise, *The Natural and Political History of the Kingdom of Siam* [1688], translated into English from the original by Herbert Stanley O'Neill (Bangkok: Siam Observer Press, 1928), pp. 67–70.

21. Ibid., pp. 74–77.

22. Simon de la Loubère, *A New Historical Relation of the Kingdom of Siam* (London, 1693; reprint, Oxford: Oxford University Press, 1986), pp. 136–39. Originally published in Paris and Amsterdam in 1691 as *De royaume de Siam.*

23. Louis le Comte, SJ, *Memoirs and Observations Topographical, Physical, Mathematical, Mechanical, Natural, Civil, and Ecclesiastical Made in a Late Journey through the Empire of China, and Published in Several Letters. Particularly upon the Chinese Pottery and Varnishing; the Silk and Other Manufactures. Description of their Cities and Publick Works; Number of People, their Language, Manners and Commerce; their Oeconomy, and Government. The Philosophy of Confucius. The State of Christianity, with Many Other Curious and Useful Remarks.* Translated from the Paris edition (London, 1697), pp. 323–25.

24. Engelbert Kaempfer, *The History of Japan, Giving an Account of the Ancient and Present* STATE *and* GOVERNMENT *of that EMPIRE; Of Its Temples, Palaces, Castles and other Buildings; Of Its Metals, Minerals, Trees, Plants, Animals, Birds and Fishes; Of the Chronology and Succession of the EMPERORS, Ecclesiastical and Secular; Of the Original Descent, Religions, Customs, and Manufactures of the natives, and of their Trade and Commerce with the Dutch and the Chinese. Together with a Description of the Kingdom of Siam. Written in High-Dutch by Engelbertus Kæmpfer, M. D. Physician to the Dutch embassy to the Emperor's Court; and translated from his Original Manuscript, never before printed by and translated by J. G. SCHEUCHZER, F. R. S. and a Member of the College of Physicians, London. With the Life of the Author, and an Introduction. ILLUSTRATED with many COPPER PLATES,* vol. 1 (London: Printed for the TRANSLATOR, 1727), pp. 34–39.

25. Ibid., 1:241–43.

CHAPTER FOUR

1. From Ippolito Desideri, SJ, *Relazione de' viaggi all' Inde e al Thibet*, in *Mission to Tibet: The Extraordinary Eighteenth-Century Account of Ippolito Desideri, S. J.*, trans. Michael J. Sweet (Boston: Wisdom Publications, 2010), pp. 394–97. I have restored Desideri's original spelling of the Tibetan terms.

2. François Valentyn [Valentijn], "The Great Buddhoo," *Asiatic Journal and Monthly Register for British India and its Dependencies* 23 (January–June, 1827): 25–26; originally published in Dutch between 1724 and 1726.

3. Bernard Picart, *The Ceremonies and Religious Customs of the Various Nations of the Known World: Together with Historical Annotations, and Several Curious Discourses Equally Instructive and Entertaining*, vol. 4 (London, 1733), pp. 101–2.

4. Ibid., 4:105–6.

5. Ibid., 4:137.

6. Ibid., 4:196.

7. Ibid., 4:291–92.

8. Jean Baptiste du Halde, SJ, *The General History of China. Containing a Geographical, Historical, Chronological, Political, and Physical Description of the Empire of China*, 3rd ed., vol. 3 (London, 1741), pp. 34–37. Originally published in French in 1735.

9. Father Adriano di St. Thecla, *Opusculum de Sectis apud Sinenses et Tunkinenses: A Small Treatise on the Sects among the Chinese and Tonkinese*, translated and annotated by Olga Dror (Ithaca, NY: Cornell Southeast Asia Program, 2002), pp. 186–87.

10. Antonio Agostino Giorgi, *Alphabetum Tibetanum: Missionum Apostolicarum Commodo Editum* (Köln: Editiones Una Voce, 1987), pp. 547–48. My thanks to Isrun Engelhardt for identifying the passage and translating it from the Latin.

11. Denis Diderot and Jean le Rond d'Alembert, *Encyclopédie, ou Dictionnaire raisonné des sciences, des arts et des métiers*, new ed., vol. 31 (Amsterdam: M. M. Rey, 1776–77), pp. 6–8. Translated from the French by Donald Lopez.

12. Translated by Peter Skilling from the 1785 edition of Voltaire's *Dictionnaire Philosophique*, vol. 43, s.v. "Sammonocodom ou Sommona-Codom"; from "Samana Gotama according to Voltaire's Dictionnaire Philosophique," in *Pakinaka lakthan prawatsat thai* [*Miscellaneous Evidence for Thai History*], ed. Mom Rajawong Suphawat Kasemsri (Bangkok, 2558 [2015]), pp. 269–79.

13. Peter Simon Pallas, *The Habitable World Described*, vol. 2 (London, 1788), pp. 242–43, 245–47; Pallas's account from August 11, 1769.

14. Guillaume Joseph le Gentil de la Galaisière, *Voyage dans les mers de l'Inde, fait par ordre du roi, à l'occasion du passage de Vénus sur le disque du soleil le 6 Juin 1761, et le 3 du*

même mois 1769, vol. 1 (Switzerland: Libraires Associés, 1780), pp. 224–25. Translated from the French by Donald Lopez. The passage had appeared in English shortly after its publication. See William Chambers, "Some Account of the Sculptures and Ruins at Mavalipuram," *Asiatick Researches* 1 (1788): 168–70.

15. William Hurd, *A New Universal History of the Religious Rites, Ceremonies, and Customs of the Whole World: Or, A Complete and Impartial View of all the Religions in the Various Nations of the Universe. Both Ancient and Modern, from the Creation down to the present Time* (London: Alexander Hogg, 1780), pp. 76–77.

16. Ibid., p. 94.

17. Abbé [Jean-Baptiste] Grosier, *A General Description of China: Containing the Topography of the Fifteen Provinces which Compose This Vast Empire; That of Tartary, the Isles, and Other Tributary Countries; The Number and Situation of the Cities, the State of its Population, the Natural History of its Animals, Vegetables and Minerals. Together with the Latest Accounts that Have Reached Europe, of the Government, Religion, Manners, Customs, Arts and Sciences of the Chinese. Illustrated by a New and Correct Map of China, and other Copper Plates*, vol. 1 (London, 1788), pp. 215–20.

18. Sir William Jones, "On the Hindus," *Asiatick Researches*, vol. 1, chap. 25 (1789; delivered February 2, 1786).

19. Sir William Jones, "On the Chronology of the Hindus," *Asiatick Researches*, vol. 2, chap. 7 (1790; written January 1788), pp. 122–25.

20. Thomas Maurice, *Indian Antiquities: or, Dissertations, Relative to the Ancient Geographical Divisions, the Pure System of Primeval Theology, the Grand Code of Civil Laws, the Original Form of Government, and the Various and Profound Literature, of Hindostan. Compared, Throughout, with the Religion, Laws, Government, and Literature, of Persia, Egypt, and Greece. The Whole Intended as Introductory to, and Illustrative of, the History of Hindostan Upon a Comprehensive Scale. Vol. V in which the Investigation of the ORIENTAL TRIADS of DEITY is continued; and the HORRIBLE PENANCES of the INDIAN DEVOTEES are detailed* (London, 1793–94), pp. 12–13.

21. Louis Langlès, ed. and trans., *Voyages de C.P. Thunberg, au Japon, par le cap de Bonne-Esperance, les îles de la Sonde, &c.: traduits, rédigés et augmentés de notes considérables sur la religion, le gouvernement, le commerce, l'industrie et les langues de ces différentes contrées, particulièrement sur le Javan et le Malai par L. Langlès* (Paris: Chez Benoît Dandré [et al.], an IV [1796]), 3:261–62, note. Cited by J. Reuilly in his notes to his translation of Pallas, entitled *Description du Tibet d'après la Relation des Lamas Tangoutes, établis parmi les Mongols* (Paris: Chez Bossange, 1808), pp. 48–49, note.

22. Paulinus a S. Bartholomaeo, *A Voyage to the East Indies, containing an account of the manners, customs, &c. of the natives, with a geographical description of the country. Collected*

from observations made during a residence of thirteen years, between 1776 and 1789, in districts little frequented by the Europeans (London: J. Davis, 1800), p. 332.

23. Lieutenant Francis Wilford, "On EGYPT and other COUNTRIES, adjacent to the CÁLÍ River, or NILE of ETHIOPIA, from the ancient BOOKS of the HINDUS," *Asiatick Researches* 3 (1796): 198–99.

24. Captain Colin McKenzie, "Remarks on Some Antiquities on the West and South Coasts of Ceylon Written in the Year 1796," *Asiatick Researches* 6 (1799): 452–53.

25. Captain Mahony, "On Singhala, or Ceylon, and the Doctrines of Bhooddha, from the Books of the Singhalais," *Asiatick Researches* 7 (1801): 33–34, 40–41.

26. Michael Symes, *An Account of an Embassy to the Kingdom of Ava, Sent by the Governor-general of India, in the Year 1795.* By Michael Symes, Esq., Major in His Majesty's 76th Regiment (London, 1800), pp. 298–303.

27. Vincenzo Sangermano, *A Description of the Burmese Empire*, 5th ed. (London: Susil Gupta, 1966), pp. 102, 107–9.

CHAPTER FIVE

1. Mr. [Joseph Endelin de] Joinville, "On the Religion and Manners of the People of Ceylon," *Asiatick Researches* 7 (1801): 397–98, 400, 413–15.

2. Francis Buchanan, "On the Religion and Literature of the Burmas," *Asiatick Researches* 6 (1801): 256–65.

3. [Alexander Hamilton?], review of *Asiatick Researches: or, Transactions of the Society instituted in Bengal, for inquiring into the History and Antiquities, the Arts, Sciences and Literature of Asia,* vol. 7, *Edinburgh Review* 9, no. 17 (1806): 97–98.

4. Edward Moor, *The Hindu Pantheon* (London, 1810; facsimile ed., New York: Garland, 1984), pp. 220–21, 231–32.

5. Captain F. Wilford, "An ESSAY on the SACRED ISLES in the West, with other Essays connected with that Work," *Asiatick Researches* 10 (1811): 94–95.

6. William Erskine, "Account of the Cave-Temple of Elephanta with a Plan of the Drawings of the Principal Figures," *Transactions of the Literary Society of Bombay,* vol. 1 (1819): 201–2.

7. George Stanley Faber, *The Origin of Pagan Idolatry Ascertained from Historical Testimony and Circumstantial Evidence* (London: F. and C. Rivingtons, 1816), 1:87, 2:42.

8. Michel-Jean François Ozeray, *Recherches sur Buddou ou Bouddou* (Paris, 1817), pp. 111–12. Translated from the French by Donald Lopez.

9. Robert Fellowes, *The History of Ceylon, from the earliest period to the year MDCCCXV; with Characteristic Details of the Religion, Laws, & Manners of the People and a Collection*

of *Their Moral Maxims & Ancient Proverbs. By Philalethes, A.M. Oxon* (London: Printed for Joseph Mawman, Ludgate Street, by J. F. Dove, St. John's Square, 1817), pp. 193–209.

10. Francis [Hamilton] Buchanan, *An Account of the Kingdom of Nepal: And of the territories Annexed to this Dominion by the House of Gorkha* (Edinburgh: A. Constable, 1819), pp. 56–58.

11. Captain R. N. Golownin, *Recollections of Japan, Comprising a Particular account of the Religion, Language, Government, Laws and Manners of the People, with Observations on the Geography, Climate, Population & Productions of the Country* (London, 1819), pp. 45–46, note.

12. John Crawfurd, *History of the Indian Archipelago. Containing an Account of the Manners, Arts, Languages, Religions, Institutions, and Commerce of its Inhabitants*, 3 vols. (Edinburgh, 1820), 2:221–22.

13. John Davy, *An Account of the Interior of Ceylon, and of its Inhabitants: With Travels in that Island* (London, 1821), pp. 230–35.

14. Julius Klaproth, "Vie de Bouddha d'après les livres Mongols (I)," *Journal Asiatique* 4 (1824): 9–10. The same biography had appeared in German in 1823 in Klaproth's *Asia Polyglotta*. The piece, entitled "Leben des Budd'a, nach Mongolischen Nachrichten," appears after page 384 in that work, but the pages are numbered 122–44. The French version is an abridged version of the German. Translated from the French by Donald Lopez.

15. Thomas Abercrombie Trant, *Two years in Ava: From May 1824, to May 1826* (London: John Murray, 1827), p. 253.

16. Samuel Davis, "Remarks on the Religious and Social Institutions of the Bouteas, or Inhabitants of Boutan, from the unpublished Journal of the late SAMUEL DAVIS, Esq. F.R.S. &c. Communicated by J.F. DAVIS, Esq. F.R.S. M.R.A.S," *Transactions of the Royal Asiatic Society of Great Britain*, vol. 2 (1830): 491.

17. John Crawfurd, *Journal of an Embassy from the Governor-General of India to the Courts of Siam and Cochin China; Exhibiting a View of the Actual State of Those Kingdoms*, vol. 2 (London: Henry Colburn and Richard Bentley, 1830), pp. 80–85.

18. Karl Friedrich Neumann, *The Catechism of the Shamans; or The Laws and Regulations of the Priesthood of Buddha, in China* (London: Oriental Translation Fund, 1831), pp. xxiii–xxiv, xxv, and xxvi–xxvii.

19. Charles Coleman, *The Mythology of the Hindus, with Notices of Various Mountain and Island Tribes, inhabiting the Two Peninsulas of India and the Neighbouring Islands; and an Appendix, Comprising the Minor Avatars, and the Mythological and Religious Terms, &c. &c. of the Hindus* (London, 1832), pp. 184–92.

20. Edward Upham, M.R.A.S. & F.S.A., ed., *THE MAHÁVANSI, THE R'AJÁ-RATNÁCARI, AND THE RÁJÁ-VALI, forming the Sacred and Historical Books of Ceylon;*

also, a Collection of Tracts illustrative of the Doctrines and Literature of Buddhism: Translated from the Singhalese, 3 vols. (London, 1833), 1:xviii–xxi.

21. Jean-Pierre Abel-Rémusat et al., *The Pilgrimage of Fa Hian; from the French edition of the Foe Koue Ki of MM. Remusat, Klaproth, and Landresse* (Calcutta: Baptist Mission Press, 1848), pp. 198–99. In the original French edition, the passage occurs at pp. 206–7.

22. Ibid., pp. 290–92. In the original French edition, the passage occurs at pp. 285–88.

23. George Turnour, "An Examination of the Páli Buddhistical Annals, No. 3," *Journal of the Asiatic Society of Bengal* 8 (1838): 687.

24. Alexander Csoma de Kőrös, "Notices of the Life of Shakya, Extracted from the Tibetan Authorities," *Asiatic Researches*, vol. 20, pt. 2 (1839): 233–38.

25. Eugène Burnouf, *Introduction to the History of Indian Buddhism*, trans. Katia Buffetrille and Donald S. Lopez Jr. (Chicago: University of Chicago Press, 2010), pp. 112–13.

26. Ibid., pp. 181–82.

Omyto, 65. *See also* Amitābha

Onân, 88–90, 92. *See also*
Ānanda

"On the Hindus" (Jones), 158

"On the Religion and Literature of the Burmas" (Bu-
chanan), 171, 178–79, 206

"On the Religion and Manners
of the People of Ceylon" (Joinville), 175

*Opusculum de Sectis apud Sin-
enses et Tunkinenses* (A Small
Treasure on the Sects among
the Chinese and Tonkinese)
(Adriano), 141

Order of Hermits of St. Augustine (Ordo Eremitarum
sancti Augustini), 44, 47

*Origin of Pagan Idolatry Ascer-
tained from Historical Testimony and Circumstantial
Evidence* (Faber), 191

Osiris, 65

Oud en Nieuw Oost-Indiën
(Old and New East Indies)
(Valentijn), 128, 194

Ovid, 17

Ozeray, Michel-Jean François,
192–93

Padmapurāṇa, as forgery, 163

Padres da Corte, 75–76

Palestine, 141

Pallas, Peter Simon, 11, 15, 149,
185–86, 206–7

Pantaenus, 20

Parke, Robert, 47

Paulinus a S. Bartholomaeo,
162–63, 179–81, 184

Pegu (Burma), 13, 48, 53, 117,
120, 153, 185–86, 237n1

Peking (China), 54

Pereira, Tomás, 4, 10, 16, 74–
76, 93

Perry, Matthew C., 1

Perseus, 146

Persia, 19, 22

Pharisees, 211

Phât, 141. *See also* Buddha

Philippines, 44, 47

Picart, Bernard, 4, 11, 115, 130–
32, 134–37, 151–52

Pisa, Rustichello da, 33

Plato, 75

Polo, Marco, 4, 8–9, 14, 33, 45

Polyglot Bible, 42

Pondicherry, 150–51

Postel, Guillaume, 42–43

Potocki, Count Jan, 214

Praària-Seria, 189

Prah Pudi Dsau, 120. *See also*
Buddha

Pra-swane, 189

Ptolemy, 60

Punjab, 8

Puraṇas, 218

Purchas, Samuel, 9–10, 16, 53

*Purchas his Pilgrimage; or,
Relations of the World and
the Religions Observed in All
Ages and Places discovered,
from the Creation unto this
Present* (Purchas), 10, 53, 130

Pygmalion, 17

Pythagoras, 22, 52, 56, 65–66,
72, 75, 87, 134, 146–47, 157;
transmigration of souls,
64, 77

Queyroz, Fernaõ de, 4, 10, 13–
14, 73, 75–76

Rada, Martín de, 44–45, 47

Radhacant, 160

Răhāns, 179–81, 183–84, 188

Rājasimha II, 68

Rakulo, 129, 177, 195–96, 202,
233

Rama, 13, 65, 118, 180, 186. *See
also* Buddha

Rashīd al-Dīn, 35–36

*Recherches sur Buddou ou
Bouddou* (Ozeray), 192, 193

*Recollections of Japan, Compris-
ing a Particular Account of
the Religion, Language, Government, Laws and Manner of
the People* (Golownin), 208

*Record of Buddhist Kingdoms
(Foguo ji)* (Faxian), 15

Recueil du Plusiers Relations
(Collection of Several Reports) (Tavernier), 66

*Relação da propagacao da fe
no reyno da China e outros
adjacentes* (Report on the
Propagation of the Faith in
the Kingdom of China and
other adjacent [lands]) (Semedo), 63

*Relazione de' viaggi all' Indie e
al Thibet* (Report on Travels
to India and Tibet) (Desideri), 124

*Religion of the Universe, The:
With Consolatory Views of a
Future State, and Suggestions
on the Most Beneficial Topics
of Theological Instruction*
(Fellowes), 194

"Remarks on the Religion and
Social Institutions of the
Bouteas, or Inhabitants of
Boutan" (Davis), 216

Rhea-Silvia, 146

Ribeiro, João, 128

Ricci, Matteo, 10, 33, 51–52, 54–
57, 113, 141

Ri-lags-skyes, 233

Robinson Crusoe (Defoe), 10

Roman Catholic Church,
145–46

Lightning Source UK Ltd.
Milton Keynes UK
UKOW05f2144191016

285648UK00003B/4/P